Dear Mom,

Maybe you would like to try this for your daily reading and meditation next year. I think it might be refreshing as an ocean breeze.

Love,
Daniel

Opened
Treasures

Frances Ridley Havergal

Frances Ridley Havergal

Opened Treasures

Compiled by William J. Pell

*"The LORD shall open unto thee
His good treasure"*
DEUTERONOMY 28:12

LOIZEAUX BROTHERS
Neptune, New Jersey

FIRST EDITION, OCTOBER 1962

FOURTH PRINTING, AUGUST 1975

ISBN 0-87213-320-6

Library of Congress Catalog Card Number: 62-21063

PRINTED IN THE UNITED STATES OF AMERICA

Preface

THE MEDITATIONS AND SONGS of Frances Ridley Havergal have provided solace, comfort, and everlasting peace to thousands of souls. Her ministry in poetry and prose is ever being used by the Spirit of God to teach, comfort, exhort, and convict.

All her poetry and prose is saturated with the living Word of God; it has a freshness and power which only the eternal dew of heavenly truth could impart. Frances always looked to the Lord for her messages before writing anything. On one occasion she wrote to her sister of her strong belief that, "If I am to write to any good, a great deal of living must go into a very little writing."

In an effort to preserve her prose for this generation this volume has been published. We have sought to include virtually all her prose writings and to couple with them selections from her poetry. The work of selecting the poetry has been done by Mabel J. Carter.

Those who have worked on the compilation and production of this book have testified to having received a great blessing from their labor of love. The book is now sent forth with the earnest desire that it, like its author, Frances Ridley Havergal, may run over all denominational barriers and be acceptable and helpful to the saints, for "In prayer and praise the saints appear as one."

WILLIAM J. PELL

Grand Rapids, Michigan

Take my life, and let it be
Consecrated, Lord, to Thee.
Take my moments and my days;
Let them flow in ceaseless praise.

Take my hands, and let them move
At the impulse of Thy love.
Take my feet, and let them be
Swift and beautiful for Thee.

Take my voice, and let me sing,
Always, only, for my King.
Take my lips, and let them be
Filled with messages for Thee.

Take my silver and my gold;
Not a mite would I withhold.
Take my intellect, and use
Every power as Thou shalt choose.

Take my will, and make it Thine.
It shall be no longer mine.
Take my heart, it is Thine own;
It shall be Thy royal throne.

Take my love; my Lord, I pour
At Thy feet its treasure-store.
Take myself, and I will be
Ever, only, all for Thee.

FRANCES RIDLEY HAVERGAL

Written February 4, 1874

Other familiar hymns by Frances Ridley Havergal:

Another Year is Dawning
I Could Not Do Without Thee
True-hearted, Whole-hearted
O Saviour, Precious Saviour
I Am Trusting Thee, Lord Jesus
Who Is on the Lord's Side?
Lord, Speak to Me
I Gave My Life for Thee
Standing at the Portal of the Opening Year

Frances Ridley Havergal

A FEW MONTHS before Princess Victoria succeeded to the throne, Frances Ridley Havergal, youngest of the six children of Rev. William Henry and Jane Havergal, was born on December 14, 1836 at her father's rectory in the little English village of Astley, in Worcestershire.

In her brief lifetime of forty-two years, Frances Havergal achieved fame and influence unusual for a woman of that era. By the time of her death one of her volumes of poetry had reached its 30th edition, *The Ministry of Song* was in its 38th edition, and her hymns and lyrics in magazines were beyond even such circulation. Publication of *Under His Shadow*, containing her last poems, exceeded 90,000 — a popularity unprecedented in English hymnody.

Yet Frances Ridley Havergal was an understandable — though exceptionally gifted — product of her time and environment. Her mother had been the "lovely Jane Head," her father was a talented, well-trained musician versed in psalmody, composer of hundreds of chants, tunes, and cathedral services, and an ardent supporter of foreign missions as well as an able preacher. Theirs was a happy home, marked by their prayers and example in searching the Scriptures, their cheery ways and godly activities.

Frances was a child of grace and beauty, fair-complexioned, sunny-haired, vivacious. In spite of her extreme precocity — she could read easy books at three, the Bible at four, and began writing verses at seven — she was full of life and spirit, distinguishing herself no less in wild tree-climbing and wall-scaling than in picking up German from overhearing the lessons given to her older brothers and sisters. She was by no means a model child — she "utterly abominated being 'talked to' " and "would do anything on earth to escape" kindly-meant admonitions. She had a very sensitive nature, especially when young, with frequent fits of unhappiness and penitence, called forth by a bit of nature, a book, or a sermon.

Frances early decided that to be a Christian was the most desirable thing in life, even while taking a "sort of savage joy" in her despondency and feelings of failure. In later years she spoke of her early spiritual experience with frankness, when persuaded it might be helpful to others, but at the time she "could as soon speak Sanscrit" as utter a word about it to any human being. She was often misjudged because of this reserve. Even her sisters did not know of her inner conflicts, her natural buoyancy of temperament enabling her to pass quickly from an agony of weeping in her room to a merry burst of laughter or a sudden lighthearted scamper up and down stairs.

"Many have thought mine a comparatively thornless path," she wrote in later years, "but often, when the path was the smoothest, there were hidden thorns within. . . ." This deep longing for a pure life, disquieted by frequent thoughts of backsliding, schooled her for the consecration evident in her writings and the understanding through which she was enabled to help countless others.

In 1845 the family moved to Worcester, where Mr. Havergal was appointed to the Rectory of St. Nicholas. Frances, scarcely ten years old, began teaching a Sunday School class of still younger children, and organized a favorite playmate and herself into "The Flannel Petticoat Society," described in *The Four Happy Days*, one of her few published books for children.

Shortly before Frances' twelfth birthday her mother went to be with the Lord. She was quite unprepared for this great sorrow. Yet her mother's words to her before she died: "Fanny dear, pray to God to prepare you for all that He is preparing for you," became a life-prayer later on. For this "preparing" went on all through her life. As one horizon was gained, another stretched on ahead. So each event prepared for the one to follow.

In boarding school in England — "That single half year was perhaps the most important of any in my life" — she began to "have conscious faith and hope in Christ," and soon after her fifteenth birthday she wrote, "I committed my soul to the Saviour . . . and earth and Heaven seemed brighter from that moment."

A few months later her father married again, and Frances expressed in poetry her loving satisfaction. Going with her parents to Germany, she attended school in Düsseldorf, learning "to think in German," and achieving first place among the 110 pupils, no small feat for an English girl whose earlier education had been so casual and intermittent. Her thirst for knowledge was lifelong. She committed to memory the entire New Testament, Psalms, Isaiah, and the Minor Prophets. She studied, and in most cases mastered, French, German, Italian, Latin, Greek, and Hebrew. In Wales she learned enough Welsh from her donkey-girl to be able to join intelligently in Sunday services. At the seashore she was eager for nautical information. She taught herself harmonics by reading a treatise. Yet she was content to sit with the smallest children in the vicar's Bible class, and often referred to the pleasure and benefit derived from his teachings.

Her confirmation in Worcester Cathedral, at 18, left deep and sacred memories. When the words, "Defend, O Lord, this Thy child with Thy heavenly grace, that she may continue Thine for ever," were solemnly pronounced over her head, "if ever my heart thrilled with earnest longing, not unmixed with joy, it did at the words, 'Thine for ever.' "

She was sensitive to Nature. "The quiet everyday beauty of the trees and sunshine was *the* chief external influence upon my early childhood. Waving boughs and golden light always touched and quieted me and spoke to me and told me about God." She was ecstatic over her first glimpse of the Alps — "that majesty of shining eternal snow" reminding her of the Psalms — remarking quaintly, "It is very difficult to believe that David never was in Switzerland."

Frances Havergal had a double talent. Although her poetry was better known, she was highly skilled in music, which she called "the only universal language, a sort of alphabet of the language of Heaven." She was a skilled pianist, proficient in Bach, Handel, Mendelssohn, Beethoven, Haydn, Schumann, and Schubert. She was a contralto soloist, later putting aside her "pleasure of public applause when singing in the Philharmonic concerts" to use her gifts solely in sacred song. She mastered harmony and counterpoint, wrote tunes for her own hymns, and prepared a volume of her father's *Psalmody* after his death.

At 21, stirred by the painting of the head of Christ, "Ecce Homo," in the Art Gallery of Düsseldorf, she composed her first real hymn, "I Gave My Life for Thee," for which her father wrote the music. A later hymn, "Take My Life," written in

1874, was virtually her autobiography in poetry, each couplet describing a definite experience in her life. The line, "Take my silver and my gold," referred to her sending "nearly fifty articles" of jewelry to the Church Missionary Society, retaining for daily wear only a brooch that was a memorial of her parents, and a locket with a portrait of her niece.

Always she sought to blend her poems and music with life. When someone described a hymn-sing as "religiously jolly," she wrote: "It is just what I wish, to get people to connect religion with all that is pleasant and joyful. *Him serve with mirth.*"

In spite of frequent illness, Frances Havergal's spare time was crowded with Bible classes, readings for the YWCA, and extensive correspondence, especially with girls who sought her spiritual counsel and help. Active to the last, she died on June 3, 1879, at Caswell Bay, Swansea, England, in her forty-third year, and was laid to rest in Astley churchyard, near the old rectory where she was born.

It has been said* of her: "Frances Ridley Havergal had none of the ordinary titles to fame. What singled her out was the note of absoluteness in her spiritual experience . . . In her consecration there was no limit and no reserve. She had learned the secret of abandonment, and she yielded herself utterly to God. By virtue of this, her writings reached and moved a multitude of souls with strange, penetrating power."

MARIE D. LOIZEAUX

* Darlow, Thomas Herbert. *Frances Ridley Havergal: A Saint of God;* A New Memoir. London, Nisbet.

January 1

For ye have not passed this way heretofore. Joshua 3:4

We have not passed this way heretofore, but the Lord Jesus has. "For we have not an high priest which cannot be touched with the feeling of our infirmities" (Hebrews 4:15). It is all untrodden and unknown ground to us, but He knows it all by personal experience; the steep bits that take away our breath, the stony bits that make our feet ache so, the hot shadeless stretches that make us feel so exhausted, the rushing rivers that we have to pass through, our Shepherd has gone through it all before us. Not some but all the many waters went over Him, and yet they did not quench His love. "All Thy waves and Thy billows are gone over Me" (Psalm 42:7). "Many waters cannot quench love, neither can the floods drown it" (Song of Solomon 8:7). He was made a perfect Leader by the things He suffered. "To make the Captain of their salvation perfect through sufferings . . . . and being made perfect, He became the Author of eternal salvation unto all them that obey Him" (Hebrews 2:10; 5:9). For now He knows all about it, and leads us softly according as we are able to endure: "For He knoweth our frame" (Psalm 103:14). And He does not only know, with that sort of up-on-the-shelf knowledge which is often guilty of want of thought among ourselves, but He *remembereth* that we are dust. "For He remembered that they were but flesh" (Psalm 78:39). Think of that when you are tempted to question the gentleness of His leading. He is remembering all the time; and not one step will He make you take beyond what your foot is able to endure. Never mind if you think it will not be able for the step that seems to come next; either He will so strengthen it that it shall be able, or He will call a sudden halt, and you shall not have to take it at all.

> I, the Lord, am with thee, be thou not afraid!
> I will help and strengthen, be thou not dismayed!
> Yea, I will uphold thee with My own right hand;
> Thou art called and chosen in My sight to stand.
> Onward then, and fear not, children of the day!
> For His word shall never, never pass away!
> For the year before us, oh, what rich supplies!
> For the poor and needy living streams shall rise;
> For the sad and sinful shall His grace abound;
> For the faint and feeble perfect strength be found.

January 2

A PURPOSEFUL PRESSURE

Thy hand presseth me sore. Psalm 38:2

Have you ever watched the exceedingly delicate and yet firm pressure of the hand of a skillful tuner of string instruments? He will make the string produce a perfectly true note, vibrating in absolute accord with his own never changing tuning-fork. The practiced hand is at one with the accurate ear, and the pressure is brought to bear with most delicate adjustment to the resistance; the tension is never exceeded, he never breaks a string; but he patiently strikes the note again and again, till the tone is true and his ear is satisfied, and then the muscles relax and the pressure ceases. The string may be a poor little thin one, yielding a very small note; but that does not matter at all; it is wanted in its place just as much as a great bass one that can yield a volume of deep sound. The tuner takes just the same pains with it, and is just as satisfied when it vibrates true to the pitch retaining its own individual tone. That string could not tune itself, and no machine was ever invented to accomplish it; nothing but the firm and sensitive pressure of the tuner's own living hand can bring it into tune.

Will you not trust your Tuner, and begin a note of praise, even under the pressure?

'Tis Thy dear hand, O Saviour, that presseth sore,
The hand that bears the nail-prints for evermore.
And now beneath its shadow, hidden by Thee,
The pressure only tells me, Thou lovest me!

January 3

IS YOUR HEART IN IT?

Whatsoever ye do, do it heartily, as to the Lord, and not unto men. Colossians 3:23

In Second Chronicles 31:21 we read of Hezekiah that in every work that he began he did it with all his heart and prospered. It is not merely much pleasanter to be bright and brisk about everything, but it is actually one of God's commands, written in His own Word. I know this is easier to some than to others. Perhaps it comes natural to you to do everything heartily. But even that is not enough. What else? "Whatsoever ye do, do it heartily *as to the Lord,* and not unto men." He knows whether you are seeking to please Him or whether He is forgotten all the while and you think only of the smiles of others. But perhaps it is hard for you to do things heartily. You like better to take your time, and so you dawdle, and do things in an idle way, especially what you do not much like doing. Is this right? Whatsoever ye do, do it heartily! Is it not just as much disobeying God as breaking any other command? Are you not *guilty* before Him? Very likely you never thought of it in this way, but there the words stand, and neither you nor I can alter them. May the Lord give us strength to obey this word of His. And *then* the last word of the verse about Hezekiah will be true of us too — we will be "prospered."

Jesus, Master! Wilt Thou use . . . One who owes Thee more than all?
As Thou wilt! I would not choose, . . . Only let me hear Thy call.
Jesus, let me always be . . . In Thy service glad and free.

January 4

LET THE LORD DO . . .

**Be of good courage, and let us behave ourselves valiantly . . .
and let the Lord do that which is good in his sight.**
1 Chronicles 19:13

Here Joab finds a double army "set against him before and behind." He makes the wisest arrangements he can think of, and encourages his brother; and then he says, ". . . And let the Lord do that which is good in His sight." And what the Lord did was to give him a splendid victory. It does not seem that he had to fight or suffer any loss at all; the Syrians and Ammonites simply fled before him (verses 15-16). "And when the children of Ammon saw that the Syrians were fled, they likewise fled before Abishai his brother, and entered into the city. Then Joab came to Jerusalem. And when the Syrians saw that they were put to the worse before Israel, they sent messengers, and drew forth the Syrians that were beyond the river." Did not these things happen unto them for ensamples? If he, in the dim old days of type and veil, could so trust the God of Israel, should we, who have the light of the knowledge of the glory of God in the face of Jesus Christ, hesitate to utter the same expression of submissive confidence?

Do what Thou wilt! Yes, only do what seemeth good to Thee:
Thou art so loving, wise, and true, it must be best for me.
Send what Thou wilt; or beating shower, soft dew, or brilliant sun;
Alike in still or stormy hour, my Lord, Thy will be done.

January 5

What is that in thine hand?   Exodus 4:2

Let us examine honestly whether it is something which He can use for His glory or not. If not, do not let us hesitate an instant about dropping it. It may be something we do not like to part with; but "the Lord is able to give thee much more than this," and the first glimpse of the excellency of the knowledge of Christ Jesus our Lord will enable us to count those things loss which were gain to us.

But if it is something which He can use, He will make us do ever so much more with it than before. Moses little thought what the Lord was going to make him do with that rod in his hand! The first thing he had to do with it was to cast it on the ground, and see it pass through a startling change. After this he was commanded to take it up again, hard and terrifying as it was to do so. But when it became again a rod in his hand, it was no longer what it was before, the simple rod of a wandering desert shepherd. Henceforth it was "the rod of God in his hand" (Exodus 4:20), wherewith he should do signs, and by which God Himself would do marvelous things (Psalm 78:12).

> The Lord commanded, "Give ye them to eat,"
> Five loaves and two small fishes all their store
> For hungering crowds. He knew they had no more,
> And He had called them to that wild retreat.
> They gave it as He gave them, piece by piece,
> Where on the green grass grouped the great and small
> Till all were filled. So not theirs at all
> But His, the glory of that grand increase.
> Master, I have not strength to serve Thee much,
> The "half-day's work" is all that I can do,
> But let Thy mighty, multiplying touch
> Even to me the miracle renew.
> Let five words feed five thousand, and Thy power
> Expand to life-results one feeble hour.

January 6

REFLECTING OR REJECTING

He will beautify the meek with salvation.   Psalm 149:4
**Thy beauty . . . was perfect through my comeliness, which
I had put upon thee, saith the Lord God.**   Ezekiel 16:14

Look at a poor little colorless drop of water, hanging weakly on a blade of grass. It is not beautiful at all; why should you stop to look at it? Stay till the sun has risen, and now look. It is sparkling like a diamond; and if you look at it from another side, it will be glowing like a ruby, and presently gleaming like an emerald. The poor little drop has become one of the brightest and loveliest things you ever saw. But is it its own brightness and beauty? No! If it slipped down to the ground out of the sunshine, it would be only a poor little dirty drop of water. So, if the Sun of Righteousness, the glorious and lovely Saviour, shines upon you, a little ray of His own brightness and beauty will be seen upon you. Sometimes we can see by the happy light on a face that the Sun is shining there; but if the Sun is really shining, there are sure to be some of the beautiful rays of holiness, love, joy, peace, gentleness, goodness, faith, meekness, making the life, even your life, very lovely.

> Jesus, Lord, I come to Thee, Thou hast said I may;
> Tell me what my life should be, take my sins away.
> Jesus, Lord, I learn of Thee, in Thy Word divine;
> Every promise there I see, may I call it mine!

January 7

TREASURES ALREADY COINED

For ye know the grace of our Lord Jesus Christ, that, though he was rich, yet for your sakes he became poor, that ye through his poverty might be rich.   2 Corinthians 8:9

Yes, through His poverty the unsearchable riches of Christ are for thee. Sevenfold riches are mentioned, and these are no unminted treasure or sealed reserve, but already coined for our use, and stamped with His own image and superscription, and poured freely into the hand of faith. The mere list is wonderful. "Riches of goodness," "riches of forbearance and longsuffering," "riches both of wisdom and knowledge," "riches of mercy," "exceeding riches of grace," and "riches of glory." And His own Word says, "All are yours." Glance on in faith, and think of eternity flowing on and on beyond the mightiest sweep of imagination, and realize that all His riches in glory and the riches of His glory are and shall be for thee. In view of this, shall we care to reserve anything that rust doth corrupt for ourselves?

> Oh, what shining revelation of His treasures God hath given!
> Precious things of grace and glory, precious things of earth and Heaven.
> Holy Spirit, now unlock them with Thy mighty golden key,
> Royal jewels of the kingdom let us now adoring see!

January 8

The Son of God, who loved me, and gave himself for me.
Galatians 2:20

Out of the realized "for me" grows the practical "for Thee."
If the former is a living root, the latter will be its living fruit.
"For Thee!" This makes the difference between forced or for-
mal, and therefore unreasonable service, and the reasonable
service, which is the beginning of the perfect service where
they see His face. This makes the difference between slave
work and free work. For Thee, my Redeemer; for Thee who
hast spoken to my heart; for Thee, who hast done for me —
what? Let us each pause, and fill up that blank with the great
things the Lord hath done for us. For Thee, who art to me—
what? Fill that up, too, before Him! For Thee, my Saviour
Jesus, my Lord and my God!

Help us lovingly to labor, looking for Thy present smile,
Looking for Thy promised blessing, thro' the brightening "little while."
Words for Thee in weakness spoken, Thou wilt here accept and own,
And confess them in Thy glory, when we see Thee on Thy throne.

January 9

GOD—CHRIST—YOU

**We have not an high priest which cannot be touched
with the feeling of our infirmities.**   Hebrews 4:15

Think of Jesus not merely entering into the fact, but into the
feeling of what you are going through. "Touched with the
feeling" — how deep that goes! When we turn away to Him
in our wordless weariness of pain which only He understands,
we find out that we have to do with Him in quite a different
sense from how we have to do with anyone else. We could not
do without Him, and thank God we shall never have to do
without Him.

And we are answerable only to Him in everything. To
our own Master we stand or fall; and that latter alternative
is instantly put out of the question, the apostle adding, "Yea,
he shall be holden up, for God is able to make him stand,"
i.e., he who is his "own Master's" servant. To Him we have
to give account, if from Him we take our orders.

We have to do with Him directly. So directly that it is
difficult at first to grasp the directness. There is absolutely

nothing between the soul and Jesus, if we will but have it
so. We have Himself as our Mediator with God, and the very
characteristic of a mediator is, as Job says, "that he might
lay his hand upon us both"; so the hand of Jesus, who is Himself "the Man of [God's] right hand," is laid upon us with
no intermediate link and no intervening distance. We do not
need any paper and print, let alone any human voice, between
us and Himself.

> *To Thee, O dear, dear Saviour,*
> *My spirit turns for rest.*

That turning is instinctive and instantaneous when we have
once learned what it is to have direct and personal dealing
with the Lord Jesus Christ. Life is altogether a different thing
then, whether shady or sunshiny, and a stranger intermeddleth
not with our hidden joy. Perhaps it is just this that makes
such a strangely felt difference between those who equally
profess and call themselves Christians.

> "My presence shall go with thee, and I will give thee rest!"
> A promise sweetly tender, soothing the anxious breast.
> He knows the lonely spirit, and all its hidden woe;
> He knows the weary yearnings no earthly friend can know.
> Encompassed by that Presence thou wilt not be alone,
> And thou may'st safely rest thee 'neath the shadow of His throne.

January 10

OLD AGE NO BARRIER

**Those that be planted in the house of the Lord shall flourish
in the courts of our God. They shall still bring forth fruit in
old age.**   Psalm 92:13-14

Some of the fruits of the Spirit seem to be especially and
peculiarly characteristic of sanctified older years; and do we
not want to bring them all forth? Look at the splendid ripe-
ness of Abraham's faith in his old age; the grandeur of Moses'
meekness when he went up the mountain alone to die; the
mellowness of Paul's joy in his later Epistles; and the wonderful gentleness of John which makes us almost forget his
early character of "a son of thunder" wanting to call down
God's lightnings of wrath. And the same Spirit is given to
us, that we, too, may bring forth "fruit that may abound,"
and always more fruit.

> Now, the pruning, sharp, unsparing;
> Scattered blossom, bleeding shoot!
> Afterward, the plenteous bearing
> Of the Master's pleasant fruit.

January 11

Father, I will that they also, whom thou hast given me, be with me where I am. John 17:24
Thou hast given him his heart's desire. Psalm 21:2
That where I am, there ye may be also. John 14:3

No more death, neither sorrow, nor crying, neither shall there be any more pain. "And the inhabitant shall not say, I am sick." No more sunsets, no more days of mourning! The troubling of the wicked and the voice of the oppressor ceased forever. No more memory of troubles; no more tears! No more anything that defileth! All this only the negative side of our dear one's present blessedness. Then, the rest for the weary one, the keeping of the Sabbath that remaineth, and yet the service free and perfect and perpetual. The crowns of life, of righteousness, and of glory! The great reward in Heaven full of love-surprises to the consciously unprofitable servant! The far more exceeding weight of glory borne by some to whom the grasshopper had been a burden! The scene of all the blessedness—the better country, the continuing city, the King's palace, the Father's house, the prepared mansions (perhaps full of contrasts to the past pilgrimage)—all summed up in the transcendent simplicity and sublimity of His words, "That where I am, there ye may be also."

> Our fairest dream can never outshine that holy light,
> Our noblest thought can never soar beyond that word of might.
> Our whole anticipation, our Master's best reward,
> Our crown of bliss, is summed in this: "Forever with the Lord!"

January 12

And the Lord passed by before him, and proclaimed, The Lord, The Lord God, merciful and gracious, longsuffering, and abundant in goodness and truth. Exodus 34:6

Every part of God's Word is a revelation, more or less clear, of Himself. When we do not see this, it is only that we miss it, not that it is not there. Do we not know how very possible it is to read the historical parts merely as history, and the prophetical merely as prophecy, and the doctrinal merely as doctrine, and miss the vision of God which everywhere shines through the glass darkly, if only His good Spirit opens our eyes to see it! And even when we do trace out God Himself in His recorded works and ways, how often we miss the personal comfort of remembering our own close and personal interest in what we see of His character and attributes. I question if there is a single chapter, from the first of Genesis to the twenty-second of Revelation, which will not reflect the light of this beautiful little lamp. Whether your gaze is turned upon a promise which reveals Him as the loving One, or a warning which reveals Him as the Just and Holy One; whether you read a history which shows His grand grasp in ordering the centuries, or a verse which shows His delicate touch upon the turn of a moment—as you admire say, "This God is *our* God." When you read, "Great things doeth He which we cannot comprehend," and the splendid variety of His Book gives a glimpse of His power and glory in upholding the things which are seen, from the hosts of million-aged stars to the fleeting flakes of the "treasures of the snow," say, "This God is *our* God."

> Glorious in holiness, fearful in praises,
> Who shall not fear Thee, and who shall not laud?
> Anthems of glory Thy universe raises,
> Holy and Infinite! Father and God!

January 13

BE FILLED

That on the good ground are they, which in an honest and good heart, having heard the word, keep it, and bring forth fruit with patience. Luke 8:15

Once I heard a beautiful prayer which I can never forget; it was this: "Lord, take my lips, and speak through them; take my mind, and think through it; take my heart, and set it on fire." And this is the way the Master keeps the lips of His servants, by so filling their hearts with His love that the outflow cannot be unloving, by so filling their thoughts that the utterance cannot be unChristlike. There must be filling before there can be pouring out; and if there is filling, there must be pouring out for He hath said, "Out of the abundance of the heart the mouth speaketh."

> He is listening; does He hear you speaking of the things of earth,
> Only of its passing pleasure, selfish sorrow, empty mirth?
> He has spoken words of blessing, pardon, peace, and love to you,
> Glorious hopes and gracious comfort, strong and tender, sweet and true;
> Does He hear you telling others something of His love untold,
> Overflowing of thanksgiving for His mercies manifold?

January 14

Upholding all things by the word of his power. Hebrews 1:3
Uphold me according to thy word. Psalm 119:116

Jesus is now "upholding all things by the word of His power."
Shall we then not say, "Uphold me according to Thy word"?
Having therefore these promises, dearly beloved, let us use
them. Let us turn them into prayers of faith. "Hold up my
goings in Thy paths, that my footsteps slip not." (Did David
add the whisper, "but nevertheless, of course, they will slip"?)
"Hold Thou me up and I shall be safe." "When I said, My
foot slippeth, Thy mercy, O Lord held me up" (not picked me
up). Then comes the New Testament echo: "Yea, he shall be
holden up; for God is able to make him stand." But take
"all the counsel of God," for this too is needed: "And thou
standest by faith. Be not high-minded, but fear." Now, if
these promises are worth the paper they are written on, ought
we not to believe and accept and give thanks for them and
go on our way rejoicing, claiming His upholding power not
once for all, not for tomorrow, but always for the next step
of the way?

> Thou knowest not how I uphold the little thou dost scan;
> And how much less canst thou unfold My universal plan,
> Where all thy mind can grasp of space is but a grain of sand—
> The time thy boldest thought can trace, one ripple on the strand!

January 15

DEBTORS TO MERCY ALONE

**I, even I, am he that blotteth out thy transgressions for mine
own sake, and will not remember thy sins.** Isaiah 43:25

There was once a deaf mute, named John. Though he never
heard any other voice, he heard the voice of Jesus, knew it,
loved it, and followed it. One day he told the lady who had
taught him, partly on his fingers and partly by signs, that
he had had a wonderful dream. God had shown him a great
black book; and all his sins were written in it, so many, so
black. And God had shown him hell, all open and fiery, waiting for him, because of all these sins. But Jesus Christ had
come and put His *red hand*, red with the blood of His Cross,
all over the page, and the red hand had blotted out all his
sins; and when God held up the book to the light, He could

not see one left! His word to us today is: "I, even I, am He that blotteth out thy transgressions." It is no fancy or mere feeling, but God's truth, that Jesus Christ's blood has been shed—nothing can alter that; and that His precious blood blotteth out our transgressions, as Paul says (Colossians 2:14), "Blotting out the handwriting of ordinances that was against us." And oh, how much there is to blot out! — sins that you have forgotten, and sins that you did not think were sins at all, besides those you know of—today, yesterday, all the past days of your life. Do you want to know them blotted out? David said, "Blot out all mine iniquities." Take God's word about it, and just believe that it is true, and true for you— "I have blotted out as a thick cloud thy transgressions, and as a cloud thy sins; return unto Me, for I have redeemed thee."

Nothing to pay; yes, nothing to pay!
Jesus has cleared all the debt away;
Blotted it out with His bleeding hand!
Free and forgiven and loved you stand.
Hear the voice of Jesus say,
"Verily thou hast nothing to pay!
Paid is the debt, and the debtor free!
Now I ask thee, lovest thou Me?"

January 16

EVEN YOU ARE A MESSENGER

Then spake Haggai the Lord's messenger in the Lord's message unto the people, saying, I am with you, saith the Lord.
Haggai 1:13

As the cold of snow in the time of harvest, so is a faithful messenger to them that send him: for he refresheth the soul of his masters.
Proverbs 25:13

We are not all called to be the King's ambassadors, but all who have heard the message of salvation for themselves are called to be the Lord's messengers, and day by day, as He gives us opportunity, we are to deliver the Lord's message unto the people. That message, as committed to Haggai, was, "I am with you, saith the Lord." Is there not work enough for any lifetime in unfolding and distributing that one message to His own people? Then, for those who are still far off, we have that equally full message from our Lord to give out, which He has condensed for us into the one word, "Come!"

Yes, we have a word for Jesus! We will bravely speak for Thee,
And Thy bold and faithful soldiers, Saviour, we would henceforth be:
In Thy name set up our banners, while Thine own shall wave above,
With Thy crimson Name of Mercy, and Thy golden Name of Love.

January 17

A FIXED GAZE MAKES A SURE STEP

For the Lord shall be thy confidence, and shall keep thy foot from being taken.   Proverbs 3:26

You cannot keep from stumbling at all, but He is "able to keep you from falling," which in the Greek is strongly and distinctly "without stumbling." The least confidence in or expectation from yourself not only leads to inevitable stumbling but is itself a grievous fall. "But, how shall I be kept?" Jesus Himself has answered: "If any man walk in the day, he stumbleth not, because he seeth the light of this world." "Walk in the light," "looking unto Jesus," and so shall we be "kept by the power of God through faith." We tell a little child to look where it steps and pick its way, but Christ's little children are to do just the opposite; they are to look away to Him. "Let thine eyes look (not down, but) right on, and let thine eyelids look straight before thee," and it is on Him, the Light of the world, that the gaze must be fixed.

> Look away to Jesus, look away from all;
> Then we need not stumble, then we shall not fall.
> From each snare that lureth, foe or phantom grim,
> Safety this ensureth: look away to Him.

January 18

HE SAID HE WOULD

Who is a God like unto thee?   Micah 7:18
God granted him that which he requested. 1 Chronicles 4:10
And I have also given thee that which thou hast not asked.
                                                  1 Kings 3:13

All God's goodness to us is humbling. The more He does for us, the more ready we are to say, "I am not worthy of the least of all the mercies, and of all the truth, which Thou hast shewed unto Thy servant." The weight of a great answer to prayer seems almost too much for us. The grace of it is "too wonderful" for us. It throws up in such startling relief the disproportion between our little, poor, feeble cry and the great, shining response of God's heart and hand, that we can only say, "Who am I, O Lord God, that Thou hast brought me hitherto? Is this the manner of man, O Lord

God?" But it is more humbling still, when we stand face to face with great things which the Lord hath done for us and given us, which we never asked for at all, never even thought of asking, with which not even a prayer had to do. It is so humbling to get a view of these, that Satan tries to set up a false humility to hinder us from standing still and considering how great things the Lord hath done for us. Thus he also contrives to defraud our generous God of the glory due unto His Name.

> I stood amazed, and whispered, "Can it be
> That He hath granted all the boon I sought?
> How wonderful that He for me hath wrought!
> How wonderful that He hath answered me!"
> O faithless heart! He said that He would hear
> And answer thy poor prayer, and He hath heard
> And proved His promise. Wherefore didst thou fear?
> Why marvel that thy Lord hath kept His word?
> More wonderful if He should fail to bless
> Expectant faith and prayer with good success!

January 19

HIS PLACE BY RIGHT

Who is gone into heaven, and is on the right hand of God; angels and authorities and powers being made subject unto him.
1 Peter 3:22

He is able even to subdue all things unto Himself *in this inner kingdom* which we cannot govern at all. We are so glad to take Him at His Word, and give up the government into His hands, asking Him to be our King in very deed, and to set up His throne of peace in the long-disturbed and divided citadel, praying that He would bring every thought into captivity to His gentle obedience. We have had enough of revolutions and revolts, of tyrants and traitors, of lawlessness and of self-framed codes. Other lords (and, oh, how many!) have had dominion over us. He has permitted us to be their servants, that now, by blessed and restful contrast, we may know His service. Now we only want "another King, one Jesus." He has made us willing in the day of His power, and that was the first act of His reign, and the token that "of the increase of His government and peace there shall be no end" in our hearts.

> Reign over me, Lord Jesus, oh, make my heart Thy throne.
> It shall be Thine forever, it shall be Thine alone.

January 20

FIRST THINGS FIRST

For if there be first a willing mind, it is accepted according to that a man hath, and not according to that he hath not.
2 Corinthians 8:12

It is important to remember that there is no much or little in God's sight, except as relatively to our means and willingness. He knows what we have not, as well as what we have. He knows all about the low wages in one sphere, and the small allowance, or the fixed income with rising prices in another. And it is not a question of paying to God what can be screwed out of these, but of giving Him all, and then holding all at His disposal, and taking His orders about the disposal of all.

> Oh, let me give
> Out of the gifts Thou freely givest;
> Oh, let me live
> With life abundantly because Thou livest;
> Oh, make me shine
> In darkest places, for Thy light is mine;
> Oh, let me be
> A faithful witness for Thy truth and Thee.

January 21

GOD'S SIDE — THE BRIGHT SIDE

And thine age shall be clearer than the noonday; thou shalt shine forth, thou shalt be as the morning.
Job 11:17

I suppose nobody ever naturally did like the idea of getting older, after he had at least left school. There is a sense of oppression and depression about it. The irresistible, inevitable onward march of moments and years without the possibility of one instant's pause—a march that even while on the uphill side of life is leading to the downhill side—casts an autumn-like shadow over even many a spring-birthday. But how surely the Bible gives us the bright side of everything. In this case it gives three bright sides of a fact which, without it, could not help being gloomy. First, it opens the sure prospect of increasing brightness to those who have begun to walk in the light. Even if the sun of our life has reached the apparent zenith and we have known a very noonday of mental and spiritual being, it is no poetic western shadows that are to lengthen upon our way but "our age is to be clearer than the noonday." The second bright side is increasing fruitfulness.

Do not let us confuse between works and fruit. Even when we come to the days when "the strong men shall bow themselves," there may be more pleasant fruits for our Master, riper, fuller, and sweeter than ever before. For "they shall still bring forth fruit in old age." The third bright side is the brightest of all, "Even to your old age, I am He" . . . "even to hoar hairs will I carry you." For we shall always be His little children and doubtless He will always be our Father. The rush of years cannot touch this.

> But when the sun draws near in westering might,
> Enfolding all in one transcendent blaze
> Of sunset glow, we trace them not, but gaze
> And wonder at the glorious holy light.
> Come nearer, Sun of Righteousness! that we,
> Whose swift short hours of day so swiftly run,
> So overflowed with love and light may be,
> So lost in glory of the nearing Sun,
> That not our light, but Thine, the world may see,
> New praise to Thee through our poor lives be won.

January 22

"AND"

Whom God hath set forth to be a propitiation through faith in his blood, to declare his righteousness . . . that he might be just, and the justifier of him which believeth in Jesus.
Romans 3:25, 26
Till heaven and earth pass, one jot or one tittle shall in no wise pass from the law, till all be fulfilled. Matthew 5:18

How precious that little word "and" becomes as we read, "He is just, *and* having salvation." "A merciful *and* faithful High Priest." "A just God *and* a Saviour." We do not half value God's little words. His justice is, if we may reverently say so, the strong point of His atoning work. The costly means of our redemption were paid for at full price. He fulfilled the Law. There was nothing wanting in all the work which His Father gave Him to do. He finished it. And His Father was satisfied. Thus He was just towards His Father, that He might be faithful and just to forgive us our sins. It is no weak compassion, merely wrought on by misery, but strong, grand, infinite, and equal justice and mercy, balanced, as they never are in human minds. For only the ways of the Lord are thus equal.

> In Thy sovereignty rejoicing, we Thy children bow and praise,
> For we know that kind and loving, just and true, are all Thy ways.
> While Thy heart of sovereign mercy, and Thine arm of sovereign might,
> For our great and strong salvation, in Thy sovereign grace unite.

January 23

Have not I written to thee excellent things? Proverbs 22:20

If I had something very special to tell you, and instead of saying it with my voice I wrote it down on a piece of paper, and gave it to you to look at, would not that be exactly the same as if I had told you with my lips? And you would take the paper eagerly to see what it was that I had said to you. So today, when you read your Bible, either alone or with the family, watch to see what Jesus will say to you in it. You will never watch in vain. You will see some word that seems to come home to you, and that you had never noticed so much before. Oh, listen lovingly to it, for *that* is what He says to you! Or if you are really watching and wishing for a word from Him, some sweet text will come into your mind, and you wonder what made you think of it! That is the voice of Jesus speaking to your heart. Listen to it, and treasure it up, and follow it; and then watch to see what else He will say to you. Say to Him, "Master, say on."

> But as I lay and waited for the sleep
> That had been asked, the Book beside my hand
> Lured me to glance at lightly opening leaves.
> Did not Thy loving Spirit guide the glance
> That fell upon the unsought word of power:
> "He is thy Lord!" So simple, yet so strong,
> So all-embracing! oh, it was enough
> To chase away all mists and glooms of life.

January 24

UNKNOWN PATHS ARE CLEAR TO HIM

And he saw them toiling in rowing; for the wind was contrary unto them. Mark 6:48

In perplexities: when we cannot understand what is going on around us, cannot tell whither events are tending, cannot tell what to do, because we cannot see into or through the matter before us, let us be calmed and steadied and made patient by the thought that what is hidden from us is not hidden from Him. If He chooses to guide us blindfold, let Him do it! It will not make the least difference to the reality and rightness of the guidance. In mysteries: when we see no clue, when we cannot understand God's partial revelation, when we cannot lift the veil that hangs before His secret counsel, when we cannot pierce the holy darkness that enshrouds His ways, or tread the great deep of His judgments where His footsteps are not known, is it not enough that even these matters are not hid from our King? "My Father will do nothing, either great or small, but He will show it me." "For the Father loveth the Son, and showeth Him all things that Himself doeth." Our King could so easily reveal everything to us, make everything so clear! It would be nothing to Him to tell us all our questions. When He does not, cannot we trust Him, and just be satisfied that He knows, and would tell us if it were best? He has many things to say unto us, but He waits till we can bear them. May we be glad that even our sins are not hid from Him? Yes, surely, for He who knows all, can and will cleanse all. He has searched us and known us, as we should shrink from knowing ourselves, and yet He has pardoned, and yet He loves!

> Not yet thou knowest how I bid each passing hour entwine
> Its grief or joy, its hope or fear, in one great love-design;
> Nor how I lead thee through the night, by many a various way,
> Still upward to unclouded light, and onward to the day.

January 25

WHAT IS HIS IS OURS

I am the vine, ye are the branches. John 15:5

Why does the sap flow from the vine to the branch? Simply because the branch is joined to the vine. Then the sap flows into it by the very law of its nature. So, being joined to our Lord Jesus by faith, that which is His becomes ours, and flows into us by the very law of our spiritual life. If there were no hindrance, it would indeed flow as a river. Then how earnestly we should seek to have every barrier removed to the inflowing of such a gift. Let it be our prayer that He will clear the way for it, that He will take away all the unbelief, all the self, all the hidden cloggings of the channel. Then He will give a sevenfold blessing: *My* peace, *My* joy, *My* love, at once and always, now and forever; *My* grace and *My* strength for all the needs of our pilgrimage; *My* rest and *My* glory for all the grand, sweet home-life of eternity with Him.

> Blessed be the God and Father of our Saviour Jesus Christ,
> Who hath blessed us with such blessings all uncounted and unpriced!
> Let our high and holy calling, and our strong salvation be,
> Theme of never-ending praises, God of sovereign grace, to Thee!

January 26

I have loved you, saith the Lord. Malachi 1:2

How different these words are from what we should have
expected! We should have expected God to say, "I will love
you, if you will love Me." But, no! He says, "I *have* loved
you." Yes, He has loved you already, poor, restless heart,
that wants to be loved! He loves you now, and will love you
always. But you say, "I wish I knew whether He loves *me!*"
Why, He *tells* you so; and what could He say more? There
it stands—"I have loved you, saith the Lord." It is true, and
you need only believe it, and be glad of it, and tell Him how
glad you are that He loves you. "God commendeth His love
toward us, in that, while we were yet sinners, Christ died for
us." He says nothing about good people, but tells you that
He loved you so much, while you were sinful, that He sent the
Lord Jesus, His own Son to die for you. Could He do more than
that? He says in the same verse (Malachi 1:2), *"Yet* ye say,
Wherein hast Thou loved us?" *Wherein?* Oh *herein!* not that
you loved God, but that He loved you, and sent His Son to
suffer instead of you. Think how many answers you can find
to that question, "Wherein hast Thou loved us?" See how
many proofs of His love you can count up; and then rest on
this soft, safe pillow, "I have loved you, saith the Lord."

Thou art Mine! oh, therefore fear not! Mine forever now;
And the flame shall never kindle on thy sealed brow.
Thou art precious, therefore fear not, precious unto Me!
I have made thee for My glory, I have loved thee.

January 27

**Awake, O sword, against my shepherd, and against the man
that is my fellow, saith the Lord of hosts: smite the shepherd.**
Zechariah 13:7

Not the hand of an impotent foe, but the sharp sword of the
omnipotent Lord of Hosts was lifted to smite His Shepherd—
our Shepherd-King, the Great, the Chief, the Good (and the
Beautiful as the original implies). Think of the words,
"stricken, smitten of God," with their unknown depths of
agony, and then of Jesus, Him whom we love, fathoming
those black depths of agony alone! "Jesus smitten of God!"

Can we even say the words, and not feel moved as no other grief could move us? Do not let us shrink from dwelling upon it; let us rather seek that the Holy Spirit, even now, might show us a little of what this awful smiting really was—to show us our dear Lord Jesus Christ, in this tremendous proving of His own and His Father's love — to whisper in our hearts as we gaze upon the Crucified One, "Behold your King." We can only stand afar off, bowed and hushed in shuddering love, as the echoes of the awful stripes that fell on Him float down through the listening centuries, while each throb of the healed heart replies, "For me! For me!" "I have trodden the wine press alone, and of the people there was none with Me."

> I suffered much for thee,
> More than thy tongue can tell
> Of bitterest agony,
> To rescue thee from hell.
> I suffered much for thee;
> What canst thou bear for Me?

January 28

ENJOYING GOD'S JOYS

Who giveth us richly all things to enjoy. 1 Timothy 6:17

"Richly." So richly, that if you tried to write down half His gifts to you, your hand would tire long before you had done. You might easily make a list of gifts given to you by others, but you could not make a list of what God gives you every day of your life. "All things." All the things you really need, and a great many more besides. All the things that will do you good, a great many more than you would ever have thought of. All the things that He can fill your hands with, and trust you to carry without stumbling and falling. All things, everything that you have. "To enjoy." Now how kind this is! Not only to do us good, but to enjoy. So you see He means you to be happy with what He gives you, and not to be dismal and melancholy. If you do not enjoy what He giveth, that is your own fault, for He meant you to enjoy it. Look up to Him with a bright smile, and thank Him for having given you richly all things to enjoy!

> My joys to Thee I bring,
> The joys Thy love hath given,
> That each may be a wing
> To lift me nearer Heaven.
> I bring them, Saviour, all to Thee,
> For Thou hast purchased all for me.

January 29

**When I remember thee upon my bed, and meditate on thee
in the night watches.**   Psalm 63:6

Memory is never so busy as in the quiet time while we are
waiting for sleep; and never, perhaps, are we more tempted
to useless recollections and idle reveries than in the night
watches. Perhaps we have regretfully struggled against them;
perhaps yielded to effortless indulgence in them and thought
we could not help it and were hardly responsible for vain
thoughts at such times. But here is full help and bright hope.
This night let us "remember Thee." We can only remember
what we already know. Oh, praise Him, then, that we have
material for memory! There is enough for all the wakeful
nights of a lifetime in the one word "Thee." It leads us straight
to "His own self." Dwelling on that one word "Thee," faith,
hope, and love wake up, and feed, and grow.

> His Spirit shines upon His Word, and makes it sweet indeed,
> Just like a shining lamp held up beside me as I read;
> And brings it to my mind again alone upon my bed,
> Till all abroad within my heart the love of God is shed.

January 30

Why should the king recompense it me with such a reward?
                                                2 Samuel 19:36

Barzillai had provided the king of sustenance while he lay
at Mahanaim, exiled from his royal city. When the day of
triumphant return came, David said to him, "Come thou over
with me, and I will feed thee with me in Jerusalem." This
was the reward. But what a privilege and delight it must
have been to the loyal old man! And to come nearer, what a
continual joy it must have been to the women who ministered
to the exiled King of Heaven of their substance. How very
much one would have liked a share in that ministry! Why
should the king recompense it me with such a reward? Why
should thy servant dwell in the royal city with thee? For
there is such a tremendous disproportion between the work
and the reward, though such a glorious proportion between
His love and His reward. And yet there is a beautiful fitness
in it. The banquet of everlasting joy for those who gave Him

meat; the river of His pleasures for those who gave Him drink; the mansions in the Father's home for those who took the stranger in; the white robes for those who clothed the naked; the tree of life and no more pain for those who visited the sick; the glorious liberty for those who came unto the prisoner; the crown of all, the repeatedly promised "with Me," for those who were content to be with His sorrowful or suffering ones for His sake. Why all this? I suppose we shall keep on asking that forever!

> What shall I render to my glorious King?
> I have but that which I receive from Thee;
> And what I give, Thou givest back to me,
> Transmuted by Thy touch; each worthless thing
> Changed to the preciousness of gem or gold,
> And by Thy blessing multiplied a thousandfold.

January 31

LOOK FULL IN HIS WONDERFUL FACE

Who will shew us any good? Lord, lift thou up the light of thy countenance upon us. Psalm 4:6

Thus the light of His countenance shall save us. In Psalm 44:3, we see it as the means of past salvation, and in Psalm 42:5, the Psalmist anticipates praise for its future help; while the two are beautifully linked by the marginal reading of the latter, which makes it present salvation: "Thy presence is salvation." Then follows peace. The waves are stilled, and the storm-clouds flee away noiselessly and swiftly and surely, when He lifts up the light of His countenance upon us, and gives us peace. For this uplifting is the shining forth of His favor — the smile instead of the frown; and as we walk in the light of it, the peace will grow into joy, and we shall be even here and now exceeding glad with His countenance, while every step will bring us nearer to the resurrection joy of Christ Himself, saying with Him, "Thou shalt make me full of joy with Thy countenance." So we shall find day by day, that in the light of the King's countenance is cleansing, salvation, peace and joy — and do not these make up life, the new life, the glad life of the children of the King?

> The fullness of His blessing encompasseth our way;
> The fullness of His promises crowns every brightening day;
> The fullness of His glory is beaming from above,
> While more and more we realize the fullness of His love.

February 1

CHRIST "IS" THE ANSWER

My soul, wait thou only upon God; for my expectation is from him. Psalm 62:5

Do not let us reserve God's promises for some far future time. In connection with chastening the Lord did not say, "a long while afterward" and do not let us gratuitously insert it. It rather implies that as soon as the chastening is over, the peaceable fruit shall appear "unto the glory and praise of God." So let us look out for the afterward as soon as the pressure is past. This immediate expectation will bring its own blessing if we can say, "My expectation is from Him," and not from any fruit-bearing qualities of our own, for only "from Me is thy fruit found." Fruit from Him will also be fruit unto Him.

> What shall Thine "afterward" be, O Lord?
> I wonder, and wait to see,
> (While to Thy chastening hand I bow,)
> What peaceable fruit may be ripening now,
> Ripening fast for me!

February 2

NOW AND AFTERWARD

My glory was fresh in me. Job 29:20

Who does not know the longing for freshness? Fresh air, fresh water, fresh flowers, the freshness of children, and of some people's conversation and writings—all illustrate or lead up to that spiritual freshness which is both pleasure and power. For it was when Job's glory was fresh in him, that his bow was renewed in his hand. Freshness and glory! and yet the brilliant music of such words is brought down to a minor strain by one little touch—it "was," not it "is"; a melancholy past instead of a bright present. Now, instead of saddening ourselves unnecessarily by sighing, "Ah, yes! that is always the way," let us see how we may personally prove that it is not always the way, and that Job's confessedly exceptional experience need not, and ought not, to be ours.

If our glory is to be fresh in us, it all depends upon what the glory in us is. If it is any sort of our own — anything connected with that which decayeth and waxeth old in us or passeth away around us—of course, it cannot be always fresh, any more than the freshness of dawn or of springtime can last. Neither material nor mental states can retain their exquisite and subtle charm, and spiritual states are no better off; "frames and feelings" have an inherent tendency to subside into flatness, dullness, staleness, or whatever else expresses the want of freshness. There is only one unfailing source of unfailing freshness—Christ Himself. "Thou hast the dew of Thy youth" — the only dew that never dries up through any heat or dust. "Christ in you, the hope of glory."

> Thy reign shall still increase!
> I claim Thy word,
> Let righteousness and peace
> And joy in the Holy Ghost be found,
> And more and more abound
> In me, through Thee, O Christ my Lord;
> Take unto Thee Thy power, who art
> My Sovereign, many crowned!
> Stablish Thy kingdom in my heart.

February 3

LET GOD GUIDE YOUR SPENDING

The silver is mine, and the gold is mine, saith the Lord of hosts. Haggai 2:8

When we have asked the Lord to take, and continually trust Him to keep our money, shopping becomes a different thing. We look up to our Lord for guidance to lay out His money prudently and rightly, and as He would have us lay it out. The gift or garment is selected consciously under His eye, and with conscious reference to Him as our own dear Master, for whose sake we shall give it, or in whose service we shall wear it, and with whose own silver or gold we shall pay for it, and then it is all right.

> What though the eastern monarch's robes are gleaming
> With gold and orient gems, each gorgeous hue
> With more than rainbow brightness in them beaming;
> The robes of Heaven are woven light, and ever new.
> All these are beautiful; and we may love them
> As His good gifts; but oh! they pass away:
> Then cling not to them; seek, far, far above them
> The joys ineffable, which fade not, nor decay.
> To see, and know, and love, and praise forever
> The Saviour who hath died that we might live,
> Where sorrow, pain, and death may enter never!
> And ever learn new cause, new songs of praise to give!
> Oh, what a prospect! How, how can we cling
> To earth's dark dream, when such a hope is given?
> Oh, may we from this hour, on faith-plumed wing,
> No longer cling to earth, but soar to yon bright Heaven!

February 4

FILLED TO OVERFLOWING

Go your way, tell . . . and she went and told. Mark 16:7, 10

Bear witness, tell it out, you with whom the King dwells in peace! Life is filled with bright interests, time is filled with happy work or peaceful waiting, the mind is filled with His beautiful words and thoughts, the heart is filled with His presence, and you abide satisfied with Him! Yes, tell it out!

> There were strange soul-depths, restless, vast and broad,
>   Unfathomed as the sea;
> An infinite craving for some infinite stilling;
> But now Thy perfect love is perfect filling!
> Lord Jesus Christ, my Lord, my God,
>   Thou, Thou art enough for me!

February 5

LIFE AND "LIPS" FOR THE MASTER

O Lord, open thou my lips; and my mouth shall shew forth thy praise. Psalm 51:15

When our lips are opened, oh, how much one does want to have them so kept for Jesus that He may be free to make the most of them, not letting them render second-rate and indirect service when they might be doing direct and first-rate service to His cause and kingdom! It is terrible how much less is done for Him than might be done, in consequence of the specious notion that if what we are doing or saying is not bad, we are doing good in a certain way, and therefore may be quite easy about it. Do we not take a lower standard, and spend our strength in just making ourselves agreeable and pleasant, creating a general good impression in favor of religion, showing that we can be all things to all men, and that one who is supposed to be a citizen of the other world can be very well up in all that concerns this world? This may be good, but is there nothing better? What does it profit if we do make this favorable impression on an outsider, if we go no farther and do not use the influence gained to bring him right inside the fold, inside the only Ark of Safety? People are not converted by this sort of work, at any rate I never met or heard of any one. "He thinks it better for his quiet influence to tell!" said an affectionately excusing relative of one who had plenty of special opportunities of soul winning, if he had only used his lips as well as his life for his Master. "And how many souls have been converted to God by his quiet influence all these years?" was my reply. And to that there was no answer! For the silent shining was all very beautiful in theory, but not one of the many souls placed specially under his influence had been known to be brought out of darkness into marvelous light. If they had, they must have been known, for such light can't help being seen.

O teach me, Lord, that I may teach
The precious things Thou dost impart;
And wing my words, that they may reach
The hidden depths of many a heart.
O fill me with Thy fullness, Lord,
Until my very heart o'erflow
In kindling thought and glowing word,
Thy love to tell, Thy praise to show.
O use me, Lord, use even me,
Just as Thou wilt, and when, and where;
Until Thy blessed face I see,
Thy rest, Thy joy, Thy glory share.

February 6

NOT SPIRED BUT INSPIRED

All this . . . the Lord made me understand in writing by his hand upon me, even all the works of this pattern.
1 Chronicles 28:19

This cannot mean that the Lord gave David a miraculously written scroll, because a few verses before, it says that he had it all by the Spirit. So what else can it mean but that as David wrote, the hand of the Lord was upon his hand, impelling him to trace, letter by letter, the right words of description for all the details of the temple that Solomon should build with its courts and chambers, its treasuries and vessels? Have we not sometimes sat down to write, feeling perplexed and ignorant, and wishing someone were there to tell us what to say? At such a moment, whether it were a mere note for post, or a sheet for press, it is a great comfort to recollect this mighty laying of a divine hand upon a human one, and ask for the same help from the same Lord. It is sure to be given!

What shall be our word for Jesus? Master, give it day by day;
Ever as the need arises, teach Thy children what to say.
Give us holy love and patience; grant us deep humility,
That of self we may be emptied, and our hearts be full of Thee;
Give us zeal and faith and fervor, make us winning, make us wise,
Single-hearted, strong and fearless—Thou hast called us, we will rise!
Let the might of Thy good Spirit go with every loving word;
And by hearts prepared and opened be our message always heard!

February 7

MANIFOLD PLEASURES UNENDING

At thy right hand there are pleasures for evermore. Psalm 16:11

You never had a pleasure that lasted. You look forward to a great pleasure, and it comes, and then, very soon it is gone, and you can only look back upon it. The very longest and pleasantest day you ever had came to an end. How different are the pleasures at God's right hand! They are for evermore, and you cannot get to the end or see to the end of evermore, for there is no end to it. And it is not one pleasure only, but *pleasures,* as manifold as they are unending. We can only tell a few things about them. They will be holy pleasures, never mingled with any sin. They will be perfect pleasures, with nothing whatever to spoil them. They will be lasting pleasures, for our text says so. They will be abundant pleasures for David says, "They shall be *abundantly satisfied* with the fatness of Thy house, and Thou shalt make them drink of the river of Thy pleasures." They will be always freshly-flowing pleasures, for they are a river, not a pool. They will be pleasures given by God Himself to us, for it does not say, "They shall drink," but *"Thou* shalt *make them* drink of the river of Thy pleasures."

> Infinite the ocean-joy
>   Opening to His children's view;
> Infinite their varied treasure,
> Meted not by mortal measure —
> Holy knowledge, holy pleasure,
> Through Eternity's great leisure,
>   Like its praises, ever new.

February 8

DISGUISED SWEETNESS

Thou holdest mine eyes waking. Psalm 77:4

If we could always say, night after night, "I will both lay me down in peace and sleep," receiving in full measure the Lord's quiet gift to His beloved, we should not learn the disguised sweetness of this special word for the wakeful ones. When the wearisome nights come, it is hushing to know that they are appointed. But this is something nearer and closer-bringing, something individual and personal; not only an appointment,

but an act of our Father: "Thou holdest mine eyes waking."
It is not that He is merely not giving us sleep; it is not a
denial, but a different dealing. Every moment that the tired
eyes are sleepless, it is because our Father is holding them
waking. It seems so natural to say, "How I wish I could go to
sleep!" Yet even that restless wish may be soothed by the
happy confidence in our Father's hand, which will not relax its
hold upon the weary eyelids until the right moment has come
to let them fall in slumber.

He hath spoken in the darkness, in the silence of the night,
Spoken sweetly of the Father, words of life and love and light.
Floating thro' the sombre stillness came the loved and loving Voice,
Speaking peace and solemn gladness, that His children might rejoice.
What He tells thee in the darkness, songs He giveth in the night—
Rise and speak it in the morning, rise and sing them in the light!

February 9

ARE YOU PLEASING GOD?

Thy will be done in earth, as it is in heaven. Matthew 6:10
Teach me to do thy will. Psalm 143:10

When you see someone doing with very great delight some
beautiful and pleasant piece of work, have you not thought,
"I should like to be able to do that!" and perhaps you have
said, "Please teach me how to do it." Can you think of anything more pleasant to do than what the very angels are full of
delight in doing? Can you think of anything more beautiful to
do than what is done in the pleasant land, the beautiful home
above? Can you fancy anything more interesting to do than
what the dwellers there will never get tired of doing for
thousands of millions of years? One version of this verse says,
"Teach me to do the thing that pleaseth Thee." So doing God's
will is just doing the things, one by one, that please Him.
Why did David ask this? He goes on to say why—"For Thou
art my God." If God is really our God, we too shall wish to
do the thing that pleaseth Him. David did not think he could
do it of himself, for he says, "Let Thy loving Spirit lead me."
That loving Spirit will lead you too, so that even on earth you
may begin to do what the angels are doing in Heaven.

It is but very little for Him that I can do,
Then let me seek to serve Him, my earthly journey through;
And without sigh or murmur, to do His holy will;
And in my daily duties His wise commands fulfill.

February 10

AN IDEAL FRIEND

I have called you friends. John 15:15

Who has not longed for an ideal and yet a real friend—one who should exactly understand us, to whom we could tell everything, and in whom we could altogether confide—one who should be very wise and very true—one of whose love and unfailing interest we could be certain? There are other points for which we could not hope—that this friend should be very far above us, and yet the very nearest and dearest, always with us, always thinking of us; always doing kind and wonderful things for us; undertaking and managing everything; forgetting nothing, failing in nothing; quite certain never to change and never to die—so that this one grand friendship should fill our lives, and that we never need trouble about anything for ourselves any more. Such is our Royal Friend, and more; for no human possibilities of friendship can illustrate what He is to those to whom He says, "Ye are my friends." We, even we, may look up to our glorious King, our Lord and our God, and say, "This is my Beloved, and this is my Friend!" And then we, even we, may claim the privilege of being the King's companion and the King's friend.

> I could not do without Thee, O Jesus, Saviour dear!
> E'en when my eyes are holden, I know that Thou art near.
> How dreary and how lonely this changeful life would be,
> Without the sweet communion, the secret rest with Thee!

February 11

REDEEMED — SEPARATED — CONFIRMED

What one nation in the earth is like thy people, even like Israel, whom God went to redeem for a people to himself, and to make him a name, and to do for you great things and terrible, for thy land, before thy people, which thou redeemedst to thee from Egypt, from the nations and their gods? For thou hast confirmed to thyself thy people Israel to be a people unto thee for ever: and thou, Lord, art become their God. 2 Samuel 7:23-24

One thought containing three thoughts seems to pervade this epitome of the history of God's people. The one thought is "Unto Thee." The three thoughts contained in it are: Redeemed, Separated, Confirmed unto Thee. (1) God went to redeem His people. It was no easy sitting still, no costless fiat:

"Thou wentest forth for the salvation of Thy people, even for salvation with Thine Anointed." These "goings forth have been from . . . the days of eternity," and we have seen by faith these "goings of my God, my King." He did it because He would do for you great things and terrible—great things in mercy, terrible things in righteousness—bringing all His sublimely balanced attributes to bear on His great work for you. "Before His people," that we might see and know and believe and praise. (2) This redemption to Himself necessarily involved separation from Egypt, from the nations and their gods. We cannot have the "to" without the "from" any more than we could go to the Equator and not come away from the Arctic regions. And the test and proof of the "to Thee" lies in the "from Egypt." (3) How magnificently God seals all His transactions! So He has not only redeemed and separated us unto Himself but "Thou hast confirmed to Thyself Thy people Israel." He, not we. His hands laid the foundation and His hands shall also finish it. He stablisheth us in Christ and He "hath also sealed us." He shall also "confirm you unto the end."

> O Thou chosen church of Jesus, glorious, blessed and secure,
> Founded on the one foundation, which forever shall endure;
> Not thy holiness or beauty can thy strength and safety be,
> But the everlasting love wherewith Jehovah loveth thee.

February 12

FIRST LEARN — THEN TELL

Now the Lord had told Samuel in his ear. 1 Samuel 9:15
What ye hear in the ear, preach ye. Matthew 10:27

It is a specially sweet part of the Lord's dealings with His messengers that He always gives us the message for ourselves first. It is what He has first told us in the darkness — that is, in the secrecy of our own rooms, or at least of our own hearts — that He bids us speak in light. And so the more we sit at His feet and watch to see what He has to say to ourselves, the more we shall have to tell to others. He does not send us out with sealed dispatches, which we know nothing about, and with which we have no concern.

> He hath spoken in the darkness, in the silence of thy grief,
> Sympathy so deep and tender, mighty for thy heart relief;
> Speaking in thy night of sorrow words of comfort and of calm,
> Gently on thy wounded spirit pouring true and healing balm.
> What He tells thee in the darkness, weary watcher for the day,
> Grateful lip and life should utter when the shadows flee away.

February 13

I have redeemed thee, I have called thee by thy name; thou art mine. Isaiah 43:1

It was not only to purchase them out of bondage and death as one might buy a captive thrush on a winter evening and let it loose into the hungry cold and think no more about it; it was to redeem them unto Himself, to be His own portion and inheritance and treasure and delight, to be a "people near unto Him," to be the objects on which all His divine love might be poured out to be the very opportunity of His joy. His glory and our good were inseparably joined in it. He did it "to make Him a name," and we may reverently say that even the very Name which is above every name could not have been the crown of the exaltation of the Son of God but for this.

> O mystery of grace,
> That chooseth us to stand before Thy face,
> To be Thy special treasure,
> Thy portion, Thy delight, Thine own;
> That taketh pleasure
> In them that fear Thy Name, that hope alone
> In Thy sweet mercy's boundless measure.

February 14

ALTOGETHER LOVELY

Yea, he is altogether lovely. Song of Solomon 5:16

We do not need to ask, "Who?" for these words could only be said of One, the Beloved One, the Holy One, the Blessed One, the Glorious One! Only of Jesus, whom having not seen we love, whom we shall see one day in all His beauty, when He shall come to be glorified in His saints, and to be admired in all them that believe! Oh! If we could see Him now, as He is at this very moment, sitting at the right hand of the Majesty on High, Himself the very brightness of God's glory, the splendor would be too great, we should fall at His feet as dead, as John did. But if He laid His right hand upon us, saying, "Fear not," and we looked again, what should we see? Oh, what loveliness! Oh, what unspeakable beauty! Fairer than the children of men, and "the chiefest among ten thousand," is our Lord Jesus! And in all the glory He is "this same Jesus"; although His countenance is now as the sun shineth in His strength, there is the gentle smile for His children, and the tender kindness for the weary, and the wonderful look of mighty love that would bring the whole world to His feet if they could only see it. And there are scars too, which make His very beauty more beautiful, for they are scars of love. He did not lose the print of the nails when He rose from the grave, and the angels and redeemed ones around Him can see them even now; for even in the midst of the throne He is the Lamb as it had been slain. So the love has overflowed the glory, and our Lord Jesus is altogether lovely. Our Lord Jesus! Yes, for the Altogether Lovely One has given Himself to us; so that the least of His saints may look up and say, "This is my Beloved, and this is my Friend."

> O Saviour, precious Saviour, my heart is at Thy feet;
> I bless Thee, and I love Thee, and Thee I long to meet.
> To see Thee in Thy beauty, to see Thee face to face,
> To see Thee in Thy glory, and reap Thy smile of grace!

February 15

INSTRUMENTS FOR GOD'S USE

Yield . . . your members as instruments of righteousness unto God.   Romans 6:13

What are your members? Hands, feet, lips, eyes, ears, and so on. What are we to do with them? "Yield" them, that is, give them up altogether, hand them over to God. What for? That He may use them as instruments of righteousness. That is, just as we should take an instrument of music, to make music with it, so He may take our hands and feet and all our members, and use them to do right and good things with. If we have given ourselves to God, every part of our body is to be God's servant, an intrument for Him to use. All our members will leave off serving Satan, and find something to do for God, for if we yield them to God, He will really take them and use them. We will be surprised to find in how many ways He will use our members, if we give them and our whole self to Him. We will never be miserable again with "nothing to do!"

> "Not your own!" but His ye are, who hath paid a price untold
> For your life, exceeding far all earth's store of gems and gold.
> With the precious blood of Christ, ransom treasure all unpriced,
> Full redemption is procured, full salvation is assured.

February 16

I . . . will watch to see what he will say unto me. Habakkuk 2:1

When the Lord Jesus said to Simon the Pharisee, "Simon, I
have somewhat to say unto thee," he answered, "Master, say
on!" When God was going to speak to Samuel, he said, "Speak,
Lord, for Thy servant heareth." Has the Lord Jesus said anything like this for us? He says, "I have yet many things to
say unto you." What things? They will be strong, helpful, life-
giving words, for He says, "The words that I speak unto you,
they are spirit and they are life." They will be loving words,
for He says, "I will speak comfortably to her" (margin, "I will
speak to her heart"). And they will be very kind and tender
words, and spoken just at the right moment, for He says He
knows "how to speak a word in season to him that is weary."
But will He really speak to me? Yes, if you will only watch
to see what He will say unto you. For it will be a still, small
voice, and you will not hear it at all if you do not listen for it.

Master, speak! I kneel before Thee, listening, longing, waiting still;
Oh, how long shall I implore Thee this petition to fulfill!
Hast Thou not one word for me? Must my prayer unanswered be?

February 17

If . . . the Lord deliver . . . shall I be your head? Judges 11:9
**Him hath God exalted with his right hand to be a Prince and
a Saviour.** Acts 5:31

When we came to Him first of all, with the intolerable burden
of our sins, there was no help for it but to come with them to
Him, and take His word for it that He would not and did not
cast us out. And so coming, so believing, we found rest to
our souls; we found that His word was true, and that His
taking away our sins was a reality.

Some give their lives to Him then and there, and go forth to
live henceforth not at all unto themselves, but unto Him who
died for them. This is as it should be, for conversion and
consecration ought to be simultaneous. But practically it is
not very often so, except with those in whom the bringing out
of darkness into marvelous light has been sudden and dazzling

and full of deepest contrasts. More frequently the work resembles the case of the Hebrew servant described in Exodus 21, who, after six years' experience of a good master's service, dedicates himself voluntarily, unreservedly, and irrevocably to it, saying, "I love my master; I will not go out free"; the master then accepting and sealing him to a lifelong service, free in law yet bound in love. This seems to be a figure of later consecration founded on experience and love.

> I love, I love my Master, I will not go out free,
> For He is my Redeemer, He paid the price for me.
> I would not leave His service, it is so sweet and blest;
> And in the weariest moments, He gives the truest rest.
> For He hath met my longing with word of golden tone,
> That I shall serve for ever Himself, Himself, alone.

February 18

DRAWN BY IRRESISTIBLE LOVE

No man can come unto me, except it were given unto him of my Father.
                                                                    John 6:65

Do not shrink from the words; do not dare to explain them away; the faithful and true Witness spoke them, the Holy Ghost has recorded them forever. There it stands; reiterated and strengthened instead of softened, because many even of His disciples murmured at it. So our coming to Jesus was not out of ourselves; it was the gift of God. How did this gift operate? Not by driving but by drawing. "No man can come to Me, except the Father which hath sent Me draw him." Here comes in the great "whosoever will." For unless and until the Father draw us, no mortal born of Adam ever wanted to come to Jesus. There was nothing else for it, He had to draw us or we never should have thought of wishing to come; nay, we should have gone on distinctly willing not to come, remaining aliens and enemies. Oh, the terrible depth of depravity revealed by that keen sword-word, "Ye will not come to Me that ye might have life." Settle it then that you never wanted to come till He drew you, and praise Him for thus beginning at the very beginning with you.

> Return!
> O chosen of My love!
> Fear not to meet thy beckoning Saviour's view;
> Long ere I called thee by thy name, I knew
> That very treacherously thou wouldst deal;
> Now I have seen thy ways, yet I will heal.
> Return! Wilt thou yet linger far from Me?
> My wrath is turned away, I have redeemed thee.

February 19

Hath he said, and shall he not do it? or hath he spoken, and shall he not make it good? Behold, I have received commandment to bless: and he hath blessed; and I cannot reverse it.   Numbers 23:19-20

"The word of our God shall stand for ever," and the hoarse recoil of every furious wave that is shattered into foam against this everlasting rock only murmurs, "I cannot reverse it." And is it not a most blessed and comforting thought that we ourselves cannot reverse it, though this is the quarter from which we are practically most tempted to dread its reversal? For, "if we believe not, yet He abideth faithful." All the earth-born or devil-breathed fogs and clouds of doubt, from the Fall till this hour, have not been able to touch the splendor of one star that He has set in the unassailable firmament of His eternal truth.

God Almighty! King of nations! earth Thy footstool, Heaven Thy throne!
Thine the greatness, power, and glory, Thine the kingdom, Lord, alone!
Life and death are in Thy keeping, and Thy will ordaineth all:
From the armies of Thy heavens to an unseen insect's fall.

February 20

WHATEVER YOUR "THIS" MAY BE

The Lord is able to give thee much more than this.
2 Chronicles 25:9

Amaziah, king of Judah, was going to war against the Edomites. He thought he would make sure of victory by hiring a hundred thousand soldiers from the king of Israel, and he paid them beforehand a hundred talents which was nearly two hundred thousand dollars of our money. But a man of God warned him not to let the army of Israel go with him, for Israel had forsaken the Lord, and so He was not with them. It seemed a great pity to waste all that money, and so Amaziah said, "But what shall we do for the hundred talents which I have given to the army of Israel? And the man of God answered, The Lord is able to give thee much more than this." So Amaziah simply obeyed, and sent the soliders away, and trusted God to help him to do without them. Was it any wonder that he gained a great victory over the Edomites? Does not this teach us that we should simply do the right thing, and trust God at any cost? When you do this, you will find that, in hundreds of ways which you never thought of, "the Lord is able to give thee much more." The trial comes in many different ways. One may be tempted to hurry over prayer and Bible reading, because there is something else that she very much wants to get done before breakfast, and she is afraid of not having time enough. Another shuts up the purse when a call comes to give something for God's work, because she is afraid she will not have enough left for another purpose. Another is tempted not to tell the exact truth, or to conceal something which he ought to tell, because he would lose something by it. Oh, resist the devil, and do what you know is right, and trust God for all the rest! For the Lord is able to give thee much more than this, whatever your *this* may be. And His smile and His blessing will always be more than this, more than anything else.

> Oh, Thou hast done far more for me
> Than I had asked or thought!
> I stand and marvel to behold
> What Thou, my Lord, hast wrought,
> And wonder what glad lessons yet
> I shall be daily taught.

February 21

GOD'S SUFFICIENCY MORE THAN ADEQUATE

Not that we are sufficient of ourselves to think any thing as of ourselves; but our sufficiency is of God.   2 Corinthians 3:5

Of ourselves we may have but little weight, no particular talents or position or anything else; but let us remember that again and again God has shown that the influence of a very average life when once really consecrated to Him may outweigh that of almost any number of merely professing Christians. Such lives are like Gideon's three hundred, carrying not even the ordinary weapons of war, but only trumpets and lamps and empty pitchers by whom the Lord wrought great deliverance while He did not use the others at all. For He hath chosen the weak things of the world to confound the things which are mighty.

> Distrust thyself, but trust His grace; it is enough for thee!
> In every trial thou shalt trace its all-sufficiency.
> Distrust thyself, but trust His love; rest in its changeless glow:
> And life or death shall only prove its everlasting flow.

February 22

Watch and pray, that ye enter not into temptation. Matthew 26:41

None of His commands clash with or supersede one another. Trusting does not supersede watching; it does but complete and effectuate it. Unwatchful trust is a delusion, and untrustful watching is in vain. Therefore let us not either willfully or carelessly enter into temptation, whether of place, or person, or topic, which has any tendency to endanger the keeping of our lips for Jesus. Let us pray that grace may be more and more poured into our lips as it was into His, so that our speech may be *alway* with grace. May they be pure, and sweet, and lovely, even as "His lips, like lilies, dropping sweet-smelling myrrh."

> Jesus, Master! I am Thine; keep me faithful, keep me near;
> Let Thy presence in me shine, all my homeward way to cheer.
> Jesus! at Thy feet I fall, oh, be Thou my All-in-all.

February 23

ALL FOR JESUS

But know that the Lord hath set apart him that is godly for himself. Psalm 4:3

It is not what we say or do, so much as what we are, that influences others. We have heard this and very likely repeated it again and again, but I do not know anything which, thoughtfully considered, makes us realize more vividly the need and the importance of our whole selves being kept for Jesus. Any part not wholly committed and not wholly kept must hinder and neutralize the real influence for Him of all the rest. If we ourselves are kept all for Jesus, then our influence will be all kept for Him, too. If not, then, however much we may wish and talk and try we cannot throw our full weight into the right scale. And just insofar as it is not in the one scale, it must be in the other; weighing against the little which we have tried to put in the right one and making the short weight still shorter. So large a proportion of it is entirely involuntary while yet the responsibility of it is so enormous that our helplessness comes out in exceptionally strong relief while our past debt in this matter is simply incalculable.

Are we feeling this a little?—getting just a glimpse, down the misty defiles of memory, of the neutral influence, the wasted influence, the mistaken influence, the actually wrong influence which has marked the ineffaceable although untraceable course? And all the while we owed Him all that influence. It ought to have been all for Him. We have nothing to say. But what has our Lord to say? "I forgave thee all that debt."

> True-hearted! Saviour, Thou knowest our story;
> Weak are the hearts that we lay at Thy feet,
> Sinful and treacherous! yet for Thy glory,
> Heal them, and cleanse them from sin and deceit.
> Half-hearted! Master, shall any who know Thee
> Grudge Thee their lives, who hast laid down Thine own?
> Nay; we would offer the hearts that we owe Thee—
> Live for Thy love and Thy glory alone.

February 24

GREAT GLADNESS IN WHATSOEVER YOU DO

Then the people rejoiced, for that they offered willingly.
1 Chronicles 29:9

See what came of offering willingly to the Lord — they rejoiced, and everything they did, even eating and drinking, was with great gladness. Never is any one so happy as those who offer their own selves willingly to the Lord. He gives them a thousandfold return for the worthless little self and weak little members which they have offered to Him. He gives them peace, and gladness, and blessing beyond what they ever expected to have. But this was not all; it was not only the people who had such a glad day, but King David also rejoiced with great joy. Those who loved their king, and recollected how much sorrow he had gone through, and how many battles he had fought for them, must have been glad indeed to see him rejoicing because they had offered willingly. And I think our King rejoices over us when He has made us able (verse 14) to offer ourselves willingly to Him. Is not this best of all? Jesus, who suffered for us, and who fought the great battle of our salvation for us, He, our own beloved King, will rejoice over thee with joy; He will rest in His love; He will joy over thee with singing.

> In full and glad surrender I give myself to Thee,
> Thine utterly, and only, and evermore to be!
> O Son of God, who lovest me, I will be Thine alone;
> And all I have, and all I am, shall henceforth be Thine own.

February 25

Our gospel came not unto you in word only, but also in power . . . and in much assurance. 1 Thessalonians 1:5

Do not let us be content with theoretically understanding and correctly holding the doctrine of justification by faith. Turn from the words to the reality, from the theory to the Person, and as a little, glad, wondering child, look at the simple, wonderful truth. That the righteousness of God (how magnificent!) is unto all and upon all them that believe; therefore, at this very moment, unto and upon you and me, instead of our filthy rags, so that we stand clothed and beautiful in the very sight of God, now; and Jesus can say, "Thou art all fair, my love, now!" That is not any finite righteousness, which might not quite cover the whole — might not be quite enough to satisfy God's all-searching eye; not a righteousness, but the righteousness of God; and this no abstract attribute, but a Person, real, living, loving — covering us with His own glorious apparel, representing us before His Father, Christ Jesus Himself made unto us righteousness! This today, and this forever, for His name shall endure forever.

Holiness by faith in Jesus, not by effort of thine own,
Sin's dominion crushed and broken by the power of grace alone,
God's own holiness within thee, His own beauty on thy brow,
This shall be thy pilgrim brightness, this thy blessed portion now.

February 26

He shall gather the lambs with his arm, and carry them in his bosom, and shall gently lead. Isaiah 40:11

One sees at a glance, by referring to a concordance, the touching fact that our Leader Himself experienced a very different leading. Never once was He gently led. He was led into the wilderness to be tempted of the devil (Matthew 4:1); He was led by men filled with wrath to the brow of the hill, that they might cast Him down headlong (Luke 4:29); He was led away to Annas, led away to Caiaphas (John 18:13, Matthew 26:57); led into the council of the elders and chief priests and scribes (Luke 22:66); led to Pontius Pilate (Matthew 27:2), and into the hall of judgment (John 18:28). And then He, our Lord Jesus Christ, was led as a sheep to the slaughter (Acts 8:32); led away to be crucified! (John 19:16). Verily, "His way was much rougher and darker than mine." That is how Jesus was led. But as for His people, He "guided them in the wilderness like a flock. And He led them on safely, so that they feared not" (Psalm 78:52-53).

> Lord Jesus, Thou hast trodden once for all
> The Via Dolorosa — and for us!
> No artist-power or minstrel-gift may tell
> The cost to Thee of each unfaltering step,
> Where love that passeth knowledge led Thee on,
> Faithful and true to God, and true to us.
> Thy ways are ways of pleasantness, and all
> Thy paths are peace; and that the path of him
> Who wears Thy perfect robe of righteousness,
> Is as the light that shineth more and more
> Unto the perfect day. And Thou hast given
> An olden promise, rarely quoted now,
> Because it is too bright for our weak faith:
> "If they obey and serve Him, they shall spend
> Days in prosperity, and they shall spend
> Their years in pleasures." All because Thy days
> Were full of sorrow, and Thy lonely years
> Were passed in grief's acquaintance — all for us!

February 27

"WONDER WORKING POWER IN THE BLOOD"

Whiter than snow.   Psalm 51:7

But snow is whiter than anything else! Especially if you saw it glittering in the sunshine on the top of a high mountain, where no dust can ever reach it. Mortal eyes have seen something as white as snow, for the raiment of the angel of the Resurrection was "white as snow"; and the shining raiment of the Lord Jesus on the Mount of Transfiguration was "exceeding white as snow." But what can be made "whiter than snow"? "Wash *me* and *I* shall be whiter than snow" if God washes me. But water will not do this, and tears will not do it. Only one thing can do it, but that does it surely and thoroughly. "The blood of Jesus Christ His Son cleanseth us from all sin." This is the fountain opened for sin and for uncleanness; and ever since the precious blood was shed, it has always been open.

> Yes, "even until now!" Then let us press
>   With free and willing feet
> Along the King's highway of holiness,
>   Until we gain the street
> O golden crystal, praising purely when
> We see our pardoning Lord; forgiven until then!

February 28

As for Mephibosheth, said the king, he shall eat at my table, as one of the king's sons.   2 Samuel 9:11

In every thought connected with the King's table we see Jesus only. He prepares the feast — "Thou preparest a table before me." He gives the invitation—"Come thou over with Me, and I will feed thee with Me." He gives the qualifying position of adoption, receiving us as the King's sons. He brings us into His banqueting house. He bids us partake, saying, "Eat, O friends, drink, yea, drink abundantly, O Beloved." He is with us at the feast, for the King sitteth at His table. He Himself is the heavenly food, the bread and the meat of His table; for He says, "The bread that I will give is My flesh"; and "My flesh is meat indeed." He Himself! Nothing less is offered to us, for nothing less can truly satisfy.

> His righteousness all glorious, thy festal robe shall be;
> And love that passeth knowledge His banner over thee.
> A little while, though parted, remember, wait, and love,
> Until He comes in glory, until we meet above.
> Till in the Father's kingdom the heavenly feast is spread,
> And we behold His beauty, whose blood for us was shed!

February 29

Write ye also for the Jews, as it liketh you, in the king's name, and seal it with the king's ring.   Esther 8:8

Does not this remind us of another writing of our King: "If ye abide in Me, and My words abide in you, ye shall ask what ye will, and it shall be done unto you." He places His own name and His own signet at the disposal of His abiding ones and says, "Ask Me of things to come concerning My sons, and concerning the work of My hands command ye Me." "Thou shalt also decree a thing, and it shall be established unto thee." Should not this encourage us in intercession? Perhaps we are saying, like Esther, "How can I endure to see the destruction of my kindred?" Have we as yet fully availed ourselves of the King's name, and the King's ring?

> For He hath given us a changeless writing,
> Royal decrees that light and gladness bring,
> Signed with His name in glorious inditing,
> Sealed on our hearts with His own signet ring.

March 1

These ought ye to have done, and not to leave the other undone.
Luke 11:42
Grant unto thy servants, that with all boldness they may speak thy word.
Acts 4:29

During a summer visit just after I had left school, a class of girls about my own age came to me a few times for an hour's singing. It was very pleasant indeed, and the girls were delighted with the hymns. They listened to all I had to say about time and expression, and not with less attention to the more shyly-ventured remarks about the words. Sometimes I accompanied them afterwards down the avenue; and whenever I met any of them I had smiles and plenty of kindly words for each, which they seemed to appreciate immensely. A few years afterwards I sat by the bedside of one of these girls—the most gifted of them all with both heart and head. She had been led by a wonderful way, and through long and deep suffering, into far clearer light than I enjoyed, and had witnessed for Christ in more ways than one, and far more brightly than I had ever done. She told me how sorrowfully and eagerly she was seeking Jesus at the time of those singing classes. And I never knew it, because I never asked, and she was too shy to speak first! But she told me more, and every word was a pang to me— how she used to linger in the avenue on those summer evenings, longing that I would speak to her about the Saviour; how she hoped, week after week, that I would just stretch out a hand to help her; just say one little word that might be God's message of peace to her, instead of the pleasant, general remarks about the nice hymns and tunes. And I never did! And she went on for months, I think for years, after, without the light and gladness which it might have been my privilege to bring to her life. God chose other means, for the souls that He has given to Christ cannot be lost because of the unfaithfulness of a human instrument. But she said, and the words often ring in my ears when I am tempted to let an opportunity slip, "Ah, Miss Frances, I ought to have been yours!"

Yours may be the joy and honor His redeemed ones to bring,
Jewels for the coronation of your coming Lord and King.
Will you cast away the gladness thus your Master's joys to share,
All because a word for Jesus seems too much for you to dare?

March 2

NOT YOUR OWN

Ye are not your own, for ye are bought with a price: therefore glorify God in your body, and in your spirit, which are God's.
1 Corinthians 6:19-20

The more we by faith and experience realize that we are His own in life and death, the more willing we shall be that He should do what He will with His own and the more sure we shall be that He will do the very best with it and make the very most of it. May we increasingly find the strength and rest of this, in our God-given claim upon God. "I am Thine, save me!" And "He will save, He will rejoice over thee with joy, He will rest in His love."

> Not your own! To Him ye owe all your life and all your love;
> Live, that ye His praise may show, who is yet all praise above.
> Every day and every hour, every gift and every power,
> Consecrate to Him alone, who hath claimed you for His own.
> Teach us, Master, how to give all we have and are to Thee;
> Grant us, Saviour, while we live, wholly, only, Thine to be.
> Henceforth be our calling high, Thee to serve and glorify;
> Ours no longer, but Thine own, Thine forever, Thine alone!

March 3

BEYOND OUR IMAGINATION!

Christ also hath once suffered for sins, the just for the unjust, that he might bring us to God.
1 Peter 3:18

If when we looked back on some terrible suffering unto death of one who loved us dearly, I really do not know how any heart could bear it, if we distinctly knew that all that prolonged agony was borne instead of us, and borne for nothing in the world but for love of us. But if to this were added the knowledge that we had behaved abominably to that dying one, done all sorts of things, now beyond recall, to grieve and vex him, not cared one bit about his love or made him any return of even natural affection, held aloof from him and sided with those who were against him; and then the terrible details of his slow agony were told, nay shown to us—well, imagine our remorse if you can, I cannot! The burden of grief and gratitude would be crushing, and if there were still any possible way in which we could show that poor, late gratitude, we should count nothing at any cost if we might but prove our tardy love. Only I think we should never know another hour's rest. But it is part of the strange power of the remembrance of our Lord's sufferings that it brings strength and solace and peace; for, as Bunyan says, "He hath given us rest by His sorrow." The bitterness of death to Him is the very fountain of the sweetness of life to us. Do the words after all seem to fall without power or reality on your heart? Is it nothing, or very little more than nothing, to you? Not that you do not know it is all true, but your heart seems cold, and your apprehension mechanical, and your faith paralyzed — does this describe you? Thank God that feelings do not alter facts! He suffered for this sinful coldness as well as for all other sins. He suffered, the Just for the unjust; and are we not emphatically unjust when we requite His tremendous love this way?

My Lord, dost Thou remember this of me,
My love, so poor, so cold?
Oh, if I had but loved Thee more,
Yet Thou hast pardoned. Let me pour
My life's best wine for Thee, my heart's best gold
(Worthless yet all I have), for very shame
That Thou shouldst tell me, calling me by name—
Thus saith Jehovah, I remember thee.

March 4

CLEAVING

The men of Judah clave unto their king. 2 Samuel 20:2

It is not a matter of course that coming is followed by cleaving Even when the King Himself, in His veiled royalty, walked and talked with His few faithful followers, many of His disciples went back, and walked no more with Him. There was no word of indignation or reproach, only the appeal of infinite pathos from His gracious lips. "Will ye also go away?" Let this sound in our ears today, not only in moments of temptation to swerve from truest-hearted loyalty and service, but all through the business of the day; stirring our too-easy-going resting into active cleaving; quickening our following afar off into following hard after Him; rousing us to add to the blessed assurance, "Thine are we, David!" the bolder and nobler position, "and on Thy side!"

In Thee I trust, on Thee I rest, O Saviour dear, Redeemer blest!
No earthly friend, no brother knows my weariness, my wants, my woes.
On Thee I call, who knowest all.
O Saviour dear, Redeemer blest, in Thee I trust, on Thee I rest.

March 5

A SURE KEEPER

He that keepeth thee will not slumber.	Psalm 121:3
I will trust, and not be afraid.	Isaiah 12:2
Thou shalt not be afraid for the terror by night.	Psalm 91:5

All through the dark hours He keepeth thee; keeps you from everything that could hurt or even frighten you. *He* keepeth thee; only think who is your Keeper! the mighty God, who can do everything, and can see everything. Why need you ever fear with such a Keeper? It is very nice to know that "He shall give His angels charge over thee to keep thee"; but it is sweeter and grander still to think that God Himself keeps us. As if He wanted us to be very sure of it, and to leave us no excuse for ever being afraid any more, He even says it three times over, "He that keepeth thee will not slumber." "Behold, He that keepeth Israel shall neither slumber nor sleep." "The Lord is thy Keeper." What could He say more?

He is speaking in the darkness, tho' thou canst not see His face,
More than angels ever needed, mercy, pardon, love and grace.
Speaking of the many mansions, where, in safe and holy rest,
Thou shalt be with Him forever, perfectly and always blest.
What He tells thee in the darkness, whispers thro' time's lonely night,
Thou shalt speak in glorious praises, in the everlasting light!

March 6

OUR SURETY

I will be surety for him.	Genesis 43:9
By so much was Jesus made a surety of a better testament.	
	Hebrews 7:22

Judah promised his father to bring Benjamin back safely from Egypt. He undertook this entirely. He said, "I will be surety for him; of my hand shalt thou require him: if I bring him not unto thee, and set him before thee, then let me bear the blame for ever." And his father trusted Judah to do as he had said, and so Judah was surety for Benjamin. The Lord Jesus is Surety for us. He undertakes to bring us safely to the house of His Father and our Father. He undertakes to present us before the presence of His glory. We are in His hand, and from His hand God will require us and receive us. Now, if God has trusted Him, will not you trust Him too? What! Hesitate about trusting Jesus? Whom else could you trust? Who else could undertake to bring you safe to Heaven? Benjamin might possibly have found his way by himself from Egypt to Canaan; but never, never could you find the way by yourself from earth to Heaven; and never could anyone but the Lord Jesus bring you there. Benjamin could not be quite certain that his brother could keep his promise, for Judah was only a man, and might have been killed in Egypt, but you may be quite certain that the Lord Jesus *can* keep His promise, for He is God as well as Man. And do you think He *would* break His promise? He, the Faithful Saviour, break His promise? Heaven and earth shall pass away, but His word shall not pass away! Then trust Him now, and never wrong His faithful love by leaving off trusting Him.

But on a higher, holier mount that Voice is pleading still;
For while one weary child of His yet wanders here below,
While yet one thirsting soul desires His peace and love to know,
And while one fainting spirit seeks His holiness to share,
The Saviour's loving heart shall pour a tide of mighty prayer;
Yes! till each ransomed one hath gained his home of joy and peace,
That fount of blessings all untold shall never, never cease.

March 7

THE TIE THAT BINDS

I am my beloved's, and my beloved is mine.
Song of Solomon 6:3

The believer's "I am Thine" is only an echo, varying in clearness according to faith's atmosphere and our nearness to the original voice. Yes, it is only the echo of "Thou art mine," falling in its mighty music on the responsive, because Spirit-prepared, heart. This note of heavenly music never originated with any earthly rock. It is only when God sends forth the Spirit of His Son in our hearts that we cry, "Abba, Father." It was when the anointed but not yet openly crowned king had gone out to meet Amasai and the Spirit came upon him that he said, "Thine we are David." Therefore do not overlook the voice in the gladness of the echo. Listen and you will hear it falling from the mysterious heights of high-priestly intercession: "They are Thine. And all Mine are Thine, and Thine are Mine."

Then bring your poor affection, and try it by this test;
The hidden depth is fathomed, you see you love Him best!
'Tis but a feeble echo of His great love to you,
Yet in His ear each note is dear, its harmony is true.

March 8

HOLINESS — CONFIDENCE — JOY

We are persuaded better things of you, and things that accompany salvation. Hebrews 6:9

There should be three practical results of our salvation: (1) *Holiness*. We must see to it that we resolutely put away all that ought not to be in His royal abode. "Having, therefore, these promises, dearly beloved, let us cleanse ourselves from all filthiness of the flesh and spirit, perfecting holiness in the fear of God." (2) *Confidence*. What does the citadel fear when an invincible general is within it? "The Lord thy God in the midst of thee is mighty; He will save." He is the wall of fire round about, and the glory in the midst of her; and he that toucheth you toucheth the apple of His eye. (3) *Joy*. Yes! "Be glad and rejoice with all the heart"; "sing and rejoice, O daughter of Zion; for, lo, I come, and I will dwell in the midst of thee, saith the Lord."

"Certainly I will be with thee!" Father, I have found it true:
To Thy faithfulness and mercy I would set my seal anew.
All the year Thy grace hath kept me, Thou my help indeed hast been,
Marvelous the loving-kindness every day and hour hath seen.

March 9

COME AND SEE

Come and see. John 1:39

The Lord Jesus said it first. He said it to the two disciples of John who heard that He was the Lamb of God. They knew very little about Him, but they followed Him. Perhaps they would not even have ventured to speak, but "Jesus turned, and saw them following," and spoke to them. Then they asked Him where He dwelt, and He said, "Come and see!" Philip said it next. He had found Christ himself, and at once he told his friend Nathanael about it, "Come and see!" Is it not said still? Oh, "come and see!" Look into the Saviour's glorious and loving face, and see what a lovely and precious Saviour He is! Come and see how ready He is to receive you, and to bless you. Come and see what He has done for you; see how He loved you and gave Himself for you; how He lived and suffered and bled and died for you! Come and see what gifts He has for you — forgiveness and peace, His Spirit and His grace, His joy and His love! Come and see where He dwelleth —see that He is ready to come in and dwell with you, to make your heart His own dwelling-place. Oh, if I could but persuade you to "come and see!" There is no other sight so glorious and beautiful. Will you not come? When you have come, when you can say, like Philip, "We have found Him!" and like Paul, "We see Jesus," will you not say to someone else, "Come and see!" You will wish every one else to come to Him, and you have His word to bid you try to bring them: "Let him that heareth say, Come!"

> Hush! while on silvery wing of holiest song
>   Floats forth the old, dear story of our peace,
> His coming, the Desire of Ages long,
>   To wear our chains, and win our glad release.
> Our wondering joy, to hear such tidings blest
> Is crowned with "Come to Him, and He will give you rest."

March 10

NOT FOR TIME — BUT FOR ETERNITY

Keep this for ever in the imagination of the thoughts of the heart of thy people, and prepare [margin, stablish] their heart unto thee. 1 Chronicles 29:18

What was to be kept forever in the imagination of the thoughts of the heart? Something that God had put there; for you cannot keep a thing in any place till it is first put there. The people had responded to the appeal of their king, "Who then is willing to consecrate his service this day unto the Lord?" As the expression of this service they had offered willingly and rejoicingly to the Lord. What they had offered was all His own: "Of Thine own have we given Thee." And David acknowledges that it was all of Him that they were enabled (margin, obtained strength) "to offer so willingly after this sort." Was all this consecration and joy to be a thing of a day? Nay! in his grand inspired prayer David, foreshadowing the Royal Intercessor by whom alone we offer up spiritual sacrifices, prays, "O Lord God, keep this *forever* in the imagination of the thoughts of the heart of Thy people."

> My Lord, art Thou indeed remembering me?
> Then let me not forget!
> Oh, be Thy kindness all the way
> Thy everlasting love today,
> In sweet perpetual remembrance set
> Before my view, to fill my marvelling gaze,
> And stir my love, and lift my life to praise,
> Because Thou sayest, "I remember Thee."

March 11

Loose him, and bring him . . . the Lord hath need of him.
Mark 11:2, 3

Perhaps we have the dreary idea, "Nobody wants me!" We never need grope in that gloom again, when the King Himself desires us! This desire is love active, love in glow, love going forth, love delighting and longing. It is the strongest representation of the love of Jesus—something far beyond the love of pity or compassion; it is the taking pleasure in His people; delighting in them; willing (i.e., putting forth the grand force of His will) that they should be with Him where He is, with Him now, with Him always. It is the love that does not end and will not endure separation—the love that cannot do without its object.

Why will you do without Him? He calls and calls again—
"Come unto Me! Come unto Me!" Oh, shall He call in vain?
He wants to have you with Him; do you not want Him too?
You cannot do without Him, and He wants — even you.

March 12

CONSIDERATION

I will lead on softly, according as the cattle that goeth before me and the children be able to endure. Genesis 33:14

The story of Jacob's thoughtfulness for the cattle and the children is a beautiful little picture. He would not let them be overdriven even for one day. "My Lord," said he (verse 13), "knoweth that the children are tender, and the flocks and herds with young are with me: and if men should overdrive them one day, all the flock will die." He would not lead on according to what Esau could do and expected them to do, but only according to what they were able to endure. "Let us take our journey, and let us go, and I will go before thee" (verse 12). He had had so much to do with them that he knew exactly how far they could go in a day; and he made that his only consideration in arranging the marches. Perhaps his own halting thigh made him more considerate for "the foot of the cattle" and "the foot of the children" (see margin). Besides, he had gone the same wilderness journey before (29:1) when they were not yet in existence, and knew all about its roughness and heat and length by personal experience. And so he said, "I will lead on softly." Is it not restful to know that you are not answerable to any Esaus for how much you get through, or how far you are led on in the day! "They" don't know, or, knowing, don't remember the weakness or drawbacks. Maybe they wonder you do not get on farther and faster, doing the work better, bearing up against the suffering or the sorrow more bravely. And maybe you feel wounded without a word being said, simply because you know they don't know. Then turn to the Good Shepherd in whose "feeble flock" you are, and remember that He remembers. Talk to Him about it for "all things are naked and opened unto the eyes of Him with whom we have to do" (Hebrews 4:13).

> Our Father, Thou carest; Thou knowest indeed
> Our inmost desires, our manifold need;
> The fount of Thy mercies shall never be dry,
> For Thy riches in glory shall mete the supply;
> Our bread shall be given, our water be sure,
> And nothing shall fail, for Thy word shall endure,
> And Thine is the power.

March 13

"IN THEM"

Is not the Lord in Zion? Is not her king in her?
Jeremiah 8:19

Waiting for a royal coming—what expectation, what preparation, what tension! A glimpse for many, a full view for some, a word for a favored few, and the pageant is over like a dream. The Sovereign may come, but does not stay. Our King comes not thus: He comes not to pass, but to "dwell in the midst of thee"; not only in His church collectively, but in each believer individually. We pray, "Abide with us," and He answers in the sublime plural of Godhead, "We will come unto him, and make our abode with him." Even this grand abiding with us does not extend to the full marvels of His condescension and His nearness, for the next time He speaks of it He changes the "with" to "in," and thenceforth only speaks of "I in you," "I in him," "I in them."

> Certainly I will be with thee! Let me feel it, Saviour dear,
> Let me know that Thou art with me, very precious, very near.
> On this day of solemn pausing, with Thyself all longing still,
> Let Thy pardon, let Thy presence, let Thy peace my spirit fill.

March 14

Thou hast given a banner to them that fear thee. Psalm 60:4

Then what is your banner, and what are you doing with it? For if you are among them that fear God, He has given you a banner that it may be displayed. Carrying a banner means something. First, it means that you belong to or have to do with those whose banner you carry, and that you are not ashamed of them. Secondly, it means that we are ready to fight, and ready to encourage others to fight under the same banner. Thirdly, it means rejoicing. You know how flags are hung out on special days, and carried in triumphal processions. Then, in the name of our God we will set up our banners *now!*

> The Master hath called us, the children who fear Him,
> Who march 'neath Christ's banner, His own little band;
> We love Him, and seek Him; we long to be near Him,
> And rest in the light of His beautiful land.

March 15

THE WAY TO PROSPERITY

The first of the firstfruits of thy land thou shalt bring unto the house of the Lord thy God. Exodus 34:26
Seek ye first the kingdom of God, and his righteousness; and all these things shall be added unto you. Matthew 6:33

Firstfruits should be specially set apart. This we find running all through the Bible. There is a tacit appeal to our gratitude in the suggestion of them—the very word implies bounty received and bounty in prospect. Bringing "the first of the first-fruits into the house of the Lord thy God" was like saying grace for all the plenty He was going to bestow on the faithful Israelite. Something of gladness, too, seems always implied. "The day of the firstfruits" was to be a day of rejoicing (compare Numbers 28:26 with Deuteronomy 16:10-11). There is also an appeal to loyalty: we are commanded to honor the Lord with the firstfruits of all our increase. And that is the way to prosper, for the next word is, "So shall thy barns be filled with plenty." The friend who first called my attention to this command, said that the setting apart firstfruits — making a proportion for God's work a first charge upon the income—always seemed to bring a blessing on the rest, and that since this had been systematically done, it actually seemed to go farther than when not thus lessened.

Presenting our firstfruits should be a peculiarly delightful act, as they are themselves the emblem of our consecrated relationship to God. For of His own will begat He us by the word of truth, that we should be a kind of firstfruits of His creatures. How sweet and hallowed and richly emblematic our little acts of obedience in this matter become, when we throw this light upon them! And how blessedly they may remind us of the heavenly company, singing, as it were, a new song before the throne; for they are the firstfruits unto God and to the Lamb.

> Set apart to praise Him, set apart for this!
> Have the blessed angels any truer bliss?
> Soft the prelude, though so clear;
> Isolated tones are trembling;
> But the chosen choir, assembling,
> Soon shall sing together, while the universe shall hear.

March 16

TAKE HIM AT HIS WORD

The people rested themselves upon the words of Hezekiah king of Judah. 2 Chronicles 32:8
We rest on thee, and in thy name we go. 2 Chronicles 14:11

If we have an entire and present belief in "My grace is sufficient for thee," or "Lo, I am with you alway," should we feel nervous at anything He calls us to do for Him? Would not that word be indeed for rest in the moment of need — rest from the hard bondage of service to which we feel unequal? Have we not sometimes found it so; and if so, why not always? I see nothing about "sometimes" in any of His promises. If we have an entire and present belief that "all things work together for good," or that He leads us forth by the right way, should we feel worried when some one thing seems to work wrong, and some one yard of the way is not what we think straightest? We lean upon the Word of the King for everlasting life, why not for daily life also? When He says perfect peace, He cannot mean imperfect peace. Just as the people rested themselves upon the words of Hezekiah, king of Judah, so simply let us rest upon the words of our King, Jesus.

> If some things were omitted or altered as we would,
> The whole might be unfitted to work for perfect good.
> Our plans may be disjointed, but we may calmly rest;
> What God has once appointed is better than our best.

March 17

For the love of Christ constraineth us. 2 Corinthians 5:14

Do you love Him? If you really do, there can surely be neither hesitation about yielding your hands to Him, nor about entrusting them to Him to be kept. Does He love you? That is the truer way of putting it; for it is not our love to Christ, but the love of Christ to us which constraineth us. And this is the impulse of the motion and the mode of the keeping. The steam-engine does not move when the fire is not kindled, nor when it is gone out; no matter how complete the machinery and abundant the fuel, cold coals will neither set it going nor keep it working. Let us ask Him so to shed abroad His love in our hearts by the Holy Ghost which is given unto us, that it may be the perpetual and only impulse of every action of our daily life.

> He loves the little children so; does darling Eric love Him?
> I think the angels must have smiled a rainbow-smile above him,
> Yet hardly brighter than his own, that lit the answer true,
> Jesus, the kind good Jesus! Me do, oh yes, me do!

March 18

HIS ETERNITY FOR THEE

For your sakes he became poor.	2 Corinthians 8:9
For their sakes I sanctify myself.	John 17:19
For their sakes therefore return thou on high.	Psalm 7:7

All we can ask Him to take are days and moments — the little span given us as it is given, and of this only the present in deed and the future in will. As for the past insofar as we did not give it to Him it is too late; we can never give it now. But His past was given to us, though ours was not given to Him. Oh, what a tremendous debt does this show us!

Away back in the dim depths of past eternity, "or ever the earth and the world were made," His divine existence in the bosom of His Father was all for thee, purposing and planning for thee, receiving and holding the promise of eternal life for thee.

Then the thirty-three years among sinners on this sinful earth; do we think enough of the slow-wearing days and nights, the heavy-footed hours, the never-hastening minutes, that went to make up those thirty-three years of trial and humiliation? We all know how slowly time passes when suffering and sorrow are near, and there is no reason to suppose that our Master was exempted from this part of our infirmities.

Then His present is for thee. Even now He liveth to make intercession; even now He "thinketh upon me"; even now He "knoweth," He "careth," He "loveth."

Then, only to think that His whole eternity will be "for thee." Millions of ages of unfoldings of all His love and of ever new declarings of His Father's names to His brethren. Think of it! and can we ever hesitate to give all our poor little hours to His service?

All His work is ended, joyfully we sing,
Jesus hath ascended! Glory to our King!
Praying for His children, in that blessed place,
Calling them to glory, sending them His grace;
His bright home preparing, faithful ones, for you;
Jesus ever liveth, ever loveth too.

March 19

CONTINUALLY CLEAN

Let thy garments be always white. Ecclesiastes 9:8

Always? Oh, how can that be? They are soiled again directly after they have been washed clean! Yet God says, "Let them be *always* white"; and He would not tell you to do what was impossible. You could not keep your garments white for five minutes; careless thoughts would come like dust upon them and wrong words would make great dark stains, and before long some unexpected deed would be like a sad fall into the mire, and you would feel sad and ashamed. But why should all this happen over and over again, till anybody but our own loving, long-suffering Saviour would be tired of us, and give up doing any more for us? Why should it be, when His precious blood cleanseth us from all sin, and "If we confess our sins He is faithful and just to forgive us our sins and to cleanse us from all unrighteousness." Perhaps you never thought of this. Trust Him today to do this, and see if it is not the happiest day you ever spent!

And He can do all this for me, because in sorrow, on the tree,
He once for sinners hung; and, having washed their sin away,
He now rejoices, day by day, to cleanse His trusting one.

March 20

HOW TO FILL AN ACHING VOID

Whosoever drinketh of this water shall thirst again: But whosoever drinketh of the water that I shall give him shall never thirst. John 4:13-14

First, you see you are quite sure to thirst again; it is no use expecting to find anything earthly that will satisfy you. Secondly, Jesus has something to give you which will make you satisfied and glad. Thirdly, as long as you go on drinking this, you will be *always* satisfied and glad. Fourthly, you cannot get it from anyone or anything else. Jesus gives it, and Jesus only. Fifthly, it must be meant for you, because He says, "whosoever," and that means anyone. And He says, "Ho everyone that thirsteth, come ye to the waters!" and "if any man thirst, let Him come unto Me and drink." And, "I will give unto him that is athirst of the fountain of the water of life freely."

Ye shall find in Him the filling of the "aching void" within;
In Him the instant antidote for anguish and for sin;
In Him the conscious meeting of the soul's unuttered need;
In Him the ALL that ye have sought, the goal of life indeed.

March 21

SEVENFOLD JUSTIFICATION

The law was our schoolmaster to bring us unto Christ, that we might be justified by faith. Galatians 3:24

This glorious justification by faith is sevenfold. We are justified:

1. "By His grace"—the grace of God the Father, one of whose most wonderful titles is "The Justifier of him which believeth in Jesus."

2. "By His blood"—that precious blood which has to do with every stage of our redemption and effectuated salvation from the writing of our names in the book of life of the Lamb slain from the foundation of the world, till the chorus of the "new song" is full in Heaven.

3. "By the righteousness of One" (of *the* One), "by the obedience of One"; by which the free gift, the unspeakable gift of eternal life—nay, of Christ Himself to be our life— "came upon all men unto justification of life."

4. By the resurrection of Jesus our Lord who was raised again for our justification, the grand token that our Substitute had indeed fulfilled all righteousness for us.

5. "By His knowledge shall My righteous Servant justify many; for He shall bear their iniquities." For true faith is founded upon the knowledge of Him and "this is life eternal."

6. "By faith"; just only believing God's Word and accepting God's way about it.

7. By works; because these are the necessary and inseparable evidence that faith is not mere fancy or talk.

By the grace of God the Father, thou art freely justified,
Thro' the great redemption purchased by the blood of Him who died;
By His life, for thee fulfilling God's command exceeding broad,
By His glorious resurrection, seal and signet of our God.

March 22

THE KEY TO GOD'S TREASURE HOUSE

Thou hast trusted in thy works and in thy treasures.
Jeremiah 48:7

It is only the continual drawing from His good treasure that will profit us, even "the light of the knowledge of the glory of God in the face of Jesus Christ." "And we have this treasure in earthen vessels, that the excellency of the power may be of God and not of us." It is only with God-given treasure that we can enrich others. When we want to give a word to another, it generally seems to come with more power if, instead of casting about for what we think likely to suit them, we simply hand over to them any treasure word which He has freshly given to us. When He opens to us some shining bit of treasure, let us not forget, "Freely ye have received, freely give." Also, let us not stand idly waiting for some further opening of treasure but "let there be search made in the king's treasure house," in the house of the rolls where the treasures are laid up, where the decrees and records of our King are to be found. They are truly hidden riches. Neither must we trust in our own store of spiritual treasures, whether of memory, experience, or even grace.

His love is the key and His glory the measure
Of grace all-abounding and knowledge and light;
To thee shall be opened this infinite treasure,
To thee, the unsearchable riches of Christ.

March 23

This also cometh forth from the Lord of hosts, which is wonderful in counsel, and excellent in working. Isaiah 28:29

Do not quarrel with the invisible dew because it is not a visible shower. The Lord would send a shower if that was the true need to be supplied to His vineyard; but as He is sending His speech in another form, you may be quite sure it is because He is supplying your true need thereby. You cannot see why it is so, and I do not pretend to explain; but what does that matter! He knows which way to water His vineyard. These words of His, which you are remembering so feebly, or reading without being able to grasp, are not going to return void. They are doing His own work on your soul, only in a quite different way to what you would choose. By and by they will sparkle out in the light of a new morning, and you will find yourself starting fresh, and perhaps wondering how it is that the leaves of life which hung so limp and drooping are so fresh and firm again on their stems.

> Tho' all is silence in my heart, I know that Thou hast heard.
> I lay my prayer before Thee, and, trusting in Thy word,
> To that blest City lead me, Lord (still choosing all my way),
> Where faith melts into vision as the starlight into day.

March 24

KEPT FOR THE MASTER'S USE

According to my earnest expectation and my hope, that . . . Christ shall be magnified in my body, whether it be by life, or by death. Philippians 1:20

Consecration is not a religiously selfish thing. If it sinks into that, it ceases to be consecration. We want our lives kept, not that we may feel happy and be saved the distress consequent on wandering and get the power with God and man, and all the other privileges linked with it. We shall have all this, because the lower is included in the higher; but our true aim, if the love of Christ constraineth us, will be far beyond this. Not "for me" at all but "for Jesus"; not for my safety, but for His glory; not for my comfort, but for His joy; not that I may find rest, but that He may see the travail of His soul, and be satisfied! Yes, for *Him* I want to be kept. Kept for His sake; kept for His use; kept to be His witness; kept for His joy! Kept for Him, that in me He may show forth some tiny sparkle of His light and beauty; kept to do His will and His work in His own way; kept, it may be, to suffer for His sake; kept for Him, that He may do just what seemeth Him good with me; kept, so that no other lord shall have any more dominion over me, but that Jesus shall have all there is to have—little enough, indeed, but not divided or diminished by any other claim. Is not this, O you who love the Lord—is not this worth living for, worth asking for, worth trusting for?

"He is thy Lord!" Oh, mine! though other lords
Have had dominion, now I know Thy name,
And its great music is the only key
To which my soul vibrates in full accord,
Blending with other notes but as they blend
With this. Oh, mine! But dare I say it, I,
Who fail and wander, mourning oftentimes
Some sin-made discord, or some tuneless string?
It would be greater daring to deny
To say, "Not mine," when Thou hast proved to me
That I am Thine, by promise sealed with blood.

March 25

A RACE TO RUN

Let us lay aside every weight. Hebrews 12:1

If you were going to run a race, you would first put down all the parcels you might have been carrying. You have a race to run today, a little piece of the great race that is set before you. God has set a splendid prize before you, "the prize of the high calling of God in Christ Jesus," a crown that is incorruptible. What are you going to do about the weights, the things that hinder you from running this race? You know some things do seem to hinder you; will you keep them or lay them aside? Will you only lay aside something that every one can see is hindering you, so that you will get a little credit for putting it down, and keep something that your own conscience knows is a real hindrance, though no one else knows anything at all about it? It may seem hard to lay our pet weight down; but oh! if you only knew how light we feel when it is laid down, and how much easier it is to run the race which God has set before us!

Unfurl the Christian Standard, with firm and fearless hands!
For no pale flag of compromise with Error's legion bands,
And no faint-hearted flag of truce with Mischief and with Wrong,
Should lead the soldiers of the Cross, the faithful and the strong.

March 26

WHEN DUTY BECOMES PLEASURE

That he may please him who hath chosen him to be a soldier.
2 Timothy 2:4

Here is something worth aiming at, worth trying for! The
Lord Jesus, the Captain of our salvation, is He who has chosen
us to be His soldiers; and now, does He only tell us that we
may do our duty—serve, obey, and fight? No; He tells us
something more, gives us a hope and an aim so bright and
pleasant, that it is like sunshine upon everything. He says
we "may *please* Him." Only one who knows what it is to
mourn for having grieved the dear Saviour, can quite understand what a happy word this is! That we, who have been
cold, and careless, and sinful, grieving His love over and over
again, should be told after all that we may *please* Him! Oh,
if we love Him, our hearts will just leap at the hope of it!
Perhaps we thought this could not be till we reached Heaven;
but His own Word says we "may please Him."

> Then every little service, of hand, or pen, or voice,
> Becomes, if He has asked it, the service of my choice,
> And from my own desires 'tis not so hard to part,
> If once I know I follow so, His wiser will and heart.

March 27

EVERYTHING FOR YOU!

Is it nothing to you? Lamentations 1:12

This was said of a great sorrow, which should have touched
the heart of every one who passed by and saw it, the terrible
troubles that came upon Jerusalem and her children. But this
was also a type of the far more terrible cup of sorrow which
the Lord Jesus drank for us, drank it willingly, so that we
might drink of the river of His pleasures. Listen! for it is
as if He said to you and me, "Is it nothing to you, all ye that
pass by? behold and see if there be any sorrow like unto My
sorrow!" Behold and see how all His life He was a Man of
Sorrows, not having where to lay His head; His own brethren
refusing to believe in Him, the wicked Jews hating Him, and
over and over again trying to kill Him, and He knowing all
the while that awful suffering was before Him. Behold and
see Him in the Garden of Gethsemane, being in an agony and
saying, "My soul is exceeding sorrowful, even unto death."

Behold and see Him, scourged and spit upon, led as a lamb to the slaughter, and then nailed to the cross; suffering even unto death, thirsting in the terrible pain, and yet not drinking to still it, and saying in the midst of it all, "My God, My God, why hast Thou forsaken Me?" Was ever any sorrow like unto the sorrow that our Lord Jesus Christ went through for love of us? Is it nothing to you? Can you look at it and not care about it? Can you pass by and go on just the same as if He had never loved and suffered? Oh, instead of nothing, let it be henceforth *everything* to you! Let it be your peace and joy, your strength and your song; let it fill your heart with love and gratitude; let it make you determined to live for Him who suffered and died for you.

> For me that full and fearful cup to drink
> Because Thou lovedst even to the end!
> "He suffered!" Saviour, was Thy love so vast
> That mysteries of unknown agony,
> Even unto death, its only gauge could be,
> Unmeasured as the fiery depths it passed?
> Lord, by the sorrows of Gethsemane
> Seal Thou my quivering love for ever unto Thee.

March 28

NO WITHHOLDINGS

He that spared not his own Son, but delivered him up for us all, how shall he not with him also freely give us all things?
Romans 8:32
All that I have is thine. Luke 15:31

He holds nothing back, reserves nothing from His dear children, and what we cannot receive now He is keeping for us. He gives us "hidden riches of secret places" now, but by and by He will give us more, and the glorified intellect will be filled continually out of His treasures of wisdom and knowledge. But the sanctified intellect will be, must be, used for Him, and only for Him, now!

> For only work that is for God alone
>   Hath an unceasing guerdon of delight,
>   A guerdon unaffected by the sight
> Of great success, nor by its loss o'erthrown.
> All else is vanity beneath the sun,
> There may be joy in **doing,** but it palls when done.
>
> For there are few who care to analyze
>   The mingled motives, in their complex force,
>   Of some apparently quite simple course;
> One disentangled skein might well surprise.
> Perhaps a "single heart" is never known,
> Save in a yielded life that lives for God alone.

March 29

He performeth the thing that is appointed for me. Job 23:14

This is wonderfully inclusive; one should read over all the
Epistles to get a view of the things present and future, seen
and unseen, the grace and the glory that He has appointed
for us. It includes also all the "good works which God hath
before ordained, that we should walk in them." It will not be
our performance of them, but His; for He "worketh in you to
will and to do," and "Thou also hast wrought all our works
in us." The beautiful old translation says, He "shall perform
the cause which I have in hand." Does not that make it very
real to us today? Just the very thing that "I have in hand,"
my own particular bit of work today—this cause that I cannot manage, this thing that I undertook in miscalculation of
my own powers—this is what I may ask Him to do "for me,"
and rest assured that He will perform it. "The wise and their
works are in the hand of God!"

> Thro' the whole of life's long way, outward, inward need we trace;
> Need arising day by day, patience, wisdom, strength, and grace.
> Needing Jesus most of all, full of need, on Him we call;
> Then how gracious His reply, God shall all your need supply!

March 30

FAITHFULNESS

Faithful over a few things. Matthew 25:21, 23

The servant who had only two talents to trade with, but traded
faithfully with them, had just the same glorious words spoken
to him as the servant who had five talents: "Well done, good
and faithful servant: thou hast been faithful over a few things
. . . enter thou into the joy of thy lord." Think what it would
be to hear the Lord Jesus saying that to you, really to you!
Oh, how sweet! how blessed! How you would listen to that
gracious voice saying those wonderfully gracious words to you!
But could He say them to you? Are you "faithful over a few
things"? He has given every one a few things to be faithful
over, and so He has to you. Your "few things" may be very
few, and very small things, but He expects you to be faithful
over them. What is being faithful over them? It means doing

the very best you can with them; doing as much for Jesus as you can with your money, even if you have very little; doing as much as you can for Him with your time. You sigh over this and think of how unfaithful you have been. You know you do not deserve for Him to call you "good and faithful servant." But come at once to your gracious Lord, and ask Him to forgive you for all the unfaithfulness and to make you faithful today. And then, even in small matters you will find it helpful to recollect, "Faithful over a few things."

Only, O Lord, in Thy dear love fit us for perfect rest above;
And help us, this and every day, to live more nearly as we pray.

In the service royal let us not grow cold;
Let us be right, loyal, noble, true and bold,
Master, Thou wilt keep us, by Thy grace divine,
Always on the Lord's side, Saviour, always Thine!

March 31

READY TO DO WHAT IS MOST NEEDED

What wilt thou that I shall do unto thee? Luke 18:41
Let your requests be made known unto God. Philippians 4:6

Only a blind beggar by the wayside! But Jesus of Nazareth stood still when he cried to Him. He could not grope his way among the crowd, but Jesus commanded him to be brought near to Him. He knew why the poor man had cried out, but He would have him tell it to Himself. So He said, "What wilt thou that I shall do unto thee?" Wonderful question, with a wonderful promise wrapped up in it! For it meant that the mighty Son of God was ready to do whatever this poor blind beggar asked. What did he ask? First, just what he most wanted! Not what he supposed he ought to ask, nor what anyone had taught him to ask, nor what other people asked; but simply *what he wanted.* Secondly, he asked straight off for a miracle! He never stopped to question whether it was likely or not, nor how Jesus of Nazareth would do it, nor whether it was too much to ask all at once, nor whether the people would think him too bold. He knew what he wanted, and he believed that Jesus of Nazareth could do it, and so he asked, and that was enough.

O Tender One, O Mighty One, who never sent away
The sinner or the sufferer, Thou art the same today!
The same in love, the same in power, and Thou art waiting still,
To heal the multitudes that come, yea, "whosoever will"!

April 1

Hold thou me up, and I shall be safe.   Psalm 119:117
And thou shalt be secure, because there is hope. Job 11:18

The path is not easy. There are rough stones over which we
may stumble, if we are not walking very carefully. There are
places which look quite smooth, but they are more dangerous
than the rough ones, for they are slippery. How are we to
walk safely along such a path? We want a strong, kind hand
to hold us up, and to hold us always; a hand that will hold
ours so tightly and lovingly, that it will be as the old Scotch-
woman said, "Not my grip of Christ, but Christ's grip of me!"
Yes, Christ's loving hand is "able to keep you from falling";
only let your hand be restfully in the hand of Jesus, and "then
shalt thou walk in thy way safely, and thy foot shall not
stumble." But do not say, "Hold Thou me up," and stop there,
or add, "But all the same, I shall stumble and fall!" Finish
with the bright words of faith that He puts into your mouth,
"Hold Thou me up, *and I shall be safe!*" So you will, if you
will trust Him to do just what you ask, and let Him hold you
up.

> We cannot see before us, but our all-seeing Friend
> Is always watching o'er us, and knows the very end.
> What though we seem to stumble, He will not let us fall;
> And learning to be humble is not lost time at all.

April 2

The Lord hath laid on him the iniquity of us all. Isaiah 53:6

Where are your sins? Wherever they are, God's terrible punishment must fall. Even if there were only one sin, and that
one hidden away down in your heart, God's wrath must find
it out, and punish it. It could not escape. But you know of
many more than one; and God knows of more still. And so
the great question for you is, Where are they? If He finds
them on you, His wrath must fall on you. But if they are put
somewhere else, you are safe, for He loves you, and only hates
your sins. Where can that wonderful "somewhere else" be?
Our text tells you that God laid them on Jesus. Why did His

terrible wrath fall on His beloved, holy Son? Because He had laid our sins on Jesus, and He took them, so that all the dreadful punishment might fall on Him instead of us. Instead of *you*. When He hung by His pierced hands and feet upon the cross, alone in the great darkness of God's wrath, it was because He was bearing *your* punishment, because *your* sins were laid upon Him, so that they might not be found upon you, and punished upon you. Satan will try to persuade you not to believe that *your* sins were laid upon Him, and will try to keep you always doubting it; but God says they were! Which will you believe? Again look at the solemn question, "Where are your sins?" and then look at Jesus, suffering and dying for you, and answer boldly, "The Lord hath laid on Him the iniquity of us all."

> "Forgiven until now!" for Jesus died
>   To take our sins away;
> His blood was shed, and still the infinite tide
>   Flows full and deep today.
> He paid the debt; we own it, and go free!
> The cancelled bond is cast in love's unfathomed sea.

April 3

HIS HANDS FOR YOU

His hands are as gold rings set with the beryl. Song of Solomon 5:14

His hands "for thee." Literal hands; literally pierced, when the whole weight of His quivering frame hung from their torn muscles and bared nerves; literally uplifted in parting blessing. Consecrated, priestly hands; "filled" hands (Exodus 28:41; 29: 9; etc., margin)—filled once with His great offering, and now with gifts and blessings "for thee." Tender hands, touching and healing, lifting and leading with gentlest care. Strong hands, upholding and defending. Open hands, filling with good and satisfying desire (Psalm 104:28 and 145:16). Faithful hands, restraining and sustaining. "His left hand is under my head, and His right hand doth embrace me."

> O waiting one, each moment's fall
> Is marked by Love that planned them all;
> Thy times, all ordered by His hand,
> In God's eternal covenant stand.
> O feeble one, look up and see
> Strong consolation sworn for thee;
> Jehovah's glorious arm is shown,
> His covenant strength is all thine own.

April 4

**And Jesus said unto him, Receive thy sight: thy faith
hath saved thee.** Luke 18:42

And that was enough, his prayer of faith, and Christ's answer
of power, for "immediately he received his sight." Was that
all? Did he go back to beg by the wayside? No; he "followed
Him, glorifying God." What a change from the cry of only
a few minutes before! "And all the people, when they saw
it, gave praise unto God." See what that first cry of "Have
mercy on me," so quickly led to! Who would have expected
a few minutes before to have seen him with his eyes open,
following Jesus, glorifying God, and causing a whole crowd
to give praise to God! I think the Lord Jesus says to you,
"What wilt *thou* that I shall do unto thee?" What will you
answer Him?

> My Saviour died in darkness that I might live in light,
> He closed His eyes in death that mine might have the heavenly sight;
> He gave up all His glory to bring it down to me,
> And took the sinner's place that He the sinner's Friend might be.
> And now my loving Jesus is my Light at eventide,
> The welcome Guest that enters in forever to abide:
> He never leaves me in the dark, but leads me all the way —
> So it is light at evening time, and soon it will be day.

April 5

AN ESTABLISHED HEART

It is a good thing that the heart be established with grace.
Hebrews 13:9

And yet some of us go on as if it were not a good thing even
to hope for it to be so. We should be ashamed to say that we
had behaved treacherously to a friend; that we had played him
false again and again; that we had said scores of times what
we did not really mean; that we had professed and promised
what all the while we had no sort of purpose of performing.
We should be ready to go off by the next ship to New Zealand
rather than calmly own to all this, or rather than ever face our
friends again after we had owned it. And yet we are not
ashamed (some of us) to say that we are always dealing
treacherously with our Lord; nay, more, we own it with an
inexplicable complacency as if there were a kind of virtue in
saying how fickle and faithless and desperately wicked our

hearts are. And we actually plume ourselves on the easy confession which we think proves our humility and which does not lower us in the eyes of others nor in our own eyes half so much as if we had to say, "I have told a story," or, "I have broken my promise." Nay, more, we have not the slightest hope and therefore not the smallest intention of aiming at an utterly different state of things. Well for us if we do not go a step farther and call those by hard and false names who do seek to have an established heart and who believe that as the Lord meant what He said when He promised, "No good thing will He withhold from them that walk uprightly," so He will not withhold this good thing.

Wholehearted! Saviour, beloved and glorious,
Take Thy great power, and reign Thou alone,
Over our wills and affections victorious,
Freely surrendered, and wholly Thine own.

Sisters, dear sisters, the call is resounding,
Will ye not echo the silver refrain,
Mighty and sweet, and in gladness abounding—
"Truehearted, wholehearted!" ringing again.

April 6

CONFIDENCE IN GOD

And the king said unto Zadok, Carry back the ark of God into the city: if I shall find favour in the eyes of the Lord, he will bring me again, and show me both it, and his habitation: But if he thus say, I have no delight in thee; behold, here am I, let him do to me as seemeth good unto him. 2 Samuel 15:25-26

Here we see David, driven from his royal home by his own son, passing amid tears over the brook Kidron, going toward the way of the wilderness, weary and weak handed," the wisest head in the land giving counsel against him, and the hearts of the men of Israel going after the traitor, and now losing the visible token of the presence of God Himself! I do not see how any of us could be brought to such a pass as all this! And yet he said, "Let Him do to me as seemeth good unto Him." But only a little while, and the Lord, whom He trusted so implicitly in such depths, restored to him all that seemed so nearly lost, and raised him again to royal heights of prosperity and praise.

Can we count redemption's treasure, scan the glory of God's love?
Such shall be the boundless measure of His blessings from above.
All we ask or think, and more, He will give in bounteous store—
He can fill and satisfy! God shall all your need supply.

April 7

ETERNAL SECURITY

Who shall also confirm you unto the end. 1 Corinthians 1:8

Your life shall be one of continual defending and strengthening and blessing; He avouching you this day and every day to be His peculiar people, as He hath promised, and establishing you an holy people unto Himself, and you avouching the Lord to be your God and to walk in His ways. Not this day only, for we are confirmed to Him "to be a people unto Thee forever." "Thine for ever!" "For I know that whatsoever God doeth, it shall be for ever"; so, having done this, it must be for ever! Fling this at the enemy when he tempts you to doubt your complete and eternal redemption—"Unto Thee for ever!" when he tempts you to regret or tamper with your separation—"Unto Thee for ever!" when he tempts you to quiver about your confirmation to the end — "Unto Thee for ever!" For "the Lord is faithful." "And now, O Lord God, the word that Thou hast spoken . . . establish it for ever, and do as Thou hast said."

> My life I bring to Thee, I would not be my own;
> O Saviour, let me be Thine ever, Thine alone.
> My heart, my life, my all
> I bring to Thee, my Saviour and my King!

April 8

BY SUBMISSION OR BY FORCE

And the vessel that he made of clay was marred in the hand of the potter: so he made it again another vessel, as seemed good to the potter to make it. Jeremiah 18:4

Just let Him do what seemeth Him good, and tell Him so! It may be you have been actually hindering deliverance and thwarting help, by not "letting" Him. Do not say, "But what difference can that make? He will do what He pleases, of course, whether I am willing or not." Not exactly that. Does it make no difference if the patient quietly lets the surgeon do what he thinks best? A remedy applied by force, or submitted to unwillingly, may be quite counteracted by fidget, or by feverishness induced or increased through setting one's self against what is prescribed or advised. The Lord's remedies do not have fair play, when we set ourselves against them. Even

Omnipotence waits for the faith that will *let* it act. If the "vessel made of clay," that was marred in the hand of the potter, could have resisted that skillful hand, how would he have been able to make it again another vessel, as it seemed good to him to make it? The unresisting clay could not help letting the potter remold it, into a better and permanent form; but we can hinder, simply by not "letting." But will you do this? For "now, O Lord, Thou art our Father, we are the clay, and Thou our Potter." Whatever may be our Potter's mysterious moldings, or our Father's mysterious dealings (I do not mean abstract, or possible, or future; but real, and present, and pressing), let us give the one sweet answer which meets everything: "Even so, Father, for so it seemed good in Thy sight."

> Hush! oh, hush! for the Father portioneth as He will,
> To all His beloved children, and shall they not be still?
> Is not His will the wisest, is not His choice the best?
> And in perfect acquiescence is there not perfect rest?

April 9

HE LISTENS PATIENTLY

And the apostles gathered themselves together unto Jesus, and told him all things.   Mark 6:30

After the apostles had been away, they "gathered themselves together unto Jesus, and told Him all things, both what they had done and what they had taught." Can you not fancy the gentle, gracious Master listening to everything so kindly, so patiently, letting them tell Him all their mistakes and all their success, all that had made them glad and all that had made them sorry? And can you not fancy the disciples sitting at His feet, and looking up into His face, and seeing how interested He was in all they had done, and not wishing to keep anything back from such a dear Master, and finding their own love to Him growing warmer and brighter for this sweet hour of talk with Him! How different if they had just said a few cold words to Him, and never *told* Him anything! Try this yourself. It will be such a help, such a comfort, and before long you will find it a great joy to tell Jesus everything.

> I came and communed with that mighty King,
> And told Him all my heart; I cannot say,
> In mortal ear, what communings were they.
> But wouldst thou know, go too, and meekly bring
> All that is in thy heart, and thou shalt hear
> His voice of love and power, His answers sweet and clear.

April 10

COUNT YOUR BLESSINGS

Forget not all his benefits. Psalm 103:2

"His benefits" means all the good things He has done for you, and all the good things He has given you. Try to count up "His benefits" of this one day; and then think of those of yesterday, and last week, and all the year, and all your life. You will soon find that there are more than you can count, and you will begin to see how very much you have to thank Him for. And then recollect His still greater benefits — the great gift of Jesus Christ Himself to be your Saviour and Redeemer, and the great gift of salvation through Him, and all His promises of grace and glory! David speaks of the multitude of His tender mercies, and Isaiah tells of "the multitude of His lovingkindnesses." Are not these true and beautiful words? Will you not turn them into a song of thanksgiving, and say, "Bless the Lord, O my soul, and forget not all His benefits:. . . . who crowneth thee with lovingkindness and tender mercies!"

So shall the father's soul be glad for him he holds so dear,
A son whose heart is truly wise in God's most holy fear;
And hallowed be our festal joy with gratitude and praise;
Forget not all His benefits, whose kindness crowns our days.

April 11

THE SPLENDOR OF HIS WILL

Now unto him that is able to do exceeding abundantly above all that we ask or think, according to the power that worketh in us, unto him be glory. Ephesians 3:20-21

Perhaps there is no point in which expectation has been so limited by experience as this. We believe God is able to do for us just so much as He has already done, and no more. We take it for granted a line must be drawn somewhere; and so we choose to draw it where experience ends, and faith would have to begin. Even if we have trusted and proved Him as to keeping our members and our minds, faith fails when we would go deeper and say, "Keep my will." And yet the only reason we have to give is, that though we have asked Him to take our will, we do not exactly find that it is altogether His, but that self-will crops up again and again. And whatever flaw there might be in this argument, we think the matter is quite settled by the fact that some whom we rightly esteem, and who are far better than ourselves, have the same experience, and do not even seem to think it right to hope for anything better. That is conclusive! And the result of this, as of every other faithless conclusion, is either discouragement and depression, or, still worse, acquiescence in an unyielded will, as something that cannot be helped. Now let us turn from our thoughts to God's thoughts. Verily, they are not as ours! He says He is able to do exceeding abundantly above all that we ask or think. Apply this here. We ask Him to take our wills and make them His. Does He or does He not mean what He says? And if He does, should we not trust Him to do this thing that we have asked and longed for, and not less but more? "Is *anything* too hard for the Lord?" "Hath He said, and shall He not do it?"

Her pencil, tracing feebly words that shall echo still,
Perchance some unknown mission may joyously fulfill:
"I think I just begin to see the splendor of God's will!"
For her, God's will was suffering, just waiting, lying still;
Days passing on in weariness, in shadows deep and chill;
And yet she had begun to see the splendor of God's will.

April 12

A LOOK THAT TRANSFORMS

Behold your God! . . . Behold the man! Isaiah 40:9; John 19:5

Look away from all "other things," look at the Crucified One, and, as you gaze, remember that He says, "Come unto Me." Is it nothing to you, all ye that pass by, that both from the depth of sorrow and from the height of glory this royal invitation comes to you? For it is the call not only of Jesus the crucified, but of Jesus reigning, and Jesus coming. "See that ye refuse not Him that speaketh," for He is coming to judge the quick and the dead. He is reigning now, and there are no neutrals in His kingdom. All are either willing and loyal subjects, or actual rebels—those who have obeyed the King's call, and come, and those who have "made light of it," and *not* come. Which are you?

Behold your King! Is it nothing to you,
That the crimson tokens of agony
From the kingly brow must fall like dew,
Thro' the shuddering shades of Gethsemane?
Jesus Himself, the Prince of Life,
Bows in mysterious mortal strife;
Oh, think of His sorrow! that we may know
The unknown love in the unknown woe!

April 13

He will keep the feet of his saints. 1 Samuel 2:9

Do not smile at a very homely thought! If our feet are not our own, ought we not to take care of them for Him whose they are? Is it quite right to be reckless about "getting wet feet," which might be guarded against either by forethought or afterthought, when there is, at least, a risk of hindering our service thereby? Does it please the Master when even in our zeal for His work we annoy anxious friends by carelessness in little things of this kind? May every step of our feet be more and more like those of our beloved Master. Let us continually consider Him in this, and go where He would have gone, on the errands which He would have done, "following hard" after Him. And let us look on to the time when our feet shall stand in the gates of the heavenly Jerusalem, when holy feet shall tread the streets of the holy city; no longer pacing any lonely path, for He hath said, "They shall walk with Me in white."

> A splendor that is shining upon His children's way,
> That guides the willing footsteps that do not want to stray,
> And that leads them ever onward unto the perfect day.

April 14

MAKE AN APPOINTMENT TO SEE HIM

Go forth, O ye daughters of Zion, and behold King Solomon.
Song of Solomon 3:11

Perhaps we have dwelt more upon the promise, "Thine eyes shall see the King in His beauty," than upon the command, "Go forth and behold" Him. We are not to be content with languidly saying, "We would see Jesus." If our eyes are too dim, let us pray, "Open Thou mine eyes"; if there is a veil upon our hearts, let us turn to the Lord, the Spirit, and it shall be taken away; if we are standing too far off to see, let us utter the cry and resolve, "Draw me, we will run after Thee"; if we are sitting still in the house, let us arise quickly and go to meet Jesus. This is neither an impossible nor a delusive command. The eye that looks away up to Jesus will behold Him now. And what shall we behold? The vision is all of beauty and glory and coronation now. The sorrow and the marred visage are past; and even when we behold Him as the Lamb of God, it is the Lamb in the midst of the throne now. O daughters of Zion, who gaze by faith upon Jesus our King, what do you see? Oh, the music of the answers!—"We see Jesus crowned with glory and honour!" "Fairer than the children of men!" "Beautiful and glorious!" "How great is His beauty!" "His countenance is as Lebanon, excellent as the cedars," and "as the sun shineth in his strength!" "Yea, He is altogether lovely."

> Thine eyes shall see! Not in a swift glance cast,
> Gleaning one ray to brighten memory,
> But while a glad eternity shall last,
>   Thine eyes shall see!
> Thine eyes shall see the King! The very same
> Whose love shone forth upon the curseful tree,
> Who bore thy guilt, who calleth thee by name;
>   Thine eyes shall see!

April 15

MAKING ANOTHER'S DAY BRIGHTER

Bear ye one another's burdens, and so fulfill the law of Christ.
Galatians 6:2
Serving the Lord with all humility of mind.   Acts 20:19

Perhaps you have never thought of the burdens of those around you. Then if you want to fulfill this law of Christ, the first thing will be to find out who has any burdens, and which of them you could bear instead. You will not have to watch long! There are very few without any. And if, for a moment a burden that you have taken up does seem rather hard, and you are tempted to drop it again, think of what the Lord Jesus bore for you! Think how He took up the heaviest burden of all for you, when He, His own self bare our sins in His own body on the tree! He did not drop that burden, but bore it till He died under it. Think of that, and it will be easy then to bear something for His sake. Now be on the watch all day for burdens to bear for others. See how many you can find out and pick up, and carry away! Depend upon it, you will not only make it a brighter day for others, but for yourself too!

> Then let it be
> The motto of our lives until we stand
> In the great freedom of eternity,
> Where we "shall serve Him" while we see His face,
> For ever and for ever "Free to serve."

April 16

If any man hear my voice, and open the door, I will come in.
Revelation 3:20

It all hinges upon Jesus coming into the heart as His own house—altogether His own. If there are some rooms of which we do not give up the key—some little sitting-room which we would like to keep as a little mental retreat, with a view from the window, which we do not quite want to give up — some lodger whom we would rather not send away just yet — some little dark closet which we have no resolution to open and set to rights—of course the King has not full possession; it is not all and really His own; and the very misgiving about it proves that He has therefore not yet come again in peace. It is no use expecting perfect peace, while He has a secret controversy with us about any withholding of what is His own by purchase. Only throw open all the doors, and the King of glory shall come in, and then there will be no craving for other guests. He will fill this house with glory, and there will be no place left for gloom.

> We cannot doubt our finding the very Key indeed,
> When Jesus fills up every void, responds to every need,
> When all the secrets of our hearts before Him are revealed,
> And all the mystery of life, alone with Him, unsealed.

April 17

PLEASED TO PLEASE

Whatsoever the king did pleased all the people. 2 Samuel 3:36

David had been giving a proof of his love for one who had long been his enemy, but whom he had received into friendship; and he had been giving a proof of his tenderheartedness and sympathy with the people, by weeping with them at the grave of Abner. "And all the people took notice of it, and it pleased them; as whatsoever the king did pleased all the people." This was because they loved their king. They watched him, not as the wicked Pharisees watched the Lord Jesus that they might find something against Him; but with the watching of admiration and love, taking notice of the kind and gracious things he did and said. Do you thus take notice of what your King does? Does it please you to hear and read of what He has done and is doing? It must be so if He really is your King. But the "whatsoever" is a little harder; and yet, if it is once really learnt, it makes everything easy. For if we learn to be pleased with *whatsoever* our King Jesus does, nothing can come wrong to us. Ask Him this day to make you so loving and loyal to Him, that *whatsoever* He does, all day long, may please you, because it has pleased Him to do it. I think He loves us so much, that He always gives us as much happiness as He can possibly trust us with, and does what is pleasantest for His dear children whenever He sees it will not hurt them; so, when He does something which at first does not seem so pleasant, we may still trust our Beloved King, and learn by His grace to be pleased with *whatsoever* He does.

Our yet unfinished story is tending all to this:
To God the greatest glory, to us the greatest bliss.
If all things work together for ends so grand and blest,
What need to wonder whether each in itself is best!

April 18

HELP OF THE HELPLESS

By thee have I been holden up. Psalm 71:6

Is it not wonderful that God should help us at all? Have we not wondered hundreds of times at the singular help He has given? If we have not, what ungrateful blindness! For He has been giving it ever since we were helpless babies. "Through Thee have I been holden up ever since I was born." How much of His help has been forgotten or altogether unnoticed. The very little things, the microscopic helpings, often seem most marvelous of all when we consider that it was Jehovah Himself who stooped to the tiny need of a moment. And the greater matters prove themselves to be the Lord's doing, just because they are so marvelous in our eyes. Why should we fear being brought to some depth of perplexity and trouble when we know He will be true to His name, and be our Help, so that we shall be even men wondered at because so marvelously helped!

Sovereign Lord and gracious Master,
Thou didst freely choose Thine own,
Thou hast called with mighty calling,
Thou wilt save, and keep from falling;
Thine the glory, Thine alone!
Yet Thy hand shall crown in heaven
All the grace Thy love hath given;
Just, though undeserved, reward
From our glorious, gracious Lord.

April 19

He shall call upon me, and I will answer him: I will be with him in trouble; I will deliver him, and honour him.

Psalm 91:15

This is the promise that he hath promised us.   1 John 2:25

Prayer must be based upon promise, but, thank God, His promises are always broader than our prayers. No fear of building inverted pyramids here, for Jesus Christ is the foundation, and this and all the other "promises of God in Him are yea, and in Him amen, unto the glory of God by us." So it shall be unto His glory to fulfill each one to us, and to answer our prayer for a "kept" or "established" heart. And its fulfillment shall work out His glory, not in spite of us, but *"by* us."

> "Tempted and tried!"
> There is One at thy side,
> And never in vain shall His children confide!
> He shall save and defend,
> For He loves to the end,
> Adorable Master and glorious Friend!
>
> "Tempted and tried!"
> The Saviour who died
> Hath called thee to suffer and reign by His side.
> His cross thou shalt bear,
> And His crown thou shalt wear,
> And forever and ever His glory shalt share.

April 20

OUR SOVEREIGN SAVIOUR

The Lord is our King; he will save us. Isaiah 33:22

The thought of salvation is constantly connected with that of kingship. Type, illustration, and prophecy combine them. "Thou shalt anoint him . . . that he may save my people." "By the hand of my servant David, I will save my people." "The king saved us." "A King shall reign; in His days, Judah shall be saved." "Thy King cometh . . . having salvation."

Because Jesus is our Saviour, He has the right to be our King; but again, because He is King, He is qualified to be our Saviour; and we never know Him fully as Saviour till we have fully received Him as King. His Kingship gives the strength to His priesthood. It is as the Royal Priest of the order of Melchizedek that He is able to save. Thus He is a Saviour, a great One, mighty to save. Our King has not only wrought and brought, and made known His salvation, but He Himself is our salvation. The very names seem used interchangeably. Isaiah says, "Say ye to the daughter of Zion, Behold, thy Salvation cometh"; Zechariah bids her rejoice, for "Behold thy King cometh." Again Isaiah says, "Mine eyes have seen the King"; and Simeon echoes, "Mine eyes have seen Thy Salvation," as he looks upon the infant Jesus, the Light to lighten the Gentiles; reminding us again of David's words, "The Lord is my Light and my Salvation."

> Worthy of adoration,
> Is the Lamb that once was slain,
> Cry, in raptured exultation,
> His redeemed from every nation;
> Angel myriads join the strain,
> Sounding from their sinless strings
> Glory to the King of kings;
> Harping, with their harps of gold,
> Praise which never can be told.

April 21

UNTO HIM

Ye have done it unto me.   Matthew 25:40
Ye did it not to me.   Matthew 25:45

Our Lord Jesus Christ has given us opportunities of showing whether we love Him or not. He tells us that what we try to do for any one who is poor, or hungry, or sick, or a lonely stranger, is just the same as doing it to Him. And when the King says, "Come, ye blessed," He remembers these little things, and says, "Ye have done it unto Me." But He tells us that if we do nothing for them, it is just the same as if He were standing there and we would do nothing for Him. And He will say, "Ye did it not to Me." One of these two words will be spoken to you in that coming day. It seems to me so very kind of the Lord Jesus to have told us this. For He knew that those who really love Him would *want* to do something for Him, and what could we do for the King of Glory in His glorious Heaven? So it was wonderfully thoughtful of Him to give to us His poor people to care for, and to say, if we have only been kind to a sick old lady or hungry little child, "Ye have done it unto Me!"

> Dear is the work He gives in many a varied way,
> Little enough in itself, yet something for every day—
> Something by pen for the distant, by hand or voice for the near,
> Whether to soothe or teach, whether to aid or cheer.

April 22

I will love thee, O Lord. Psalm 18:1

I will love Thee, Lord Jesus, because Thou hast loved me, and because Thou art loving me now, and wilt love me to the end. How could I have helped loving Thee, when Thou wast waiting all the time for me, waiting patiently while I did not care about Thee! Oh, forgive me, and now I will love Thee always; for Thou wilt take my love, and fix it on Thyself, and keep it for Thyself. I will love Thee, O Lord Jesus; I will not listen to Satan, who tries to keep me from loving Thee; I will not ask myself anything about it, lest I should begin to get puzzled about whether I do love Thee or not. Thou knowest that I do want to love Thee; and now, blessed Lord Jesus, hear me say that I will love Thee, and that I will trust Thee to make me love Thee more and more, always more and more. Thou hast heard me say it. And I am so glad I have said it. I do not want ever to take it back, and Thou wilt not let me take it back. Fill me so full of Thy love that it may run over into everything I do, and that I may love everybody, because I love Thee. Yes, I will love Thee, blest Lord Jesus!

> Jesus, Master, whose I am, purchased Thine alone to be,
> By Thy blood, O spotless Lamb, shed so willingly for me;
> Let my heart be all Thine own, let me live to Thee alone.

April 23

Ask, and ye shall receive, that your joy may be full. John 16:24

Why ask a little when we may ask much? The very next time we want to speak or write a word for Jesus (and of course that ought to be today), let us ask Him to give us not merely a general idea what to say, but to give us literally every single word, and "they shall be withal fitted in thy lips." For He will not say, "Thou hast asked a hard thing," though it is far more than asking for the mantle of any prophet. He says, "Behold, I have put My words in thy mouth." This was not for Jeremiah alone, for soon after we read, "He that hath My word, let him speak My word faithfully" (for we must not overlook our responsibility in the matter) ; and then follows the grand declaration of its power, even when spoken by feeble human lips: "Is not My word like as a fire? saith the Lord; and like a hammer that breaketh the rock in pieces?" "Behold, I will make My words in thy mouth fire." If we are not even sufficient of ourselves to think anything as of ourselves, how much less to speak anything! "Have I now any power at all to say anything? The word that God putteth in my mouth, that shall I speak." We would rather have it so, that the excellency of the power may be of God, and not of us. Our ascended Lord has said, "All power is given unto Me. Go ye therefore . . . and lo I am with you alway." This is enough for me; and I trust His word.

He is with thee! In thy service He is with thee "certainly,"
    Filling with the Spirit's power.
Giving in the needing hour His own messages by thee.
He is with thee! With thy spirit, with thy lips and with thy pen;
    In the quiet preparation,
In the heart-bowed congregation, nevermore alone again.

April 24

WHEN WEAK THEN STRONG

Beware . . . Lest when thou hast eaten and art full . . . and all that thou hast is multiplied; then thine heart be lifted up.
Deuteronomy 8:11-14

The times of marvelous help are times of danger. Unclasp the ivy from the elm and it is prostrate at once. Thank God if He keeps us realizing amid the busiest work and the pleasantest success that we have no power at all of ourselves to help ourselves. Then there will be nothing to hinder His continual help. As long as we say quite unreservedly, "My help cometh from the Lord," the help will come. As long as we are saying, "Thou art my help," He is our help—a very present help. Then we shall not be helped with a little help, which is too often all we really expect from our Omnipotent Helper, just because we do not feel that we have no might. Peter was a good swimmer but he did not say, "Lord, help me to swim." He said, "Lord, save me." And so the Master's help was instant and complete. "Most gladly therefore will I rather glory in my infirmities, that the power of Christ may rest upon me."

I am so weak, dear Lord, I cannot stand
    One moment without Thee!
But oh, the tenderness of Thine enfolding,
And oh! the faithfulness of Thine upholding,
And oh! the strength of Thy right hand!
    That strength is enough for me.

April 25

ACTIONS SPEAK LOUD

Neither yield ye your members as instruments of unrighteousness unto sin. Romans 6:13

Quick, angry motions of the heart will sometimes force themselves into expression by the hand, though the tongue may be restrained. The very way in which we close a door or lay down a book may be a victory or a defeat, a witness to Christ's keeping or a witness that we are not truly being kept. How can we expect that God will use our hand as an instrument of righteousness unto Him, if we yield it thus as an instrument of unrighteousness unto sin? Therefore, let us see to it, that it is at once yielded to Him whose right it is; and let our sorrow that it should have been even for an instant desecrated to Satan's use, lead us to entrust it henceforth to our Lord, to be kept by the power of God through faith "for the Master's use." For when the gentleness of Christ dwells in us, He can use the merest touch of a finger. Have we not heard of one gentle touch on a wayward shoulder being the turning-point of a life? I have known a case in which the Master made use of less than that — only the quiver of a little finger being made the means of touching a wayward heart.

Only a look and a motion! Yes, but we little know
How from each dwarf-like "only" a giant of power may grow;
The thundering avalanche crushes, loosened by only a breath,
And only a colorless drop may be laden with sudden death.

April 26

"I WILL FORGIVE BUT I CAN'T FORGET!"

First be reconciled to thy brother, and then come and offer thy gift. Matthew 5:24

Someone may have somewhat against you—an old quarrel, or a fresh misunderstanding—and you are too proud to acknowledge your fault, or your share in it; or you are too timid, or even too idle to do so. When there are faults on both sides, it is pretty often the one most in fault who is the least ready to forgive. Now do look into the matter, and see if you are truly in love and charity with all men. It is no use trying to explain away the words, "Forgive us our trespasses as we forgive them that trespass against us," for Christ Himself has explained and emphasized them. He said, "But if ye forgive not men their trespasses, neither will your Father forgive your trespasses." There is no evading this. There is absolutely *no* forgiveness for you if you do not forgive; for who can forgive sins but God only? And it is no use saying, "Well I will forgive but I can't forget!" You know quite well in your heart that the very tone in which you say that, shows that you are not really forgiving, and God knows what is at the bottom of your "can't forget!" Don't turn round fiercely, and say, "But if I can't, I can't!" For the things which are impossible with men, are possible with God.

> Our Father, forgive us for we have transgressed,
> Have wounded Thy love, and forsaken Thy breast;
> In the peace of Thy pardon henceforth let us live,
> That through Thy forgiveness we too may forgive.
> The Son of Thy love, who hath taught us to pray,
> For Thy treasures of mercy hath opened the way,
>   And Thine is the power.

April 27

A CHANNEL FOR GOD'S POWER

Most gladly therefore will I rather glory in my infirmities, that the power of Christ may rest upon me.   2 Corinthians 12:9

When there are great natural gifts people give the credit to them instead of to the grace which alone did the real work, and thus God is defrauded of the glory. So that, to say it reverently, God can get more glory out of a feeble instrument because then it is more obvious that the excellency of the power is of God and not of us.

Do you not really believe that the Holy Spirit is just as able to draw a soul to Jesus if He will by your whisper of the one word, "Come," as by an eloquent sermon an hour long? I do. At the same time, as it is evidently God's way to work through these intellects of ours, we have no more right to expect Him to use a mind which we are willfully neglecting and taking no pains whatever to fit for His use than I should have to expect you to write a beautiful inscription with my pen if I would not take the trouble to wipe it and mend it.

> Oh, sometimes strangely I forget, and, learning o'er and o'er,
> A lesson all with tear-drops wet, which I had learnt before.
> He chides me not, but waits awhile, then wipes my heavy eyes:
> Oh, what a Teacher is our God, so patient and so wise!
> If others sadly bring to me a lesson hard and new,
> I often find that helping them has made me learn it too.
> Or, had I learnt it long before, my toil is overpaid,
> If so one tearful eye may see one lesson plainer made.

April 28

And he shall put his hand upon the head of the burnt offering; and it shall be accepted for him.   Leviticus 1:4
Thou wilt keep him in perfect peace, whose mind is stayed on thee.   Isaiah 26:3

After all this, their hands were filled with consecrations for a sweet savor, so, after laying the hand of our faith upon Christ, suffering and dying for us, we are to lay that very same hand of faith, and in the very same way, upon Him as consecrated for us, to be the source and life and power of our consecration. And then our hands shall be filled with consecration, filled with Christ, and filled with all that is a sweet savor to God in Him.

Peace, peace!
Yea, peace to him that is near.
The crown is set on the Victor's brow,
For thy warfare is accomplished now;
And for thee eternal peace is made
By the Lord on whom thy sins were laid:
Then why shouldst thou fear?

Peace, peace!
Wrought by the Spirit of Might.
In thy deepest sorrow and sorest strife,
In the changes and chances of mortal life,
It is thine, beloved! Christ's own bequest,
Which vainly the tempter shall strive to wrest;
It is now thy right.

April 29

A MIND AT PERFECT PEACE WITH GOD

Shew my people their transgression, and the house of Jacob their sins.   Isaiah 58:1

He does not merely show us; it is something more than that. It is not merely an invisible hand drawing away a veil from hidden scenes, and a light brought to bear upon them, so that we can see them if we will; it is more personal, more terrible, and yet more tender than that. He tells us what we have done, and, if we listen, the telling will be very clear, very thorough, very unmistakable. At first we are tempted not to listen at all; we shrink from the still, small voice which tells us so startlingly unwelcome things. Many feel what one expressed: "Whenever I do think about it, I feel so horribly bad that I don't like to think any more." Ah, "if thou hadst known, even thou, at least in this thy day" that it was not mere thinking about it, but the voice of the Saviour beginning to tell thee what would have cleared the way for "the things which belong unto thy peace," what blessing might not the patient and willing listening have brought! Oh, do not stifle the voice, do not fancy it is only uncomfortable thoughts which you will not encourage lest they should make you low-spirited. Instead of that, ask Him to let His voice sound louder and clearer, and believe "that the goodness of God leadeth thee to repentance."

Peace, peace!
The word of the Lord to thee.
Peace, for thy passion and restless pride,
For thy endless cravings all unsupplied,
Peace for thy weary and sinworn breast;
He knows the need who has promised rest,
And the gift is free.

April 30

HIS THRONE BY RIGHT

He shall bear the glory, and shall sit and rule upon his throne; and he shall be a priest upon his throne.   Zechariah 6:13

The heart that is established in Christ is also established for Christ. It becomes His royal throne, no longer occupied by His foe, no longer tottering and unstable. And then we see the beauty and preciousness of the promise, "He shall be a Priest upon His throne." Not only reigning, but atoning. Not only ruling, but cleansing. Thus the throne is established in mercy but by righteousness.

I think we lose ground sometimes by parleying with the tempter. We have no business to parley with an usurper. The throne is no longer his when we have surrendered it to our Lord Jesus. And why should we allow him to argue with us for one instant as if it were still an open question? Do not listen; simply tell him that Jesus Christ is on the long-disputed throne and no more about it, but turn at once to your King and claim the glorious protection of His sovereignty over you. It is a splendid reality, and you will find it so. He will not abdicate and leave you kingless and defenseless. For verily, "The Lord is our king; He will save us" (Isaiah 33:22).

Look to Him who ever liveth, interceding for His own:
Seek, yea, claim the grace He giveth freely from His priestly throne.
Will He not thy strength renew with His Spirit's quickening dew?

May 1

Prove what is that good, and acceptable, and perfect, will of God.
Romans 12:2

The will of God which has seemed in old far-off days a stern and fateful power, is only love energized; love saying, "I will." And when once we really grasp this (hardly so much by faith as by love itself), the will of God cannot be otherwise than acceptable, for it is no longer a question of trusting that somehow or other there is a hidden element of love in it, but of understanding that it is love; no more to be dissociated from it than the power of the sun's rays can be dissociated from their light and warmth. And love recognized must surely be love accepted and reciprocated. So, as the fancied sternness of God's will is lost in His love, the stubbornness of our will becomes melted in that love, and lost in our acceptance of it.

> With quivering heart and trembling will
>   The word hath passed thy lips,
> Within the shadow, cold and still,
>   Of some fair joy's eclipse.
> "Thy will be done!" Thy God hath heard,
> And He will crown that faith-framed word.
>
> Thy prayer shall be fulfilled: but how?
>   His thoughts are not as thine;
> While thou wouldst only weep and bow,
>   He saith, "Arise and shine!"
> Thy thoughts were all of grief and night,
> But His of boundless joy and light.

May 2

INCREASING JOY

These things write we unto you, that your joy may be full.
1 John 1:4

Never in His Word are we told anything contradicting or explaining away this precious and reiterated promise. All through we are brightly pointed not merely to hope of permanent joy, but an increase of joy. "The meek shall increase [not merely shall keep up] their joy in the Lord." There are mingled promises and commands as to growth and increase in grace, knowledge, love, strength and peace, and does not increase of these imply and insure joy? It is suggested that we cannot expect to be always joyful, but it is written, "Rejoice in the Lord [not 'sometimes,' but] alway." "As sorrowful, yet alway rejoicing." When we are told that it would not even be good for us, remember that it is written again, "The joy of the Lord is your strength." Perhaps in that word "of" lies the whole secret of lasting joy, for it is even more than joy in the Lord; it is His own joy flowing into the soul that is joined to Himself which alone can remain in us, not even our joy in Him. "That they might have my joy fulfilled in themselves." Let us, then, seek not the stream but the fountain; not primarily the joy but that real and living union with Jesus by which His joy becomes ours.

> Thy love, Thy joy, Thy peace,
> Continuously impart
> Unto my heart;
> Fresh springs, that never cease,
> But still increase.

May 3

ON "FALLING"

Thy foot shall not stumble. Proverbs 3:23

Many a Christian says, "I shall be kept from falling at last, but, of course, I shall stumble continually by the way." But have ye not read this Scripture, "Thy foot shall not stumble"? And if you have only once read it, ought not the "of course" to be put over on the other side? For "hath He spoken, and shall He not make it good?" "And the Scripture cannot be broken." But as a matter of fact man does stumble, and though he riseth again, yet even the "just man falleth seven times." Of course we do, and this is entirely accounted for by the first "of course." God gives us a promise and instead of humbly saying, "Be it unto me according to Thy word," we either altogether overlook or deliberately refuse to believe it. And then, of course, we get no fulfillment of it. The measure of the promise is God's faithfulness, the measure of its realization is our faith. Perhaps we have not even cried, "Help Thou mine unbelief" as to this promise, much less said, "Lord, I believe."

Increase our faith that we may claim each starry promise sure,
And always triumph in Thy name, and to the end endure.
Increase our faith, that never dim or trembling it may be,
Crowned with the "perfect peace" of Him "whose mind is stayed on Thee."
Increase our faith, for Thou hast prayed that it should never fail;
Our steadfast anchorage is made with Thee, within the veil.

May 4

**So teach us to number our days, that we may apply our
hearts unto wisdom.**   Psalm 90:12

It is not so often a whole sermon as a single short sentence in
it, that wings God's arrow to a heart. It is seldom a whole
conversation that is the means of bringing about the desired
result, but some sudden turn of thought or word, which comes
with the electric touch of God's power. Sometimes it is less
than that; only a look (and what is more momentary?) has
been used by Him for the pulling down of strongholds. Again,
in our own quiet waiting upon God, as moment after moment
glides past in the silence at His feet, the eye resting upon a
page of His Word, or only looking up to Him through the darkness, have we not found that He can so irradiate one passing
moment with His light that its rays never die away, but shine
on and on through days and years? Are not such moments
proved to have been kept for Him? And if some, why not all?
This view of moments seems to make it clearer that it is impossible to serve two masters, for it is evident that the service
of a moment cannot be divided. If it is occupied in the service
of self, or any other master, it is not at the Lord's disposal;
He cannot make use of what is already occupied.

> The weary waiting times are but the muffled peals
> Low preluding celestial chimes, that hail His chariot-wheels.
> Trust Him to tune Thy voice to blend with seraphim;
> His "Wait" shall issue in "Rejoice"! Wait patiently for Him.

May 5

A new heart also will I give you. Ezekiel 36:26

Why does God promise this? Because our old hearts are so
evil that they cannot be made any better; and so nothing will
do any good but giving us a new heart. Because we cannot
make a new heart for ourselves; the more we try, the more
we shall find we cannot do it; so God, in His great pity and
kindness says He will give it to us. Because, unless we have
a new heart we cannot enter the kingdom of God, we cannot
even see it! Without this gift we must be left outside in

the terrible darkness when the door is shut. There is a great difference between the old heart and the new one. The old heart is afraid of God, and does not love Him, and would much rather He were not always seeing us. The new heart loves God and trusts what He says, and loves to think that He is always watching it. Oh, how happy and blessed to have this new heart! All God's children receive it, for He has said, "I will give them one heart"; that is, all the same new heart. Do you not want to have it too? You must come to Him for it, for He hath said, "A new heart also will I give you!"

> My heart to Thee I bring, the heart I cannot read;
> A faithless, wandering thing, an evil heart indeed.
> I bring it, Saviour, now to Thee
> That fixed and faithful it may be.

May 6

INFLUENCE OF THE KING

I will be thy king. Hosea 13:10

He knows our need of a King. He knows the hopeless anarchy, not only of the world, but of a heart without a king. Is there a more desolate cry than, "We have no king"?—none to reverence and love, none to obey, none to guide and protect us and rule over us, none to keep us in that truest freedom of wholehearted loyalty? Have we not felt that we really want a strong hand over our hearts? That having our own way is not so good as another way if only that other is one to whom our hearty and entire confidence and allegiance can be and are given? Has there not been an echo in our souls of the old cry, "Give me a king"?—a cry nothing can still but this divine promise, "I will be thy King!" But the promise has been given; and now, if the old, desolate wail of a kingless heart comes up in an hour of faithless forgetfulness, His word comes like a royal clarion, "Now, why dost thou cry out aloud? Is there no king in thee?" And then the King's gracious assurance falls with hushing power, "I will be thy King."

> "He is thy Lord!" Oh, I am glad of this,
> So glad that Thou art Master, Sovereign, King!
> Only I want Thy rule to be supreme
> And absolute; no lurking rebel thought,
> No traitor in disguise to pass its bounds.
> So glad — because it is such rest to know
> That Thou hast ordered and appointed all,
> And wilt yet order and appoint my lot.

May 7

PURGING MUST COME

**And thou shalt . . . anoint them, and consecrate them, and
sanctify them, that they may minister unto me.** Exodus 28:41

If we look at any Old Testament text about consecration, we
shall see that the marginal reading of the word is "fill the
hand." Now, if our hands are full of "other things," they
cannot be filled with "the things that are Jesus Christ's"; there
must be emptying before there can be any true filling. So if
we are sorrowfully seeing that our hands have not been kept
for Jesus, let us humbly begin at the beginning, and ask Him
to empty them thoroughly, that He may fill them completely.
For they must be emptied. Either we come to our Lord willingly about it, letting Him unclasp their hold, and gladly
dropping the glittering weights they have been carrying, or,
in very love, He will have to force them open, and wrench
from the reluctant grasp the "earthly things" which are so
occupying them that He cannot have His rightful use of them.
There is only one other alternative, a terrible one—to be let
alone till the day comes when not a gentle Master, but the re-
lentless king of terrors shall empty the trembling hands as
our feet follow him out of the busy world into the dark valley,
for "it is certain we can carry nothing out."

> Take all Thy vessels, O glorious Finer,
> Purge all the dross, that each chalice may be
> Pure in Thy pattern, completer, diviner,
> Filled with Thy glory and shining for Thee.

May 8

THINE, LORD

I am thine. Psalm 119:94

This is a wonderful stone for the sling of faith. It will slay
any Goliath of temptation, if we only sling it out boldly and
determinately at him. When self tempts us (and we know
how often that is), let it be met with "not your own," and
then look straight away to Jesus with "I am Thine." If the
world tries some lure, old or new, remember the words of the
Lord Jesus, how He said, "If ye were of the world, the world
would love his own; . . . But I have chosen you out of the
world"; and lest the world should claim us as its own, look

away to Jesus and say, "I am Thine." Is it sin, subtle and strong and secret, that claims our obedience? Acknowledge that "ye were the servants of sin"; but now, "being made free from sin, ye became the servants of righteousness," and conquer with the faith-shout, "I am Thine." Is it a terrible hand-to-hand fight with Satan himself making a desperate effort to reassert his old power? Tell the prince of this world that he hath nothing in Jesus and that you are "in Him that is true," a member of His body, His very own, and see if he is not forced to flee at the sound of your confident "I am Thine"?

> He is thy Lord! Thyself, O Saviour dear,
> And not another. Whom have I but Thee
> In Heaven or earth? And whom should I desire!
> For Thou hast said, "So shall the King desire thee!"
> And well may I respond in wondering love,
> "Thou art my Lord, and I will worship Thee."

May 9

HIS HEART FOR THEE

Behold . . . he is mighty . . . in heart. Job 36:5, margin

And this mighty and tender heart is for thee! If He had only stretched forth His hand to save us from bare destruction, and said, "My hand for thee!" how could we have praised Him enough? But what shall we say of the unspeakably marvelous condescension which says, "Thou hast ravished [margin, *taken away*] my heart, my sister, my spouse!" The very fountain of His divine life, and light, and love, the very center of His being, is given to His beloved ones, who are not only "set as a seal upon His heart," but taken into His heart, so that our life is hid there, and we dwell there in the very center of all safety, and power, and love, and glory. What will be the revelation of that day, when the Lord Jesus promises, "Ye shall know that I am in My Father, and ye in Me"? For He implies that we do not yet know it, and that our present knowledge of this dwelling in Him is not knowledge at all compared with what He is going to show us about it. Now shall we, can we, reserve any corner of our hearts from Him?

> We thirst for God, our treasure is above;
> Earth has no gift our one desire to meet,
> And that desire is pledge of His own love.
> Sweet question; with no answer! oh how sweet!
> My heart in chiming gladness o'er and o'er
> Sings on — God's everlasting love!
> What wouldst thou more?

May 10

NO CONVENIENT SEASON

Son, go work to day in my vineyard. Matthew 21:28

The Lord's work is always pressing, and may never be put off. Much of it has to do with souls which may be in eternity tomorrow; and with opportunities which are gone forever if not used then and there; there is no convenient season for it but today. Often it is not really done at all, because it is not done in the spirit of holy haste. We meet an unconverted friend again and again, and beat about the bush, and think to gain quiet influence and make way gradually, and call it judicious not to be in a hurry, when the real reason is that we are wanting in holy eagerness and courage to do the King's true business with that soul, and in nine such cases out of ten nothing ever comes out of it; but "As thy servant was busy here and there, he was gone." Have we not found it so? Delay in the Lord's errands is next to disobedience, and generally springs out of it or issues in it. "God commanded me to make haste." Let us see to it that we can say, "I made haste, and delayed not to keep Thy commandments."

> Have you not a word for Jesus? Some, perchance, while you are dumb,
> Wait and weary for your message, hoping you will bid them come;
> Never telling hidden sorrows, lingering just outside the door,
> Longing for your hand to lead them into rest for evermore.

May 11

YOU ARE NEVER FORGOTTEN

Not one of them is forgotten before God. Luke 12:6

When you come to those parts of the Bible which are too often undervalued and left out of the daily reading, still, though it may be through a less transparent veil, God will reveal Himself. For instance, when you come to the genealogies in Chronicles, consider how His individual care is illustrated by the otherwise unknown names, noted in His book because of their connection with Christ; no matter how remote that connection, through the distant generations and collateral branches, might seem to human ways of thinking. And then remember that "this God," who thus inscribed their individual names for Christ's sake, is "our God" who has inscribed our individual names in the book of life for Christ's sake, because we are chosen in Him. And when we read the life of His dear Son, and see what that beloved Son, in the infinite lovableness of His exquisite perfection, must have been to the Father who yet spared Him not; and, most of all, when we read of the hand of God being laid upon the Man of His right hand, when He made the iniquities of us all to meet on Him, and let Him suffer unto death for us men and for our salvation, then, above all, let us turn to God the Father and say, "This God, who so loved the world, is our God!" It seems as if this personal relationship to us as our "God," were one in which He specially delights, and which He would have us keep continually in mind.

It is so sweet to trust Thy Word alone:
I do not ask to see
The unveiling of Thy purpose, or the shining
Of future light on mysteries untwining:
Thy promise-roll is all my own —
Thy Word is enough for me.

May 12

ROYAL BOUNTY

Thou openest thine hand, they are filled with good. Psalm 104:28
According to thine own heart, hast thou done all this greatness.
1 Chronicles 17:19
Thou hast dealt well with thy servant, O Lord, according unto thy word. Psalm 119:65

His hand, His heart, His word—what an immeasurable measure of His bounty! The great *hand* that holds the ocean in its hollow is opened to satisfy our desire, and to go beyond that exceeding abundantly, giving us according to the *heart* that so loved the world, and according to the *word* which is so deep and full that all the saints that ever drew their hope and joy from it cannot fathom its ever-upspringing fountain. Perhaps nobody knows the Bible well enough to know the full significance of saying, "Be it unto me *according to Thy word*"; how much less can we imagine what shall be the yet unrevealed royal bounty *according to His heart* of infinite love and hand of infinite power. "What I do thou knowest not now, but thou shalt know hereafter." "And ye shall . . . be satisfied, and praise the name of the Lord your God, that hath dealt wondrously with you."

Great our need, but greater far, is our Father's loving power;
He upholds each mighty star, He unfolds each tiny flower.
He who numbers every hair, earnest of His faithful care,
Gave His Son for us to die; God shall all your need supply.

May 13

HE GIVETH AND GIVETH AND GIVETH

Every good gift and every perfect gift is from above, and cometh down from the Father of lights. James 1:17

Think a little this morning of God's great kindness to you. How very good He is to you! I know one of His dear children who looks up many, many times a day, and says, "Good Lord Jesus!" or "Kind Lord Jesus!" She does not set herself to say it, but it seems as if she could not help saying it, just because He is so good and kind. And then it seems only natural to look up again and say, "Dear Lord Jesus!" How can anybody go on all day long, and never see how good He is, and never look up and bless Him? Most especially on bright, pleasant days, when He giveth us more even than usual to enjoy! He "giveth." Not one single pleasant thing, not one single bit of enjoyment comes to us but what He giveth. We cannot get it, we do not earn it, we do not deserve it; but He *giveth* lovingly, and kindly, and freely. Suppose He stopped giving, what would become of us?

> No valley-life but hath some mountain days,
> Fair sunlit memories of joy and praise.
> Grave on thy heart each past "red letter day"!
> Forget not all the sunshine of the way
> By which the Lord hath led thee; answered prayers,
> And joys unasked, strange blessings, lifted cares,
> Grand promise-echoes. Thus thy life shall be
> One record of His love and faithfulness to thee.

May 14

CONFESSION IS GOOD FOR THE SOUL

We have sinned: do thou unto us whatsoever seemeth good unto thee; deliver us only, we pray thee, this day. Judges 10:15

The children of Israel were sold for their evil deeds into the hands of the Philistines and Ammonites, and vexed and oppressed for eighteen years. ("Vexed and oppressed"—does that describe your case?) They come to the Lord with bare excuseless confession, "We have sinned," and then they cast themselves on bare undeserved mercy: "Do Thou unto us whatsoever seemeth good unto Thee." And what then? "His soul was grieved for the misery of Israel." Could anything be more humanly tender, as well as divinely magnanimous! Is it not a lesson to come straight to His heart with any misery of which the sting is that we have brought it on ourselves, and deserved it a thousandfold? First confess the sin, and then leave the sorrows wholly in His hands, and we find Him verily "the same Lord, whose property is always to have mercy." And mercy includes help, for the Lord did not stop short at grieving over their misery; He sent Jephthah to deliver them, so that they "dwelled safe" for about thirty years. (Compare Judges 11:33 and 1 Samuel 12:11.)

> "Thou hast forgiven — even until now!"
> We bless Thee, Lord, for this,
> And take Thy great forgiveness as we bow
> In depth of suffering bliss;
> While over all the long, regretful past
> This veil of wondrous grace Thy sovereign hand doth cast.

May 15

TIDINGS MAKE THE FEET

How beautiful upon the mountains are the feet of him that bringeth good tidings, that publisheth peace.   Isaiah 52:7

"How beautiful are the feet of them that bring glad tidings of good things!" That is the best use of all; and I expect the angels think those feet beautiful, even if they are cased in muddy boots or galoshes.

Once the question was asked, "Wherefore wilt thou run, my son, seeing that thou hast no tidings ready?" So if we want to have these beautiful feet, we must have the tidings ready which they are to bear. Let us ask Him to keep our hearts so freshly full of His good news of salvation that our mouths may speak out of their abundance. "If the clouds be full of rain they empty themselves upon the earth." The two olive branches empty the golden oil out of themselves. May we be so filled with the Spirit that we may thus have much to pour out for others!

> "Such as I have I sow, it is not much,"
> Said one who loved the Master of the field;
> "Only a quiet word, a gentle touch,
> Upon the hidden harp strings, which may yield
> No quick response; I tremble, yet I speak
> For Him who knows the heart, so loving, yet so weak."
> And so the words were spoken, soft and low,
> Or traced with timid pen; yet oft they fell
> On soil prepared, which she would never know,
> Until the tender blade sprang up, to tell
> That not in vain her labor had been spent;
> Then with new faith and hope more bravely on she went.

May 16

The king also himself passed over the brook Kidron. 2 Samuel 15:23
And Jesus went before them.   Mark 10:32

Jesus went forth with His disciples over the brook Cedron.
How precisely the Old Testament shadow corresponds with the
New Testament fulfillment! The king in sorrow and humiliation, is here brought before us, passing from his royal home,
from all its glory and gladness — passing over into exile and
unknown distresses. There is no need for imagination in dwelling on His sorrows. The pathos of the plain words is more
than enough; no pen has power to add to it. Do we know anything of fellowship with Him in His sorrow? All the people,
except the rebels passed over with the king. Do we know anything of this passage over Cedron, the brook of sadness with
Him? Possibly it seems presumptuous to think of sharing the
fellowship of His sufferings, that mysterious privilege! But
mark, it was not only the mighty Ittai and all his men, the
nobles and the veterans, that passed over, but all the "little
ones" that were with him too. And so the little ones, the
weak ones, the least member of his body may thus continue
with Jesus; and nothing brings one closer to another than
a shared sorrow.

> Thy claim to rest on Jesus' breast all weariness shall be,
> And pain thy portal to His heart of boundless sympathy.
> No conflict, but the King's own hand shall end the glorious strife;
> No death, but leads thee to the land of everlasting life.

May 17

WILLINGNESS — THE SECRET OF KNOWING

Whatsoever he saith unto you, do it.   John 2:5

How are you to know what He says to you? Ah, it is so easy
to know if we are really willing to know, and willing to obey
when we do know! He has spoken so plainly to us in His
Word! In that He tells us exactly what to do. It is most wonderful how He has said everything there for us, told us everything we ought to do. When you read a chapter, listen and
watch to see what He saith unto you in it. There is another
way in which He tells us what to do. He speaks to you through

your conscience. Now "whatsoever He saith unto you, do it!" Whether easy or hard, do it because He tells you; do it for love of Him, and it will be much better and happier to obey the Lord than to please yourself. "Whatsoever He saith unto you, *do* it!" "Do *it!*" Do the exact thing He would have you do, not something a little bit different, or something which you think will be nearly the same, but do "*it.*" And do it at once. It is so true, that the very first moment is the easiest for obedience. Every minute that you put off doing the right thing makes it harder. Do not let your Lord have to "speak twice" to you. "Whatsoever He saith unto you, do it" cheerfully, exactly, instantly.

> Master, speak! and make me ready, when Thy voice is truly heard,
> With obedience glad and steady, still to follow every word.
> I am listening, Lord, for Thee; Master, speak, oh, speak to me!

May 18

HE IS KING! . . . IS HE YOURS?

Thou art my King.   Psalm 44:4

Can I say it? Ought I to say it? Do I say it? Is Jesus in very deed and truth my King? Where is the proof of it? Am I living in His kingdom of righteousness and peace and joy in the Holy Ghost now? Am I speaking the language of that kingdom? Am I following the customs of the people which are not His people, or do I diligently learn the ways of His people? Am I practically living under the rule of His laws? Have I done heart homage to Him? Am I bravely and honestly upholding His cause, because it is His, not merely because those around me do so? Is my allegiance making any practical difference to my life today? He came Himself to purchase me from my tyrant and His foe; He laid aside His crown and His royal robes, and left His kingly palace, and came down Himself to save a rebel; though He was rich, yet for my sake became poor, that I "through His poverty might be rich." God has called me unto His Kingdom and glory; He hath translated me into the kingdom of the Son of His love; and shall the loyal words falter or fail from my lips, "Thou art my King"?

> O Saviour, precious Saviour, whom yet unseen we love;
> O Name of might and favor, all other names above!
> We worship Thee, we bless Thee, to Thee alone we sing;
> We praise Thee, and confess Thee our holy Lord and King!

May 19

SUPERABOUNDING COMPENSATION

The hand of the Lord shall be known toward his servants.
Isaiah 66:14

"All that see them shall acknowledge them, that they are the seed which the Lord hath blessed." More than that, the whole world shall "know that Thou hast loved them as Thou hast loved Me," and "I will make them . . . to know that I have loved thee." Is not this superabounding compensation for any tiny share we may now have in the world-wide misunderstanding of our Father's wisdom and our Saviour's love? "And they shall know," is not only for those who do not know at all; for "at that day ye shall know that I am in My Father, and ye in Me, and I in you"—revelations of the mysteries of Godhead and of the ineffable union of Christ with His people, which have not yet entered into our hearts to conceive. "Then shall we know [if we follow on to know] the Lord." "For now I know in part; but then shall I know even as also I am known."

> Yes, work by faith and not by sight, fast clinging to My hand;
> Content to feel My love and might, not yet to understand.
> A little while thy course pursue, till grace to glory grow;
> Then what I am and what I do, hereafter thou shalt know.

May 20

NO RETIREMENT FROM HIS SERVICE

He loveth thee and thine house, because he is well with thee.
Deuteronomy 15:16

The Hebrew servant had trial of his master's service for six years, and in the seventh he might go out free if he would. But then, "if the servant shall plainly say, I love my master . . . I will not go out free," then publicly and legally, he was sealed to his service forever. It all depended on the love. He would say, "I will not go away from thee; because he loveth thee and thine house, because he is well with thee." How this meets our case, dear fellow-servants! We do not want to go away from Jesus, because we love Him; and we love His house too, the spiritual house, the blessed company of the faithful. And are we not well with Him? Where else so well? Where else anything but ill? Has He not dealt well with His servants? What a chorus it would be if we all spoke out, and said, "I love my Master, and it hath been well for me with Him!" Why don't we speak out, and let people know what a Master He is, and what a happy service His is? Who is to speak out, if we have not a word to say about it? Let us stand up for Jesus and His service, every one of us! Perhaps, when we do speak out, we shall realize the joy of His promise as never before. It was not till the servant had owned his love, and given up "the rest of his time in the flesh," and had his ear bored, that the word was spoken, "He shall serve him for ever"; and it is only the loving and consecrated heart that leaps up for joy at the heavenly prospect: "And his servants shall serve Him."

> How can the lip be dumb,
> The hand all still and numb,
> When Thee the heart doth see and own
> Her Lord and God alone?
> Tune for Thyself the music of my days,
> And open Thou my lips that I may show Thy praise.
> Yea, let my whole life be
> One anthem unto Thee,
> And let the praise of lip and life
> Outring all sin and strife.
> O Jesus Master! by Thy name supreme
> For Heaven and earth the one, the grand eternal theme.

May 21

CHRIST JESUS SAVES FROM SIN AND SINS

Christ Jesus came into the world to save sinners. 1 Timothy 1:15

In death we would cling to these words. Why not in life equally cling to, and equally make real use of the promise, "He shall save His people from their sins"—not merely from sin in general, but definitely from their sins, personal and plural sins? "Is My hand shortened at all that it cannot redeem? or have I no power to deliver?" His salvation is indeed finished, His work is perfect; and yet our King is still working salvation in the midst of the earth, applying the reality of His salvation (if we will only believe His power) to the daily details of our pilgrimage and our warfare. We need it not only at last, but now—every hour, every minute. And the King "shall deliver the needy when he crieth," "and shall save the souls of the needy." May He say to your soul this day, "I am thy salvation."

> On Thee the Lord
> My mighty sins hath laid;
> And against Thee Jehovah's sword
> Flashed forth its fiery blade.
> The stroke of justice fell on Thee,
> That it might never fall on me.

May 22

GOD'S TREASURE HOUSE IS OURS

The Lord shall open unto thee his good treasure. Deuteronomy 28:12

When the wise men opened their treasures, they brought out gold and frankincense and myrrh. When Jehovah opens unto us His good treasure, we shall see greater things than these. The context of this rich promise seems to make the Heaven the treasure house; and in its primary and literal sense, the fertilizing rain is the first outpouring of the opened treasure, soon after expanded into beautiful details of "the precious things of heaven and . . . the precious things of the earth." But the spiritual blessings are closely interwoven with the temporal in the whole passage, and the faithful Israelites who did not "look only for transitory promises" may well have claimed the opening of heavenly treasure through this promise.

Nor withhold we glad thanksgiving for His mercies ever new,
Precious things of earth and Heaven, sun and rain and quickening dew;
Precious fruits and varied crowning of the year His goodness fills,
Chief things of the ancient mountains, precious things of lasting hills.

May 23

GIVING WHAT WAS GIVEN

Freely ye have received, freely give. Matthew 10:8

The context shows that we must not content ourselves with applying this only to silver and gold. Those to whom the command was spoken neither possessed nor provided any. Far greater gifts had they received, far greater gifts were they to give. What have we freely received? Our Bibles give us a threefold answer. (1) Love: God our Father says, "I will love them freely." (2) Justification: for we are "justified freely by His grace" and "by His blood." (3) Life: for He says, "I will give unto him that is athirst of the fountain of the water of life freely." And unto us has been preached this "gospel of God freely."

We are responsible not only for having received such gifts, but for knowing that we have received them, for "we have received . . . the Spirit which is of God, that we might know the things that are freely given to us of God." The whole Bible is one long inventory of the things that are freely given to us, and yet we cannot reckon our wealth, for "all things are yours." Possessing the one unspeakable gift, Jesus Christ Himself, is "possessing all things."

"As every man hath received the gift, even so minister the same." How will you do this? Can you make it a question of dollars and cents? Is *that* what you have received? Is that *as* you have received? Will you not say, "I will freely sacrifice unto Thee"? Sacrifice! What? "I beseech you therefore, brethren, by the mercies of God, that ye present your bodies a living sacrifice." There are so many who would delight to go, but whose way God has entirely hedged up. Are there none whose way is not so hedged up? He who spared not His own Son, but with Him freely gives us all things, is saying very clearly and loudly, "Whom shall I send, and who will go for us?" Will any one who might say, "Here am I, send me," refuse to say it?

> What hast Thou done for me, O mighty Friend
> Who lovest to the end!
> Reveal Thyself, that I may now behold
> Thy love unknown, untold.
> Bearing the curse, and made a curse for me,
> That blessed and made a blessing I might be.

May 24

HE DID WHAT HE CAME TO DO

I have finished the work. John 17:4

His great promise has had its first fulfillment "unto Thee." It is a finished fact of sevenfold grace. The Lord has come, and His own voice has given the objects of His coming—"to do Thy will, O God"; to fulfill the law; "to call sinners to repentance"; "to seek and to save that which was lost"; "that they might have life, and that they might have it more abundantly"; "a light into the world, that whosoever believeth on me should not abide in darkness." What He came to do He has done, for "He faileth not." On this we may and ought to rest quietly and undoubtingly, for "the Lord hath done it."

> For I know that what He doeth stands forever, fixed and true;
> Nothing can be added to it, nothing left for us to do;
> Nothing can be taken from it, done for me and done for you,
>   Evermore and evermore.
> Listen now! the Lord hath done it! for He loved us unto death;
> It is finished! He has saved us! Only trust to what He saith.
> He hath done it! Come and bless Him, spend in praise your
>   ransomed breath
>   Evermore and evermore.

May 25

Our light affliction, which is but for a moment, worketh for us a far more exceeding and eternal weight of glory.
2 Corinthians 4:17

We think of trials as intended to do us good in the long run and in a general sort of way, but the Lord says of each one, "It yieldeth." Apply this to the present. The particular annoyance which befell you this morning, the vexatious words which met your ear, and grieved your spirit, the disappointment which was His appointment for you today, the slight but hindering ailment, the presence of someone who is a grief of mind to you, whatever this day seemeth not joyous but grievous is linked in "the good pleasure of His goodness" with a corresponding afterward of peaceable fruit, the very seed from which if you only do not choke it shall spring up and ripen. If we set ourselves to watch the Lord's dealings with us, we shall soon be able to detect a most beautiful correspondence and proportion between each individual chastening and its own resulting afterward. The habit of thus watching and expecting will be very comforting and a great help to quiet trust when some new chastening is sent, for then we shall simply consider it as the herald and earnest of a new afterward.

What shall Thine "afterward" be, O Lord?
How long must Thy child endure?
Thou knowest! 'Tis well that I know it not!
Thine "afterward" cometh, I cannot tell what,
But I know that Thy Word is sure.

May 26

Put that on mine account. Philemon 18

When Paul asked Philemon, in a most beautiful letter, to take back Onesimus who had run away from him, he said, "If he hath wronged thee, or oweth thee ought, put that on my account." Onesimus had been a bad servant to Philemon; and being willing to come back and do better, would not pay for what he had wronged him in before, and would not pay his old debts. And he evidently had nothing himself to pay them with. But Paul offered to pay all, so that Onesimus might be

received, "not now as a servant," but as a "brother beloved."
This is an exquisite picture of what the Lord Jesus Christ does.
He not only intercedes for us with Him from whom we have
departed, and against whom we have sinned; but, knowing to
the full how much we have wronged God, and how much we
owe Him, He says, "Put that on Mine account." And God has
put it all on His account, and the account has been paid, paid
in blood. When the Lord "laid on Him the iniquity of us all,"
Jesus saw and knew all your sins; and He said, "Put that on
Mine account." Oh, what wonderful "kindness and love of God
our Saviour"!

> Nothing to pay! the debt is so great;
> What will you do with the awful weight?
> How shall the way of escape be made?
> Nothing to pay! yet it must be paid!
> Hear the voice of Jesus say,
> "Verily thou hast nothing to pay!
> All has been put to My account,
> I have paid the full amount."

May 27

FOREVER SATISFIED

He did eat continually at the king's table. 2 Samuel 9:13
**And his allowance was a continual allowance given him of
the king, a daily rate for every day, all the days of his life.**
2 Kings 25:30

It is not occasional but continual feeding on Christ that really
satisfies the longing soul, and fills the hungry soul with goodness. "He did eat *continually* at the king's table." It is "he
that *cometh* to Me" who "shall never hunger," not "he who
did come." "To whom coming," always coming, never going
away, because we "have tasted that the Lord is gracious," we
shall be "built up." If we really are guests at the King's table
in its fullest sense — if we are feeding upon Christ Himself,
and not on any shadow of the true substance — we must be
satisfied. Here is a strong, severe test. Christ *must* satisfy;
then, if we are not satisfied, it must be because we are not
feeding on Him wholly and only. The fault is not in the pro-
vision which is made—"For all that came unto King Solomon's
table, they lacked nothing."

> God doth not bid thee wait to disappoint at last;
> A golden promise, fair and great, in precept-mold is cast.
> Soon shall the morning gild the dark horizon rim,
> Thy heart's desire shall be fulfilled, "Wait patiently for Him."

May 28

CHRIST IN YOU DAY AND NIGHT

We will come unto him, and make our abode with him.

John 14:23

Do not let us say, "How can this be?" but, like Mary, "How shall this be?" The means, though not the mode, of the mystery is revealed for our grasp of adoring wonder: "That Christ may dwell in your heart by faith." It is almost too wonderful to dare to speak of. Christ Himself, my King, coming to me, into me! abiding, dwelling in my very heart! Really staying there all day, all night, wherever I am, whatever I am doing; here in my poor, unworthy heart at this very moment! And this only because the grace that flowed from His own love has broken the bars of doubt, and because He has given the faith that wanted Him and welcomed Him. Let us pause a little to take it in!

Again that holy Breeze swept by in might,
And fanned each faint desire to stronger flame;
He said, "O bid me come to Thee!" He came,
Just as he was, that memorable night;
And lo! the King, who waited at the door,
Entered to save, to reign, and to go out no more.

May 29

POSSESSING THE TREASURE OF TREASURES

Yea, let him take all, forasmuch as my lord the king is come again in peace unto his own house.   2 Samuel 19:30

It is when the King has really come in peace to His own home in the "contrite and humble spirit" (not before) — when He has entered in to make His abode there (not before) — that the soul is satisfied with Him alone, and is ready to let any Ziba take all else, because all else really seems nothing at all in comparison to the conscious possession of the Treasure of treasures. Sometimes this is reached at once, in the first flush of wondering joy at finding the King really "come in peace" to the empty soul which wanted to be "His own house." Sometimes very gradually—as year after year we realize His indwelling more and more, and find again and again that He is quite enough to satisfy us in all circumstances; that the empty corners of the house are filled one after another; that the old longings have somehow gone away, and the old ambitions vanished; that the old tastes and interests in the things of the world are superseded by stronger tastes and interests in the things of Christ; that He is day by day more really filling our lives—we "count" (because we really find) one thing after another "but loss for the excellency of the knowledge of Christ Jesus my Lord," till He leads us on to the rapturous joy of the "Yea, doubtless," and "all things!"

> Take what Thou wilt, beloved Lord,
> For I have all in Thee!
> My own exceeding great reward,
> Thou, Thou Thyself shalt be!

May 30

SILENCE IS GOLDEN

There was silence, and I heard a voice.   Job 4:16
The words of wise men are heard in quiet. Ecclesiastes 9:17

Who hears the dew fall? What microphone could reveal that music to our "gross unpurged ears"? The dew distills in silence. So does the speech of our God. Most frequently in the silence of trust. In that stillness God's silent love can be condensed into dewlike communications; not read, not heard, but made known by the direct power of the Spirit upon the soul. Most often He does this by thrilling into remembrance something from the written Word, already learnt, but now flashing out in the quickened memory as if it had never been heard before. We do not get much of this if we are always in the midst of noise and turmoil and bustle. He can, and now and then He does, send this "speech" through a very chaos of bustle or trouble. He can make a point of silence in the very center of a cyclone, and speak there to our hearts. But the more usual way is to make a wider silence for His dew to fall, by calling us apart into some quiet place of sorrow or sickness. So when we find ourselves thus led into a wilderness, let us forthwith look out for the dew, and it will not fail. Then our desert will rejoice and blossom as the rose; very likely much more so than the hot harvest fields, or the neat gardens from which we have been called away.

> There are songs which only flow in the loneliest shades of night,
> There are flowers which cannot grow in a blaze of tropical light,
> There are crystals which cannot form till the vessel be cooled and stilled;
> Crystal, and flower, and song, given as God hath willed.

May 31

I pray for them.   John 17:9

He ever liveth to make intercession for us; and so while you have been silent to Him, He has been praying for you. If His hand has been upon you so that you could not pray, why need you be mourning over this, when your merciful and faithful High Priest has been offering up the pure and sweet and costly incense of His own intercession? But if your heart condemns you, and you know you gave way to indolent coldness when you might have roused yourself to more prayer, will it not touch you to recollect that, in His wonderful long-suffering, Jesus has been praying instead! What confident and powerful petitions for His disciples He was pouring out when He said, "I pray for them." And how gracious of Him to let us over-hear such breathings of Almighty love on their behalf. If He had said no more than this, we might have tremulously inferred that, being always the same Lord, He might give us a remote share of some reflected blessing from this prayer. But He anticipates a wish that we should hardly have been bold enough to form, and says: "Neither pray I for these alone, but for them also which shall believe on Me through their word." Have you believed on Him through their word? Then you have His plain and positive assurance that He was praying for you then, that verse by verse you may take that prayer of prayers and say, "Jesus prayed this for *me*." And now that He is the center of the praises of Heaven, whence no other echo floats down to us, what is our one permitted glimpse of the continual attitude and occupation of this same Jesus? "Who is even at the right hand of God, who also maketh intercession for us." That is what He is doing for you *now*.

> He prayeth. — But for whom? For Himself He needeth nought;
> Nor strength, nor peace, nor pardon, where of sin there is no spot;
> But 'tis for us in powerful prayer He spendeth all the night,
> That His own loved ones may be kept and strengthened in the fight;
> That they may all be sanctified, and perfect made in one;
> That they His glory may behold where they shall need no sun;
> That in eternal gladness they may be His glorious bride:
> It is for this that He hath climbed the lonely mountain side.
> It is for this that He denies His weary head the rest
> Which e'en the foxes in their holes, and birds have in their nest.

June 1

He was marvellously helped. 2 Chronicles 26:15

The help with which God makes us to prosper is literally "marvelous." We do wonder at it, or ought to wonder at it. Wonder is one of the God-given faculties which distinguishes us from the beasts that perish. And He gives us grand scope for its happy exercise not merely in His works in general, but in His dealings with us in particular. But wonder is always founded upon observation. We do not wonder at that which we do not observe. So, if we have not wondered very much at the help He has given us, it is because we have not noticed, nor considered very much, how great things He hath done for us.

> The Lord **hath** done great things for thee!
> All through the fleeted days
> Jehovah hath dealt wondrously;
> Lift up thy heart and praise!
> For greater things thine eyes shall see,
> Child of His loving choice!
> The Lord **will** do great things for thee;
> Fear not, be glad, rejoice!

June 2

Lo, I am with you alway. Matthew 28:20

Some of us think and say a good deal about a sense of His presence; sometimes rejoicing in it, sometimes going mourning all the day long because we have it not; praying for it, and not always seeming to receive what we ask; measuring our own position, and sometimes even that of others by it; now on the heights, now in the depths about it. All our trouble and disappointment about it is met by His own simple word, and vanishes in the simple faith that grasps it. For if Jesus says simply and absolutely, "Lo, I am with you alway," what have we to do with feeling or "sense" about it? We have only to believe it, and to recollect it. And it is only by thus believing and recollecting that we can realize it.

> He is with thee! — thine own Master,
> Leading, loving to the end;
> Brightening joy and lightening sorrow,
> All today, yet more tomorrow,
> King and Saviour, Lord and Friend.

June 3

SAVIOUR OR JUDGE?

If thou forbear to deliver them that are drawn unto death, and those that are ready to be slain . . . doth not he that pondereth the heart consider it . . . and shall not he render to every man according to his works? Proverbs 24:11-12

When one has even a glimmer of the tremendous difference between having Christ and being without Christ; when one gets but one shuddering glimpse of what eternity is, and of what it must mean, as well as what it may mean, without Christ: when one gets but a flash of realization of the tremendous fact that all these neighbors of ours, rich and poor alike, will have to spend that eternity either with Him or without Him—it is hard, very hard indeed, to understand how a man or woman can believe these things at all, and make no effort for anything beyond the temporal elevation of those around, sometimes not even beyond their amusements! "People must have entertainment," they urge. I do not find that "must" in the Bible, but I do find, "We must all stand before the judgment seat of Christ." And if you have any sort of belief in that, how can you care to use those lips of yours, which might be a fountain of life to the dying souls before you, merely to entertain them. As you sow, so you reap.

> Will you not sow that song?
> Will you not drop that word
> Till the coldest heart be stirred
> From their slumber deep and long?
> Then your harvest shall abound,
> With rejoicing full and grand,
> Where the heavenly summer-songs resound,
> And the fruits of faithful work are found,
> In the glorious Holy Land.

June 4

AS PRAYERS GO UP BLESSINGS COME DOWN

See, I have hearkened to thy voice, and have accepted thy person.
1 Samuel 25:35

We must be accepted in the Beloved before we can expect to be answered through the Beloved. Is there a doubt about this, and a sigh over the words? There need not be; for now, at this moment, the old promise stands with its unchangeable welcome to the weary; "Him that cometh to Me I will in no wise cast out." Then, if you come now, at this moment, on the strength of His word, you cannot be rejected, there is nothing but one blessed alternative—accepted. Then come the answers! As surely as the prayers go up from the accepted one, so surely will blessings come down. When Esther had touched the golden scepter, then said the king unto her, "What wilt thou Queen Esther, and what is thy request? it shall be given thee to the half of the kingdom." But there is no half in our King's promise. He says, "All things," and "Whatsoever." And He does do exceeding abundantly above all that we ask or think, and more than fulfills our little scanty requests. And then, by every fresh fulfillment we should receive ever new assurance of our acceptance — then (shall it not be today?) as we give thanks for each gracious answer, we may look up confidingly and joyfully, and say, "Thy servant knoweth that I have found grace in Thy sight" (2 Samuel 14:22).

Accepted, perfect and complete,
For God's inheritance made meet!
How true, how glorious, and how sweet!
In the Beloved — by the King
Accepted, though not anything
But forfeit lives had we to bring.

June 5

UNDIVIDED ATTENTION

I am come into my garden, my sister, my spouse. Song of Solomon 5:1

Hush! Listen! Believe! for the King speaks to you. Do not miss the unspeakable blessing and joy of meeting Him and resting in His presence, by hurrying away to anything else, by listening to any outward call. Stay *now*, lay the little book aside, kneel down at your King's feet, doubt not His word, which is "more sure" than even the "excellent glory" that the apostles beheld, and thank Him for coming to you. Commune with Him now of all that is in your heart, and "rejoice greatly," for, "Behold, thy King cometh unto thee."

O Prince's daughter, whom I see in bridal garments, pure as light,
Betrothed forever unto Me, on thee My own new name I write,
It is Humility, who sees herself unworthy of such grace,
Who dares not hope her Lord to please, who dares not look upon His face?
Nay, where that mantle fleeting gleams, 'tis Unbelief who turns aside,
Who rather rests in self-spun dreams, than trust the love of Him who died.
Faith casts away the fair disguise, she will not doubt her Master's voice,
And droop when He hath bid her rise, or mourn when He hath said,
    "Rejoice!"

June 6

NOW OR NEVER

They that were ready went in . . . and the door was shut.
Matthew 25:10
When once the master of the house is risen up, and hath shut to the door . . . he shall answer and say unto you, I know you not.
Luke 13:25

There are plenty of things besides immediate death which may just as effectually prevent your ever coming to Christ at all, if you do not come now. This might be your last free hour for coming. Tomorrow the call may be less urgent, and the other things entering in may deaden it, and the grieved Spirit may withdraw and cease to give you even your present inclination to listen to it, and so you may drift on and on, farther and farther from the haven of safety (into which you may enter *now* if you will), till it is out of sight on the horizon. And then it may be too late to turn the helm, and the current may be too strong; and when the storm of mortal illness at last comes, you may find that you are too weak mentally or physically to rouse yourself even to hear, much less to come. What can one do when fever or exhaustion are triumphing over mind and body? Do not risk it. Come now! And "though your sins be as scarlet, they shall be as white as snow; though they be red like crimson, they shall be as wool."

What will you do without Him, in the long and dreary day
Of trouble and perplexity, when you do not know the way,
And no one else can help you, and no one guides you right,
And hope comes not with morning, and rest comes not with night?

June 7

GIVING DETERMINES VALUE

The children of Israel brought a willing offering unto the Lord.
Exodus 35:29
And he brought into the house of God the things that his father had dedicated . . . and there was no more war.
2 Chronicles 15:18, 19

There is no bondage in consecration. The two things are opposites and cannot co-exist, much less mingle. We should suspect our consecration and come afresh to our great Counselor about it directly we have any sense of bondage. As long as we have an unacknowledged feeling of fidget about our account book and a smothered wondering what and how much we ought to give and a hushed-up wishing the thing had not been put quite so strongly before us, depend upon it we have not said unreservedly, "Take my silver and my gold." And how can the Lord keep what He has not been sincerely asked to take?

Ah! if we had stood at the foot of the cross and watched the tremendous payment of our redemption with the precious blood of Christ — if we had seen that awful price told out, drop by drop, from His own dear patient brow and torn hands and feet until it was all paid and the central word of eternity was uttered, "It is finished," should we not have been ready to say, "Not a mite will I withhold!"

Halfhearted, falsehearted! Heed we the warning!
  Only the whole can be perfectly true;
Bring the whole offering, all timid thought scorning,
  Truehearted only if wholehearted too.
Halfhearted! Saviour, shall aught be withholden,
  Giving Thee part who hast given us all?
Blessings outpouring, and promises golden
Pledging, with never reserve or recall.

June 8

WE SEE JESUS . . .

As seeing him who is invisible. Hebrews 11:27

If we were always doing everything just as if we saw Him, whom having not seen we love, how different our lives would be! How much happier too! These words were said of Moses; and this seeing Him by faith had three effects. (1) "He forsook Egypt"; it made him ready to give up anything for his God, and God's people. It made him true and loyal to God's cause. What did he care for anything else, so long as he saw "Him who is invisible"? (2) It took away all his fear. What was "the wrath of the king" to him, when Jehovah was by his side? Of what should he be afraid? (3) It enabled him to "endure," to wait patiently for forty years in the desert, and then to work patiently for forty years in the wilderness; and only think how strength-giving that sight of faith must be which enabled him to endure everything for eighty years! Try for yourself today what was such great help to Moses.

"From glory unto glory!" Though tribulation fall,
It cannot touch our treasure, when Christ is all in all!
Whatever lies before us, there can be nought to fear,
For what are pain and sorrow when Jesus Christ is near?

June 9

Under his wings shalt thou trust. Psalm 91:4

When the little eaglets, that have not yet a feather to fly with, are under the great wings of the parent eagle, how safe they are! Who would dare touch them? If a bold climber put his hand into the nest, then those powerful wings would beat him in a minute from his hold, and he would fall down the rocks and be dashed to pieces. So safe shall you be under His wings, nothing shall by any means hurt you there. When the wild snowstorms rage around the eyrie, that is death to an unprotected sleeper, how warm the little eaglets are kept! Not an arrow of the keen blast reaches them, poor little featherless things, not a snowflake touches them. So warm shall you be kept under His wings when any cold and dark day of trouble comes, or even any sudden little blast of unkindness or loneliness. Under His wings shalt thou *trust!* Not shalt thou *see!* If one of the eaglets wanted to see for itself what was going on, and thought it could take care of itself for a little while, and hopped from under the shadow of the wings, it would be neither safe nor warm. The sharp wind would chill it, and the cruel hand might seize it then. So you are to *trust,* rest quietly and peacefully under His wings; stay there, not be peeping out and wondering whether God really is taking care of you! You may be always safe and happy there. Safe, for in the shadow of Thy wings will I make my refuge. Happy, for "in the shadow of Thy wings will I rejoice."

> Upon Thy word I rest, so strong, so sure;
> So full of comfort blest, so sweet, so pure.
> The word that changeth not, that faileth never!
> My King! I rest upon Thy word forever.

June 10

THE UNKEPT PLEDGE

As many as I love, I rebuke and chasten: be zealous therefore, and repent. Revelation 3:19

But have you found out that it is one of the secrets of the Lord, that when any of His dear children turn aside a little bit after having once entered the blessed path of true and conscious consecration, He is sure to send them some little punishment? He will not let us go back without a sharp, even if quite secret, reminder. Go and spend ever such a little without reference to Him after you have once pledged the silver and gold entirely to Him, and see if you are not in some way rebuked for it! Very often by being permitted to find that you have made a mistake in your purchase, or that in some way it does not prosper. If you observe these things, you will find that the more closely we are walking with our Lord, the more immediate and unmistakable will be His gracious rebukes when we swerve in any detail of the full consecration to which He has called us. And if you have already experienced and recognized this part of His personal dealing with us, you will know also how we love and bless Him for it.

> Yes! there is tribulation, but Thy power
> Can blend it with rejoicing. There are thorns,
> But they have kept us in the narrow way,
> The King's highway of holiness and peace.
> And there is chastening, but the Father's love
> Flows through it; and would any trusting heart
> Forego the chastening and forego the love?
> And every step leads on to "more and more,"
> From strength to strength Thy pilgrims pass and sing
> The praise of Him who leads them on and on,
> From glory unto glory, even here!

June 11

NOT PROMISED BUT GIVEN

The Good Shepherd giveth his life for the sheep. John 10:11

Oh, wonderful gift! not promised, but *given;* not to friends, but to enemies. Given without condition, without reserve, without return. Himself unknown and unloved, His gift unsought and unasked, He gave His life for thee; a more than royal bounty—the greatest gift that Deity could devise. Oh, grandeur of love! "I lay down My life for the sheep!" And we for whom He gave it have held back, and hesitated to give our lives, not even *for* Him (He has not asked us to do that), but *to* Him! But that is past, and He has tenderly pardoned the unloving, ungrateful reserve, and has graciously accepted the poor little fleeting breath and speck of dust which was all we had to offer. And now His precious death and His glorious life are all "for thee."

> Look to Him, the Lord of Glory, tasting death to win thy life;
> Gazing on that wondrous story, canst thou falter in the strife?
> Is it not new life to know that the Lord hath loved thee so?

June 12

Rest in [margin, Be silent to] the Lord. Psalm 37:7

An invalid was left alone one evening for a little while. After many days of acute pain there was a lull. "Now," she thought, "I shall be able to pray a little." But she was too wearied out and exhausted for this; feeling that utter weakness of mind and body which cannot be realized without actual experience, when the very lips shrink from the exertion of a whisper, and it seems too much effort of thought to shape even unspoken words. Only one whisper came: "Lord Jesus, I am so tired!" She prayed no more; she could not frame even a petition that, as she could not speak to Him, He would speak to her. But the Lord Jesus knew all the rest; He knew how she had waited for and wanted the sweet conscious communing with Him, the literal talking to Him and telling Him all that was in her heart. And He knew that, although a quiet and comparatively painless hour had come, she was "so tired" that she could not think. Very tenderly did He, who knows how to speak a word in season to the weary, choose a message in reply to that little whisper. "Be silent to the Lord!" It came like a mother's "hush" to one whom his mother comforteth. It was quite enough, as every Spirit-given word is; and the acquiescent silence was filled with perfect peace. Only real friends understand silence.

> I am too weak for effort, so let me rest,
> In hush of sweet submission, on Thine own breast.
> I take this pain, Lord Jesus, as Thine own gift;
> And true through tremulous praises I now uplift.
> I am too weak to sing them, but Thou dost hear
> The whisper from the pillow, Thou art so near!

June 13

Thy holy child Jesus. Acts 4:30

God's Word has only told us this one thing about the early years in the life of the Lord—He was a *holy* child. What is holy? It is everything that is perfectly beautiful and good and lovable, without anything to spoil it. This is what He was as a child. He was gentle and brave, considerate and unselfish, noble and truthful, obedient and loving, kind and forgiving—

everything you can think of that you ever admired or loved in any one else was all found together in Him, and all this not only outside but inside, for He was holy. And all His goodness and holiness may be reckoned to you, for you have none of your own. God desires to smile on you for His sake, just as if you had been perfectly obedient and truthful and unselfish and good and to give you Jesus Christ's reward, which you never deserved at all, but which He deserved for you. On the cross He took your sins, and now He gives you His righteousness; He took your punishment and gives you His reward; it is just changed over, if you will accept the exchange!

> Thine was the chastisement with no release,
>   That mine might be the peace;
> The bruising and the cruel stripes were Thine
>   That healing might be mine;
> Thine was the sentence and the condemnation.
>   Mine the acquittal and the full salvation.
>
> For Thee revilings, and a mocking throng,
>   For me the angel-song;
> For Thee the frown, the hiding of God's face,
>   For me the smile of grace;
> Sorrows of hell and bitterest death for Thee,
>   And heaven and everlasting life for me.

June 14

TREASURES RARE AWAIT YOU

In whom are hid all the treasures of wisdom and knowledge.
Colossians 2:3

And the Lord shall open these treasures unto thee. Riches of goodness, and forbearance, and long-suffering shall be meted out in infinitely gracious proportion to our sins, and provocations and repeated waywardness; exceeding riches of grace for all our poverty now, and riches in glory enough and to spare for all the needs of glorified capacities through all eternity. "All are yours" in Him. Faith is the key to this infinite treasury, and in giving us faith He gives us treasure for treasure. He is ready to make us "rich in faith," and then still to "increase our faith" "unto all riches of the full assurance of understanding." Ask for this golden key, and then put it into the Lord's hand, that He may turn it in the lock.

> As the key is to the lock, when it enters quick and true,
> Fitting all the complex wards that are hidden from the view,
> Moving all the secret springs that no other finds or moves,
> So is Jesus to the soul, when His saving power He proves.

June 15

THE WAY OF ESCAPE

And Noah went . . . into the ark.   Genesis 7:7
By me if any man enter in, he shall be saved. John 10:9

Noah did not put it off. He and his family entered the self-same day into the ark. I wonder if any of Noah's acquaintances were thinking about coming when the flood overtook them, and even coming gradually nearer! We are told that Noah *only* remained alive, and they that were with him *in* the ark. Then, come thou into the Ark, that when the great and terrible day comes, you may be found of Him in peace, found in Him.

> *The rising tempest sweeps the sky,*
> *The rain descends, the winds are high;*
> *The waters swell and death and fear*
> *Beset thy path, no refuge near:*
>   *Haste, traveler, haste!*
>
> *Oh, haste! a shelter you may gain,*
> *A covert from the wind and rain,*
> *A hiding-place, a rest, a home,*
> *A refuge from the wrath to come:*
>   *Haste, traveler, haste!* —W. B. COLLYER

He who brings the flood has provided the Ark. And the door is open. It will be shut some day—it may be shut tomorrow. What will you do if you find yourself not shut in, but shut out? Whose fault is it if you do not enter in and be saved?

> Will you not come to Him for life?
> Why will ye die, oh why?
> He gave His life for you, for you!
> The gift is free, the word is true!
> Will you not come? oh, why will you die?

June 16

THE MAGNET OF LOVE

Draw me, we will run after thee. Song of Solomon 1:4

There is no love so deep and wide as that which is kept for Jesus. It flows both fuller and farther when it flows only through Him. Then, too, it will be a power for Him. It will always be unconsciously working for Him. In drawing others to ourselves by it, we shall be necessarily drawing them nearer to the fountain of our love, never drawing them away from it. It is the great magnet of His love which alone can draw any heart to Him; but when our own are thoroughly yielded to its mighty influence, they will be so magnetized that He will condescend to use them in this way. Is it not wonderful to think that the Lord Jesus will not only accept and keep, but actually use our love? "Of Thine own have we given Thee," for "we love Him because He first loved us."

Set apart to love Him, and His love to know!
Not to waste affection on a passing show.
Called to give Him life and heart,
Called to pour the hidden treasure,
That none other claims to measure,
Into His beloved hand! thrice-blessed "set apart!"

June 17

LOVE SO AMAZING

Our Lord Jesus Christ, who died for us. 1 Thessalonians 5:9-10

Died for us? Who else did as much for you? Who else ever loved you so much? Only think now what it really means, because it is really true; and surely it is most ungrateful, when one for whom such a great thing has been done does not even think about it. It was the very most He could do to show His exceeding love to you. He was not obliged to go through with it; He might have come down from the cross any moment. The nails could not have kept Him there an instant longer than He chose; His love and pity were the real nails that nailed Him fast to the cross till the very end, till He could say, "It is finished," till He "died for us." It was not only because He loved His Father that He did it, but because He loved us; for the text goes on, "Who died for us, that, whether we wake or sleep, we might live together with Him." So He loved us so much that He wanted us to live together with Him; and as no sin can enter His heavenly Home, He knew our sins must be taken away before we could go there. And only His blood could take sin away, only death could atone for it; and so He bled that we might be washed in His most precious blood; He died, "that, whether we wake or sleep, we might live together with Him."

Then glory in the highest be to Him, our Strength and Song;
May every heart uplift its part, in blessings deep and long.
Thro' Him who died that we might live, our thanks to God ascend,
The King of kings and Lord of lords, our Saviour and our Friend.

June 18

DRESSED IN BEAUTY NOT OUR OWN

Let the beauty of the Lord our God be upon us. Psalm 90:17

"How great is His beauty!" said Zechariah. How can His beauty be upon us? In two ways; try to understand them, and then ask that in both ways the beauty of the Lord our God may be upon you. One way is by His covering you with the robe of Jesus Christ's righteousness, looking upon you not as you are in yourself, all sinful and unholy, but as if all the Saviour's beautiful and holy life were yours, reckoning it to you for His sake. In this way He can call us "perfect through My comeliness which I had put upon thee." The other way is by giving you the beauty of holiness, for that is His own beauty; and though we never can be quite like Him till we see Him as He is, He can begin to make us like Him even now.

> Shall not longsuffering in thee be wrought,
>   To mirror back His own?
> His gentleness shall mellow every thought,
>   And look and tone.
> And all around shall praise Him as they see
>   The meekness of Thy Lord;
> Thus, even here and now, how blest shall be
>   Thy sure reward!

June 19

THE TOUCH OF HIS HAND

And he touched her hand, and the fever left her. Matthew 8:15

What must the touch of the Master's own hand have been! One imagines it very gentle, though so full of power. Can He not communicate both the power and the gentleness? When He touched the hand of Peter's wife's mother, she arose and ministered unto them. Do you not think the hand which Jesus had just touched must have ministered very excellently? As we ask Him to touch our lips with living fire, so that they may speak effectively for Him, may we not ask Him to touch our hands, that they may minister effectively, and excel in all that they find to do for Him? Then our hands shall be made strong by the hands of the mighty God of Jacob.

It is very pleasant to feel that if our hands are indeed our Lord's, we may ask Him to guide them, and strengthen them, and teach them. I do not mean figuratively, but quite literally.

In everything they do for Him (and that should be everything we ever undertake) we want to do it well — better and better. "Seek that ye may excel." We are too apt to think that He has given us certain natural gifts, but has nothing practically to do with the improvement of them, and leaves us to ourselves for that. Why not ask Him to make these hands of ours more handy for His service, more skillful in what is indicated as the "next thynge" they are to do? The "kept" hands need not be clumsy hands. If the Lord taught David's hands to war and his fingers to fight, will He not teach our hands, and fingers too, to do what He would have them do?

The Spirit of God must have taught Bezaleel's hands as well as his head, for he was filled with it not only that he might devise cunning works, but also in cutting of stones and carving of timber. And when all the women that were wisehearted did spin with their hands, the hands must have been made skillful as well as the hearts made wise to prepare the beautiful garments and curtains.

> Master, to do great work for Thee, my hand
> Is far too weak! Thou givest what may suit—
> Some little chips to cut with care minute,
> Or tint, or grave, or polish. Others stand
> Before their quarried marble fair and grand,
> And make a life work of the great design
> Which Thou hast traced; or, many-skilled, combine
> To build vast temples, gloriously planned.
> Yet take the tiny stones which I have wrought,
> Just one by one, as they were given by Thee,
> Not knowing what came next in Thy wise thought.
> Set each stone by Thy master-hand of grace,
> Form the mosaic as Thou wilt for me,
> And in Thy temple-pavement give it place.

June 20

MAGNIFICENTLY PRECIOUS

For God so loved the world. John 3:16

Which is the more wonderful—the love that devised such a gift, or the gift that was devised by such love! Oh, to realize the glorious value of it! May we, who by His grace know something of God's gift of His Son as our Saviour, learn day by day more of the magnificent preciousness of His gift of His anointed One as our King!

> But with Him—oh! with Jesus! Are any words so blest?
> With Jesus, everlasting joy and everlasting rest!
> With Jesus—all the empty heart filled with His perfect love;
> With Jesus—perfect peace below, and perfect bliss above.

June 21

HE DINES WITH US

This man receiveth sinners, and eateth with them. Luke 15:2

When we feel that "we are not worthy so much as to gather up the crumbs under His table," how precious are these words! When we remember that we were dead in trespasses and sins, we may recollect that Lazarus, the raised one, "was one of them that sat at the table with Him." When we come back from the battlefield, weary yet victorious, we may look for our King of Peace coming to meet us with bread and wine and His own priestly blessing, that we may be strengthened and refreshed by Himself.

> Who shall tell our untold need,
> Deeply felt, though scarcely known!
> Who the hungering soul can feed,
> Guard and guide, but God alone?
> Blessed promise! while we see
> Earthly friends must powerless be,
> Earthly fountains quickly dry:
> "God" shall all your need supply.

June 22

PUT YOUR CASE IN YOUR FATHER'S HAND

Let him do what seemeth him good. 1 Samuel 3:18

Eli spoke these words under the terrible certainty of heavy judgments upon his house, because the Lord had spoken it. But how often God's dear children tremble to say an unreserved "Let Him do what seemeth Him good," though they are under no such shadow of certainly coming events! It is almost easier to say it when a crushing blow has actually fallen, than when there is suspense and uncertainty as to what the Lord may be going to do. There is always more or less of this element of suspense and uncertainty. One can hardly imagine a life in which there are no clouds, little or great, within the horizon, even when the sky is clearest overhead. We hold not a treasure on earth which we are sure of keeping; and we never know whether gain or loss, failure or success, ease or pain, lies before us. And if we were allowed to put our finger on the balance of uncertainties and turn it as we chose, we should be sure to defeat some ultimate aim by securing a nearer one, and prevent some greater good by grasping a lesser. I think if we were permitted to try such an experiment, we should soon grow utterly puzzled and weary, and find ourselves landed in complications of mistakes; and if we had any sense left, we should want to put it all back into our Father's hands, and say, "Let Him do what seemeth Him good," then we should feel relieved and at rest.

Then why not be relieved and at rest at once? For "It is the Lord," who is going to do, we know not what. That is a volume in itself — the Lord who loves you, the Lord who thinks about you and cares for you, the Lord who understands you, the Lord who never makes a mistake, the Lord who spared not His own Son but gave Him up for you! Will you not let Him do what seemeth Him good? Then think what it is you are to let Him do. Something out of your sight, perhaps, but not out of His sight. For the original word in every case is "what is good in His eyes." Those eyes see through and through, and all around and beyond everything. So what is good in His eyes must be absolutely and entirely good, a vast deal better than our best! There is great rest in knowing that He will do what is right, but He crowns the rightness with the goodness; and when we see this, the rest is crowned with gladness. Ought it, then, to be so very hard to say, "Let Him do what seemeth Him good"?

Yet we often vainly plead for a fancied good denied,
What we deemed a pressing need still remaining unsupplied.
Yet from dangers all concealed, thus our wisest Friend doth shield;
No good thing will He deny, God shall all your need supply.

June 23

SIGNED—SEALED—HELD—CONFIRMED

For all the promises of God in him are yea, and in him Amen, unto the glory of God by us.   2 Corinthians 1:20

Where? In Him, the Son of God. He holds these stars in His right hand; He has held the great promise of eternal life for us since God gave it to Him for us before the world began, and every other is subincluded. And it is one of His offices to confirm the promises. Signed, sealed, held, and confirmed thus, should not "It is written" be enough for our present "light, and gladness, and joy, and honor"?

Then let our hearts be surely fixed where truest joys are found,
And let our burning, loving praise, yet more and more abound;
And, gazing on the "things not seen," eternal in the skies,
"From glory unto glory," O Saviour, let us rise!

June 24

THANK HIM FOR THE GIFT

The gift of God is eternal life through Jesus Christ our Lord.
Romans 6:23
Be thankful unto him, and bless his name.   Psalm 100:4

Will you not now prove your acceptance of the great gift of eternal life by pouring out your thanks at once for it, and prove your trust in the finished work by praising the Saviour who died to finish it for you?

> Rest, by His sorrow! Bruised for our sin,
> Behold the Lamb of God! His death our life.
> Now lift your heads, ye gates! He entereth in,
> Christ risen indeed, and Conqueror in the strife.
> Thanks, thanks to Him who won, and Him who gave
> Such victory of love, such triumph o'er the grave.

June 25

CHERISHED AND PILLOWED TO REST

Cherisheth it, even as the Lord the church. Ephesians 5:29

The Church is not only "one body," but also "many members"; "for the body is not one member, but many." And what is true for the whole is true also for the smallest part. Lest any one should think the individual is rather lost in the great whole, the gracious word of our God comes down to meet the possible or passing tremor, and says: "Ye are," not only the body of Christ, but "members in particular." Do not hesitate to take all the revelation of love that shines softly through this one word "cherisheth," for your own self; for the more you feel yourself to be the weakest imaginable member of Christ, unworthy to be a member at all of His glorious body, the more closely and sweetly will it apply to you.

For it necessarily implies, on the one side, weakness and inferiority and need. It would be nothing to us if we felt extremely strong and capable and self-contained. The Lord would never have taken the trouble to cause it to be written for such people. They would neither want it nor thank Him for it. We do not talk about "cherishing" an oak tree, or an athlete, or even a "strong-minded woman." Our heart-welcome to this beautiful word, and our sense of its preciousness, will be just in proportion to our sense of being among the Lord's little ones, or weak ones, no matter what others suppose us to be. After all, are not even those who are chasing thousands, but little ones; and those who are slaying Goliaths, but weak ones; in their real and hidden relationship to their own great and mighty Saviour and Lord? Even a father in Christ, or a mother in Israel may turn with the heart of a little child, lovingly and gratefully, and perhaps very wearily too, to their cherishing Lord, to be comforted afresh with the old comforts, and hushed to rest on the little pillow of some very familiar text.

> I never thought it could be thus—month after month to know
> The river of Thy peace without one ripple in its flow;
> Without one quiver in the trust, one flicker in its glow.

June 26

THIS SAME JESUS

Christ also hath loved us, and hath given himself for us.
Ephesians 5:2

Yes, Himself! What is the Bride's true and central treasure? What calls forth the deepest, brightest, sweetest thrill of love and praise? Not the Bridegroom's priceless gifts, not the robe of His resplendent righteousness, not the dowry of unsearchable riches, not the magnificence of the palace home to which He is bringing her, not the glory which she shall share with Him, but HIMSELF! Jesus Christ, "who His own self bare our sins in His own body on the tree"; "this same Jesus," "whom having not seen, ye love"; the Son of God, and the Man of Sorrows; my Saviour, my Friend, my Master, my King, my Priest, my Lord and my God — He says, "I also for thee!" What an "I"! What power and sweetness we feel in it, so different from any human "I," for all His Godhead and all His manhood are concentrated in it, and all "for thee!" And not only "all" but "ever" for thee! His unchangeableness is the seal upon every attribute; He will be "this same Jesus" for ever. How can mortal mind estimate this enormous promise? How can mortal heart conceive what is enfolded in these words, "I also for thee"?

> "This same Jesus!" Oh! how sweetly fall these words upon the ear,
> Like a swell of far-off music, in a nightwatch still and drear!
> He who gently called the weary, "Come and I will give you rest!"
> He who loved the little children, took them in His arms and blest;
> He, the lonely Man of Sorrows, 'neath our sin-curse bending low;
> By His faithless friends forsaken in the darkest hours of woe.

June 27

The Lord shall establish thee an holy people unto himself, as he hath sworn unto thee.   Deuteronomy 28:9

Can there be a stronger promise? Just obey and trust His word *now*, and yield yourselves *now* unto God, "that He may establish thee *today* for a people unto Himself." Commit the keeping of your souls to Him in well-doing, as unto a faithful Creator, being persuaded that He is ABLE TO KEEP that which you commit to Him.

> Now, Lord, I give myself to Thee;
> I would be wholly Thine,
> As Thou hast given Thyself to me,
> And Thou art wholly mine.
> Oh, take me, seal me as Thine own,
> Thine altogether — Thine alone!

June 28

OUR LIPS FOR HIM

The lips of the righteous feed many. . . . The lips of the righteous know what is acceptable.   Proverbs 10:21, 32

The days are past forever when we said, "Our lips are our own." Now we know that they are not our own. And yet how many of my readers often have the miserable consciousness that they have "spoken unadvisedly with their lips!" How many pray, "Keep the door of my lips," when the very last thing they think of expecting is that they will be kept! They deliberately make up their minds that hasty words, or foolish words, or exaggerated words, according to their respective temptations, must and will slip out of that door, and that it can't be helped. The extent of the real meaning of their prayer was merely that not quite so many might slip out. As their faith went no farther, the answer went no farther, and so the door was not kept. Do let us look the matter straight in the face. Either we have committed our lips to our Lord, or we have not. This question must be settled first. If not, oh, do not let another hour pass! Take them to Jesus, and ask Him to take them. But when you have committed them to Him, it comes to this—is He able or is He not able to keep that which you have committed to Him? If He is not able, of course you may as well give up at once, for your own experience has abundantly proved that you are not able, so there is no help for you. But if He is able—nay, thank God there is no if on this side!—say, rather, as He is able, where was this inevitable necessity of perpetual failure? You have been fancying yourself virtually doomed and fated to it, and therefore you have gone on in it, while all the time His arm was not shortened that it could not save, but you have been limiting the Holy One of Israel. Honestly, now, have you trusted Him to keep your lips this day? Trust necessarily implies expectation that what we have intrusted will be kept. If you have not expected Him to keep, you have not trusted. You may have tried and tried very hard, but you have not trusted, and therefore you have not been kept and your lips have been the snare of your soul (Proverbs 18:7).

> Read to him, Connie! Read of the One
> Who loves him most, yes more than you!
> Read of that love, so great, so true,
> Love everlasting, yet ever new;
> For who can tell but his heart may be won!
> Read to him, Connie. For it may be
> That your Sunday book, like a silver bar
> Of steady light from a guiding star,
> May gleam in memory, clear and far,
> Across the waves of a wintry sea.

June 29

HIS FEET FOR YOU

His legs are as pillars of marble, set upon sockets of fine gold. Song of Solomon 5:15

His feet for thee! They were weary very often, they were wounded and bleeding once. They made clear footprints as He went about doing good and as He went up to Jerusalem to suffer; and these "blessed steps of His most holy life," both as substitution and example, were for thee. Our place of waiting and learning, of resting and loving, is at His feet. And still those blessed feet are, and shall be, for thee, until He comes again to receive us unto Himself, until and when the word is fulfilled, "They shall walk with Me in white."

> O Saviour, fix my wayward, wandering heart
> Upon Thyself, that I may closely cling
> To Thy blest side, and never more depart
> From Thee, my loved Redeemer, Thee, my heart's own King.
> And grant me daily grace to follow Thee
> Through joy and pleasure, or through grief and sadness,
> Until an entrance is vouchsafed to me
> In Thy bright home of holiness and gladness.

June 30

THE LESS INCLUDES THE GREATER

But this I say, brethren, the time is short. 1 Corinthians 7:29
See then that ye walk circumspectly . . . redeeming the time.
Ephesians 5:15, 16

When we take a wide sweep, we are so apt to be vague. When we are aiming at generalities we do not hit the practicalities. We forget that faithfulness to principle is only proved by faithfulness in detail. Has not this vagueness had something to do with the constant ineffectiveness of our feeble desire that our time should be devoted to God? In things spiritual, the greater does not always include the less, but, paradoxically, the less more often includes the greater. So in this case, time is entrusted to us to be traded with for our Lord. But we cannot grasp it as a whole. We instinctively break it up ere we can deal with it for any purpose. So when a new year comes round, we commit it with special earnestness to the Lord. But as we do so, are we not conscious of a feeling that even a year is too much for us to deal with? And does not this feeling, that we are dealing with a larger thing than we can grasp, take away from the sense of reality? Thus we are brought to a more manageable measure; and as the Sunday mornings or the Monday mornings come round, we thankfully commit the opening week to Him and the sense of help and rest is renewed and strengthened. But not even the six or seven days are close enough to our hand; even tomorrow exceeds our tiny grasp, and even tomorrow's grace is therefore not given to us. So we find the need of considering our lives as a matter of day by day, and that any more general committal and consecration of our time does not meet the case so truly. Here we have found much comfort and help, and if results have not been entirely satisfactory, they have, at least, been more so than before we reached this point of subdivision. But if we have found help and blessing by going a certain distance in one direction, is it not probable we shall find more if we go farther in the same? And so, if we may commit the days to our Lord, why not the hours, and why not the moments? And may we not expect a fresh and special blessing in so doing?

> Make Thy members every hour
> For Thy blessed service meet;
> Earnest tongues, and arms of power,
> Skillful hands, and hastening feet,
>   Ever ready to fulfill
> All Thy word and all Thy will.

July 1

Ye belong to Christ. Mark 9:41

There is no vague and general belonging to Christ. This relationship is full of specific realities. "I am Thine" means, "Truly I am Thy servant. I am one of Thy dear children. I am Thy chosen soldier. I am Thy ransomed one. I am Thy own sheep. I am Thy witness. I am Thy friend." And all these are but Amens to His own condescending declarations. He says we are all these, and we have only to say, "Yes, Lord, so I am." Why should we ever contradict Him?

> "Not your own!" but His by right, His peculiar treasure now,
> Fair and precious in His sight, purchased jewels for His brow.
> He will keep what thus He sought, safely guard the dearly bought,
> Cherish that which He did choose, always love and never lose.
>
> "Not your own!" but His, the King, His, the Lord of earth and sky,
> His, to whom archangels bring homage deep and praises high.
> What can royal birth bestow? Or the proudest titles show?
> Can such dignity be known as the glorious name, "His own!"

July 2

ONLY FOR JESUS

He is thy Lord; and worship thou him. Psalm 45:11

Do my lips say, "My Lord and my God"? Does my life say, "Christ Jesus, *my* Lord"—definitely and personally, *"my"* Lord"? Can I share in His last sweet commendation to His disciples, the more precious because of its divine dignity, "Ye call me Master and Lord, and ye say well, for so I am"? Am I ashamed or afraid to confess my allegiance in plain English among His friends or before His foes? Is the seal upon my brow so unmistakable that always and everywhere I am known to be His subject? Is "He is thy Lord" blazoned, as it ought to be, in shining letters on the whole scroll of my life, so that it may be "known and read of all men"? "Search me and try me," and show me the true state of my case, and then for Thine own sake pardon all my past disloyalty, and make me by Thy mighty grace from this moment totally loyal!

> Only for Jesus! Lord, keep it forever
> Sealed on the heart and engraved on the life!
> Pulse of all gladness and nerve of endeavor,
> Secret of rest, and the strength of our strife.

July 3

THE OLD WAY THE ONLY WAY

O ye of little faith, why reason ye . . . ? Matthew 16:8

Did we ever receive the powerful fulfillment of any promise so long as we argued and reasoned, whether with our own hearts or with others, and said, "How can these things be?" Has it not always been that we had to lay down our arms and accept God's thought and God's way instead of our own ideas, and be willing that He should "speak the word only," and believe it as little children believe our promises? Then, *never* till then, the promise and the privilege became ours not only in potentiality but in actuality. While "the riches of His glory in Christ Jesus" is the measure of the fullness of God's promises; "according to your faith" is the appointed measure of their reception and benefit by ourselves. "Lord, increase our faith." . . . Before the triumph-leading of every thought can take place, there is the "casting down imaginations," or, as in the more correct margin, "reasonings." As long as we are reasoning about a promise, we never know its reality. It is not God's way. It is the humble who hear thereof and are glad. Have we not found it so? Then, how is it that we do not understand, and apply the same principle to every promise or privilege which as yet we see only afar off? It is the old way and the only way: "Who through faith . . . obtained promises."

> Reason unstrings the harp to see wherein the music dwells;
> Faith pours a Hallelujah song, and heavenly rapture swells.
> While Reason strives to count the drops that lave our narrow strand,
> Faith launches o'er the mighty deep, to seek a better land.

July 4

THE SEARCHER OF HEARTS

Come, see a man, which told me all things that ever I did: is not this the Christ? John 4:29

Yes! it is not merely a vague general belief in Christ as the Teacher who "will tell us all things" which suffices for heart conviction of "the reality of Jesus Christ," but the individual knowledge of Him as the Searcher who "told me all things that ever I did." This was what led the woman of Samaria to exclaim, "Is not this the Christ?" This was to her the irresistible proof of His Messiahship. What about ourselves? If we know anything of true intercourse with the Lord Jesus, our experience will not be unlike hers. When He who "searches Jerusalem with candles" turns the keen flame of His eyes upon the dark corners of our hearts, and flashes their far-reaching, all-revealing beam upon even the far-off and long-forgotten windings of our lives, when in His light we see the darkness, and in His purity we see the sin that has been, or that is; when He "declareth unto man what is his thought," and then convinces that "as a man thinketh in his heart, so is he," then we know for ourselves that He "with whom we have to do" is indeed the Christ.

O happy end of every weary quest!
He told me all I needed graciously—
Enough for guidance and for victory
O'er doubts and fears, enough for quiet rest;
And when some veiled response I could not read,
It was not hid from Him — this was enough indeed.

July 5

RUNNING OR REELING

When thou runnest, thou shalt not stumble. Proverbs 4:12

This promise does not stand alone; it is reiterated and varied. He knew our constant, momentary need of it. He knew that without it we *must* stumble, and fall too; that we have not the least power to take one step without a stumble—or rather, that we have no power to take one single onward step at all. And He knew that Satan's surest device to make us stumble would be to make us believe that it can't be helped. We have thought that, if we have not said it. But "what saith the Scripture?" "When thou runnest" (the likeliest place for a slip), "thou shalt not stumble." "He will not suffer thy foot to be moved." "He will keep the feet of His saints." "He led them . . . that they should not stumble." Can we say, "Yea, hath God said?" to all this? Leave that to Satan; it is no comment for God's children to make upon His precious promises. If we do not use the power of faith, we find the neutralizing power of unbelief.

Yes! He knows the way is dreary,
Knows the weakness of our frame,
Knows that hand and heart are weary;
He, in all points, felt the same.
He is near to help and bless;
Be not weary, onward press.

July 6

A man is justified by faith without the deeds of the law.
                                          Romans 3:28

"Therefore, being justified by faith," what then? 1. We have
peace with God. 2. We shall be saved from wrath through Him.
3. We are made heirs of eternal life. 4. We shall be glorified
by Him and with Him for ever. What about my own part and
lot in the matter? Whom does God thus justify? And may I
hope to be among them? He begins indeed at the lowest depth,
so that none may be shut out; for He would "justify the heathen
through faith," and He "justifieth the ungodly." The publican
who could only cry, "God be merciful to me the sinner," was
justified. I can come in here, at all events. But how shall I
be actually and effectually justified now? Let God speak and
I will listen: "Even the righteousness of God which is by faith
of Jesus Christ unto *all* and upon *all* them that believe: for
there is no difference," "By Him all that believe *are* justified."
"Knowing that a man is not justified by the works of the law,
but by the faith of Jesus Christ, even we have believed in
Jesus Christ, that we might be justified by the faith of Christ."
And now, "He is *near* that justifieth me." "Who shall lay
anything to the charge of God's elect? It is God that justifieth."

> Israel of God, awaken! Church of Christ, arise and shine!
> Mourning garb and soiled raiment henceforth be no longer thine!
> For the Lord thy God hath clothed thee with a new and glorious dress,
> With the garments of salvation, with the robe of righteousness.

July 7

IS HE YOURS?

**This God is our God for ever and ever: he will be our
guide even unto death.**   Psalm 48:14

In Deuteronomy, that wonderful book of remindings, God has
caused this gracious name, "the Lord thy God," or "the Lord
your God," to be written no less than two hundred and twenty-
seven times. What a name for Him to be revealed by to the
wayward wanderers of Israel! And what comfort to us that He
is the same God to us! When you want a helpful Bible subject
to work out, suppose you take this, and trace out all through
the Bible under what circumstances or with what context of
precious teaching He gives these words, and let the gladness

of the search be "This God is *our* God." And then trace out (with your concordance if you like) the responses to this constantly repeated and heart-strengthening Name, noting and arranging the passages that speak of "Our God." Between these you will find every soul need for time and eternity supplied, from the first great need of the awakened sinner who is met with the words "He that is our God is the God of salvation," to the fullness of present blessing, "God, even our own God, shall bless us," and the fullness of future joy when "thy God [shall be] thy glory." As you study, the claim will grow closer, and the response will intensify from the wide chorus of "Our God" to the fervent thrill of the whisper, "O God, Thou art my God."

What know we, Holy God, of Thee, Thy being and Thy essence pure?
Too bright the very mystery for mortal vision to endure.
We only know Thy word sublime, Thou art a Spirit! Perfect! One!
Unlimited by space or time, unknown but through the eternal Son.

July 8

FROM FAITH TO FAITH

For therein is the righteousness of God revealed from faith to faith. Romans 1:17

We go forth from faith to forgetfulness, and there seems no help for it. Neither is there, in ourselves. But "in Me is thine help." Jesus Himself had provided against this before He gave the promise. He said that the Holy Spirit should bring all things to our remembrance. It is no use laying the blame on our poor memories, when the Almighty Spirit is sent that He may strengthen them. Let us make real use of this promise, and we shall certainly find it sufficient for the need it meets. He can, and He will give us that holy and blessed recollectedness, which can make us dwell in an atmosphere of remembrance of His presence and promises, through which all other things may pass and move without removing it.

Oh, her heart can see, her heart can see!
And its sight is strong and swift and free.
Never the ken of mortal eye
Could pierce so deep and far and high
As the eagle vision of hearts that dwell
In the lofty, sunlit citadel
Of faith that overcomes the world,
With banners of hope and joy unfurled,
Garrisoned with God's perfect peace,
Ringing with paeans that never cease,
Flooded with splendor bright and broad,
The glorious light of the love of God.

July 9

THE PROPER ANSWER

Rise up, my love, my fair one, and come away.
Song of Solomon 2:10

In deeper humility and stronger faith let us listen to the voice of our Beloved as He breathes names of incomprehensible condescension and love. Shall we contradict Him here, in the tenderest outflow of His divine affection, and say, "Not so, Lord"? Shall we not rather adoringly listen and let Him say even to us in our depths of utter unworthiness, "My sister, My spouse, My love, My dove, My undefiled," answering only with a wondering, yet unquestioning, "I am Thine," "I am all that Thou choosest to say that I am"? The echo may vary and falter (though it is nothing short of atrocious ingratitude and unbelief when it does), but the Voice never varies or falters. He does not say, "Thou art Mine" today, and reverse or weaken it tomorrow. We are "a people unto Thee for ever," and why grieve His love by doubting His word, and giving way to a very fidget of faithlessness? Love that is everlasting cannot be ephemeral; it is everlasting, and what can we say more?

For infinite outpourings of Jehovah's love and grace,
And infinite unveilings of the brightness of His face,
And infinite unfoldings of the splendor of His will.
Meet the mightiest expansions of the finite spirit still.

July 10

A BLESSED NECESSITY

Pray ye therefore the Lord of the harvest, that he would send forth labourers into his harvest.   Luke 10:2

Most likely we never went to a missionary meeting in our lives but what we were told to pray for the work. We are quite used to it; we take it as a matter of course, and as the right and proper thing to be said. Nobody disputes for an instant that it is a Christian duty. But—*are we doing it?*

As it is an acknowledged obligation upon all who profess to love the Lord Jesus Christ that they should obey His commandments, it is clearly a real obligation upon us, upon you and me, to obey *this* commandment. And if we are not doing it, we are equally clearly directly disobeying our dear Master, and failing in the one test of personal love to Himself which He gave us in the same night in which He was betrayed.

Yes, *are we doing it?* Did you pray this morning what He bade you pray? Did you yesterday? Or last week? Surely it is no light thing to go on from day to day leaving undone a thing which we ought to have done, and about which His own lips gave the most explicit direction! How often we have sorrowfully felt that "we know not what we should pray for as we ought"! Now here is something that we *know* we are to pray for. We know that it is according to His will, or He would not have bidden us ask it. And "if we ask anything according to His will, He heareth us." And if we know that He hears us in whatsoever we ask, we know that we have the petitions that we desired of Him. See what a splendid conclusion we reach! Oh, "pray ye therefore"! And if we thus pray, like little children, exactly what Jesus bids us pray, see if we do not find a real and probably conscious and immediate blessing in the very act—the floodgates opened, the spirit of grace and of supplication poured out, and the parched tongue filled with prayer and praise!

> There is no holy service but hath its secret bliss:
> Yet, of all blessed ministries, is one so dear as this?
> The ministry that cannot be a wondering seraph's dower,
> Enduing mortal weakness with more than angel-power;
> The ministry of purest love uncrossed by any fear,
> That bids us meet at the Master's feet and keeps us very near.

July 11

IT'S ALL DIFFERENT NOW!

Woe to the rebellious children, saith the Lord . . . that walk to go down into Egypt.   Isaiah 30:1-2

But what do we want with Egypt? What is there to attract us to the house of bondage and its old taskmasters? Did we not have enough of them? And shall we not gratefully accept redemption "from the nations," "out of" them, from the tyranny of "the customs of the people," "from our vain conversation," and say henceforth, "Thy people shall be my people"? "What have I to do any more with idols?" when God Himself has redeemed me from their gods? Yes, *has* redeemed me, for He says so. "Sing, O ye heavens; for the Lord hath done it!" He "gave Himself for us, that He might redeem us from all iniquity."

> Other lords have long held sway; now, Thy name alone to bear,
> Thy dear voice alone obey, is my daily, hourly prayer.
> Whom have I in Heaven but Thee? Nothing else my joy can be.

July 12

WHICH SHALL IT BE?

Leaving us an example, that ye should follow his steps.
1 Peter 2:21

Now what are those steps? Following steps is quite a different thing from thinking to follow one's own idea of the general direction of a course. If you would only take one Gospel, and read it through with the earnest purpose of noting, by the Holy Spirit's guidance, what the steps of Jesus are, you would soon see clearly whether you are following or not, far more clearly than by reading any amount of books about it, or consulting any number of human counselors. Take for today only one indication of what those steps were. "Who went about doing good." Do your steps correspond with that? It is not, "went about doing no harm," but actively and positively "doing good."

> Lord, speak to me, that I may speak
> In living echoes of Thy tone;
> As Thou hast sought, so let me seek
> Thy erring children, lost and lone.
>
> O lead me, Lord, that I may lead
> The wandering and the wavering feet;
> O feed me, Lord, that I may feed
> Thy hungering ones with manna sweet.

July 13

REFLECTING LIGHT

For with thee is the fountain of life: in thy light shall we see light.
Psalm 36:9

We see something of God's infinite greatness and wisdom when we try to fix our dazzled gaze on infinite space. But when we turn to the marvels of the microscope, we gain a clearer view and more definite grasp of these attributes by gazing on the perfection of His infinitesimal handiworks. Just so, while we cannot realize the infinite love which fills eternity, and the infinite vistas of the great future are "dark with excess of light" even to the strongest telescope of faith, we see that love magnified in the microscope of the moments, brought very close to us, and revealing its unspeakable perfection of detail to our wondering sight.

But we do not see this as long as the moments are kept in

our own hands. We are like little children closing our fingers over diamonds. How can they receive and reflect the rays of light, analyzing them into all the splendor of their prismatic beauty, while they are kept shut up tight in the dirty little hands? Give them up; let our Father hold them for us, and throw His own great light upon them, and then we shall see them full of fair colors of His manifold loving-kindnesses; and let Him always keep them for us, and then we shall always see His light and His love reflected in them.

> Jesus, grace for grace outpouring,
> Show me ever greater things;
> Raise me higher, sunward soaring,
> Mounting as on eagle-wings,
> By the brightness of Thy face,
> Jesus, let me grow in grace.

July 14

THE KING KNOWS

There is no matter hid from the king. 2 Samuel 18:13

The very attributes which are full of terror to the King's enemies, are full of comfort to the King's friends. Thus His omniscience is like the pillar, which was "a cloud and darkness" to the Egyptians, but "gave light by night" to the Israelites. The king's own general complained of a man who did not act precisely as he himself would have acted. In his reply he uses these words, "There is no matter hid from the king." The appeal was final, and Joab had no more to say. When others say, like Joab, "Why didst thou not do so and so?" and we know or find that full reasons cannot be given or cannot be understood, what rest it is to fall back upon the certainty that our King knows all about it! When we are wearied out with trying to make people understand, how restful it is that no explanations are wanted when we come to speak to Him! "All things are naked and opened unto the eyes of Him with whom we have to do"; and the more we have to do with Him, the more glad and thankful we shall be that there is not anything hid from the King.

> Oh, let our adoration for all that He hath done
> Peal out beyond the stars of God, while voice and life are one!
> And let our consecration be real, and deep, and true;
> Oh, even now our hearts shall bow, and joyful vows renew!
>   .   .   .
> To Thee who hast so helped me, to Thee who hast so blessed,
> The only Friend who knows my heart, the nearest and the best.

July 15

ALL THINGS ARE READY

Come; for all things are now ready. Luke 14:17

All things! God the Father is ready to save you. Jesus Christ is ready to receive you. The Holy Spirit is ready to dwell in you. Are you ready? *All* things. The "great salvation" is ready for you. The full atonement is made for you. The eternal redemption is obtained for you. Are you ready? *All* things. The cleansing fountain is opened for you. The robe of righteousness is wrought for you. The way into the holiest is consecrated for you. Are you ready? *All* things. All things that pertain unto life and godliness are given you by His divine power. Exceeding great and precious promises are given you. The supply of all your need is guaranteed to you. Strength and guidance, teaching and keeping, are provided for you. A Father's love and care and a Saviour's gift of peace are waiting for you. The feast is spread for you. All these things are ready for you. Are you ready for them?

> Will you not come to Him for all?
> Will you not "taste and see"?
> He waits to give it all to you,
> The gifts are free, the words are true!
> Jesus is calling, "Come unto Me!"

July 16

IS ROYAL LIKENESS RECOGNIZABLE?

Whosoever shall do the will of my Father which is in heaven, the same is my brother, and sister, and mother. Matthew 12:50

"How beautiful to be Christ's little sister!" said a young disciple. For of course He really means it. Will not this make our prayer more fervent, "Teach me to do Thy will"? If the King is indeed near of kin to us, the royal likeness will be recognizable. Can it be said of us, "As thou art, so were they; each one resembled the children of a King"? Nor let us shrink from aiming at the still higher standard, "The King's daughter is all glorious within." We must not dwell only on a one-sided kinship. If He is not ashamed to call us brethren, shall we ever be ashamed to call Him Master? If He is ready to give us all that is implied or involved in near kinship, should we fail to reciprocate with all the love and sympathy and faithfulness which the tie demands on our side? Also, let us prove our loyal love by "looking for and hasting unto the coming of the day" of His return. Let us not incur the touching reproach, "Ye are my brethren, ye are my bones and my flesh: wherefore then are ye the last to bring back the King?"

Joined to Christ in mystic union,
 We Thy members, Thou our Head,
Sealed by deep and true communion,
 Risen with Thee, who once were dead—
Saviour, we would humbly claim
All the power of this Thy name.

Instant sympathy to brighten
 All their weakness and their woe,
Guiding grace their way to lighten,
 Shall Thy loving members know;
All their sorrows Thou dost bear,
All Thy gladness they shall share.

July 17

A MAGNIFICENT GLIMPSE OF JOY

It is the voice of my beloved that knocketh, saying, Open to me, my sister, my love. Song of Solomon 5:2

It was the literal voice of the Lord Jesus which uttered that one echoless cry of desolation on the cross "for thee," and it will be His own literal voice which will say, "Come, ye blessed!" to thee. And that same tender and glorious voice has literally sung and will sing for thee. I think He consecrated song for us, and made it a sweet and sacred thing for ever when He Himself "sang an hymn" the very last thing before He went forth to consecrate suffering for us. That was not His last song. "The Lord thy God . . . will joy over thee with singing." And the time is coming when He will not only sing "for thee" or "over thee" but with thee. He says He will! "In the midst of the church will I sing praise unto Thee." Now what a magnificent glimpse of joy this is! "Jesus Himself leading the praises of His brethren," and we ourselves singing not merely in such a chorus, but with such a leader! If "singing for Jesus" is such delight here, what will this "singing *with* Jesus" be? Surely song may well be a holy thing to us henceforth.

The hour is come; but ere they meet its terrors—yet once more
Their voices blend with His who sang as none e'er sang before.
Why do they linger on that note? Why thus the sound prolong?
Ah! 'twas the last! 'Tis ended now, that strangely solemn song.
And forth they go—the song is past; but like the rose-leaf, still,
Whose fragrance doth not die away, its soft low echoes thrill
Thro' many a soul, and there awake new strains of glowing praise
To Him who, on that fateful eve, that last sweet hymn did raise.

July 18

DIVINE REASON FOR DIVINE DOINGS

And they shall know that I am the Lord. Ezekiel 6:10

It is one of the shining threads that run all through the Bible, a supply indeed for the heart's desire of those who delight in the Lord. It is never long out of sight, judgments and mercies being alike sent for this great purpose. For this the waters of the Red Sea receded and returned again; for this the Jordan was dried up; for this Goliath was delivered into David's hand; for this 185,000 of the Assyrians were smitten by God's angel; and many more instances. Throughout Ezekiel it seems to be the very key-word, recurring seventy-five times as the divine reason of divine doings, that they may "know that I am the Lord." Is there not a peculiar solace in this?

> Reigning, guiding, all-commanding, ruling myriad worlds of light;
> Now exalting, now abasing, none can stay Thy hand of might!
> Working all things by Thy power, by the counsel of Thy will,
> Thou art God! enough to know it, and to hear Thy word: "Be still!"

July 19

OUR EVER-PRESENT COUNSELOR

And his name shall be called . . . Counsellor. Isaiah 9:6
Is thy counsellor perished? Micah 4:9

Nothing is more practically perplexing to a young Christian, whose preparation time is not quite over, or perhaps painfully limited, than to know what is most worth studying, what is really the best investment of the golden hours, while yet the time is not come for the field of active work to be fully entered and the "thoroughly furnishing" of the mind is the evident path of present duty. Is not His name called "Counsellor"; and will He not be faithful to the promise of His name in this, as well as in all else? The same applies to every subsequent stage. Only let us be perfectly clear about the principle that our intellect is not our own, either to cultivate, or to use, or to enjoy, and that Jesus Christ is our real and ever-present Counselor; and then there will be no more worry about what to read, and how much to read, and whether to keep up one's accomplishments, or one's languages, or one's *"ologies"!* If the Master has need of them, He will show us; and if He has not, what need have we of them? If we go forward without

His leading, we may throw away some talent, or let it get too rusty for use, which would have been most valuable when other circumstances arose or different work was given. We must not think that "keeping" means not using at all! What we want is to have all our powers kept for His *use*.

In this they will probably find far higher development than in any other sort of use. I know cases in which the effect of real consecration on mere mental development has been obvious and surprising to all around. Yet it is only a confirmation of what I believe to be a great principle, viz., that *the Lord makes the most of whatever is unreservedly surrendered to Him*. There will always be plenty of waste in what we try to cut out for ourselves. But He wastes no material!

> Where are our early lessons, the teachings of our youth,
> The countless words forgotten of knowledge and of truth?
> Not lost! for they are living still, as power to think, and do, and will.
> Where, where are all God's lessons, His teachings dark or bright?
> Not lost! but only hidden, till in eternal light,
> We see, while at His feet we fall, the reasons and results of all.

July 20

HE REMEMBERS . . . SHALL WE?

Thus saith the Lord; I remember thee, the kindness of thy youth, the love of thine espousals.   Jeremiah 2:2

Forgetting all the sin, all the backsliding, all the coldness, casting all that into the unreturning depths of the sea, He says He remembers that hour when we first said, "Take my love." He remembers it now, at this minute. He has written it for ever on His infinite memory, where the past is as the present. His own love is unchangeable, so it could never be His wish or will that we should thus drift away from Him. Oh, "Come and let us return unto the Lord"! But is there any hope that, thus returning, our flickering love may be kept from again failing? Hear what He says: "And I will betroth thee unto Me for ever." And again: "Thou *shalt* abide *for Me* many days; so will I also be for thee." Shall we trust His word or not? Is it worthy of our acceptation or not? Oh, rest on this word of the King, and let Him from this day have the keeping of your love, and He will keep it!

> Whom He calleth He preserveth, and His glory they shall see;
> He is faithful that hath called you; He will do it, fear not ye!
> Therefore, holy brethren, onward! thus ye make your calling sure;
> For the prize of this high calling, bravely to the end endure.

July 21

We which have believed do enter into rest. Hebrews 4:3

He hath given us rest by *His* sorrow, and life by His death; "rest from thy sorrow and from thy fear, and from thy hard bondage wherein thou wast made to serve" (Isaiah 14:3). Come and take the gift! It is gloriously real. It is no mere slight and temporary sense of relief. And He gives us rest on every side—complete rest, guarded and sheltered all around. It is not only rest *from* all weariness and burdens, but rest *in* Himself. Jesus is spoken of in type as "the Man of Rest," "and His rest shall be glorious." It is this, His own divine rest, that He will give. "This is the rest wherewith ye may cause the weary to rest." Is it worth having? Will you not come for it? You cannot have it without coming to Jesus; but only come, and it shall be yours—for there stands His word—and "in returning and rest shall ye be saved."

> Yes, "even until now!" And so we stand,
>   Forgiven, loved, and blessed;
> And covered in the shadow of God's hand,
>   Believing, are at rest.
> The one great load is lifted from the soul,
> That henceforth on the Lord all burdens we may roll.

July 22

PREPARED FOR HIS APPOINTMENTS

Thy servants are ready to do whatsoever my lord the king shall appoint. 2 Samuel 15:15

This is the secret of steady and unruffled gladness in "the business of the Lord, and the service of the King," whether we are "over the treasures of the house of God," or, "for the outward business over Israel." It makes all the difference! If we are really, and always, and equally ready to do *whatsoever* the King appoints, all the trials and vexations arising from any change in His appointments, great or small, simply do not exist. If He appoints me to work there, shall I lament that I am not to work here? If He appoints me to wait indoors today, am I to be annoyed because I am not to work out-of-doors? If I meant to *write* His messages this morning, shall I grumble because He sends interrupting visitors, rich or poor, to whom I am to *speak* them, or "show kindness" for

His sake, or at least obey His command, "Be courteous"? If all my members are really at His disposal, why should I be put out if today's appointment is some simple work for my hands or errands for my feet, instead of some seemingly more important doing of head or tongue? The "whatsoever" is not necessarily active work. It may be waiting (whether half an hour or half a lifetime), learning, suffering, sitting still. But, dear fellow-servants of "my Lord the King," shall we be less ready for these, if any of them are His appointments for today? "Whatsoever the king did pleased all the people." "Ready" implies something of preparation—not being taken by surprise. So let us ask Him to prepare us for all that He is preparing for us. And may "the hand of God give" us "one heart to do the commandment of the King"!

> Speak to me by name, O Master, let me know it is to me;
> Speak, that I may follow faster, with a step more firm and free,
> Where the Shepherd leads the flock, in the shadow of the Rock.

July 23

WHERE THERE'S LIFE THERE'S RENEWING

My speech shall distil as the dew, as the small rain upon the tender herb, and as the showers upon the grass. Deuteronomy 32:2

Sometimes God's dew goes on falling through many hours of the night. But none of it is lost; some is already doing a hidden work as it falls around the very roots of our being, and some is ready to be revealed in sparkling brightness when the night is over. Lessons learnt among the shadows will be lived out in the sunshine. The object of the dew is to maintain life in dry places and seasons. Dew does nothing for the stones. You would not know there ever was any at all if you only look at the gravel path. And it makes no difference at all to a dead leaf. But if it falls on the little fading plant that could hardly have lived through many more days of July sunshine, the weak little stem straightens up as the leaves absorb the life-renewing moisture, and the closed blossom can open out again with fresher fragrance than before. So God keeps on distilling His speech into our frail spiritual life, or it would soon wither up. Dryness is more to be dreaded than darkness.

> Master, speak, though least and lowest, let me not unheard depart;
> Master, speak, for oh, Thou knowest all the yearning of my heart,
> Knowest all its truest need; speak and make me blest indeed.

July 24

THIS DAY

**Consecrate yourselves to day to the Lord . . . that he may
bestow upon you a blessing this day.** Exodus 32:29

Not a long time hence, not even tomorrow, but "this day." Do
you not want a blessing? Is not your answer to your Father's
"What wilt thou?" the same as Achsah's "Give me a blessing!"
Here is His promise of just what you so want; will you not
gladly fulfill His condition? A blessing shall immediately follow. He does not specify what it shall be; He waits to reveal
it. You will find it such a blessing as you had not supposed
could be for you — a blessing that shall verily make you rich,
with no sorrow added — a blessing *this day.*

> One the channel, deep and broad, from the Fountain of the Throne,
> Christ the Saviour, Son of God, blessings flow through Him alone.
> He, the Faithful and the True, brings us mercies ever new:
> Till we reach His home on high, God shall all your need supply.

July 25

THE ADEQUACY OF CHRIST

Him with whom we have to do. Hebrews 4:13
For in him we live, and move, and have our being. Acts 17:28

These words seem to meet every sort of need of comfort. If
it is perplexity, or oppressive puzzle what to do, when we cannot see through things—or if it is being unable to explain
yourself to others, and trials or complications arising out of
this: just fall back upon "Him with whom we have to do,"
to whose eyes all things are naked and opened. He is your
Guide—why need you puzzle? He is your Shield—why need
you try so hard or wish so much to explain and vindicate
yourself?

If it is sense of *sin* which does not let you be comfortable, turn *at once* to "Him with whom you have to do." Remember, it is not with Satan that you have to do, nor with
your accusing conscience, but with Jesus. He will deal with
all the rest; you only have to deal with Him. And He is your
great High Priest. He has made full Atonement for you; for
the very sins that are weighing on you now.

If it is *temptation* that will not let you rest, come straight
away out of the very thick of it; it may be with fiery darts
sticking in you. Come with all the haunting thoughts that you

hate, just as you are, to "Him with whom you have to do." You would not or could not tell the temptations to any one else; but then you have not got to do with any one else in the matter, but *only* with Jesus. And He "suffered, being tempted."

If it is *bodily weakness, sickness, or pain,* how very sweet it is to know that we have to do with Jesus, who is "touched with the feeling of our infirmities." (The word is the same that is elsewhere translated sickness: John 11:2-4.) Don't you sometimes find it very hard to make even your doctor understand *what* the pain is like? Words don't seem to convey it. And after you have explained the trying and wearying sensation as best you can, you are convinced those who have not felt it do not understand it. But He does.

> Just to leave in His dear hand little things,
> All we cannot understand, all that stings!
> Just to let Him take the care sorely pressing,
> Finding all we let Him bear, changed to blessing.
> This is all! and yet the way marked by Him who loves thee best!
> Secret of a happy day, secret of His promised rest.

July 26

GOING AND GROWING

Ye shall go forth, and grow up. Malachi 4:2

All our natural delight in progress finds satisfaction here—no stagnation, no reaching a dead level; we are on an ever-winning side, bound up with an ever-progressing cause. A typical light on this point flashes from the story of David. He "went on and grew great," or, as the margin has it, "going and growing"; which we cannot forbear connecting with the promise to ourselves. And then we are told that he "waxed greater and greater" (margin), "went on going and *increasing.*" But we must not be merely onlookers. Let us see to it, first, that there be increasing prosperity in His kingdom in our hearts. Pray that He may not only reign, but prosper in that domain. And next, let us see to it that we are doing all we can to further His prosperity all around us. Translate our daily prayer, "Thy kingdom come," into daily, burning, glowing action for its prosperity.

> That "greater things," far greater, our longing eyes shall see!
> We can but wait and wonder what "greater things" shall be!
> But glorious fulfillments rejoicingly we claim,
> While pleading in the power of the All-prevailing Name.

July 27

PERPETUAL CLEANSING

In the light of the king's countenance is life. Proverbs 16:15

But first fell the solemn words, "Thou hast set our secret sins in the light of Thy countenance." That was the first we knew of its brightness; and to some its revelation has been so terrible, that they can even understand how the Lord "shall destroy" the wicked "with the brightness of His coming." Yet, though we feel that "His eyes were as a flame of fire," we found also that our "King that sitteth in the throne of judgment, scattereth away all evil with His eyes"; and that it was when we stood in that light, that we found the power of the precious blood of Jesus, the Anointed One, to cleanse us from all sin. This gives new value to the promise, "They shall walk, O Lord, in the light of Thy countenance"; for it is when we walk in the light that we may claim and do realize the fullness of its power and preciousness — not for fitful and occasional cleansing, but for a glorious, perpetual, present cleansing from all sin.

> Abiding in His presence, and walking in the light,
> And seeking to "do always what is pleasing in His sight,"
> We look to Him to keep us "all glorious within,"
> Because "the blood of Jesus is cleansing from all sin."

July 28

THE ONLY ALTERNATIVE

For rebellion is as the sin of witchcraft, and stubbornness is as iniquity and idolatry. 1 Samuel 15:23

Presumptuous are they, selfwilled, they are not afraid to speak evil of dignities. 2 Peter 2:10

We have asked many a time without, perhaps, realizing how great a petition we were singing, "Guard my first springs of thought and will!" That goes to the root of the matter, only it implies that the will has been already surrendered to Him, that it may be wholly kept and guarded. It may be that we have not sufficiently realized the sin of the only alternative. Our wills belong either to self or to God. It may seem a small and rather excusable sin in man's sight to be self-willed, but see in what a category of iniquity God puts it (2 Peter 2:10).

And certainly we are without excuse when we have such a promise to go upon as, "It is God that worketh in you both to *will* and to do of His pleasure." How splendidly this meets our very deepest helplessness—"worketh in you to will"! Oh, let us pray for ourselves and for each other, that we may know "What is the exceeding greatness of His power to usward who believe." It does not say, "To usward who fear and doubt"; for if we will not believe, neither shall we be established. If we will not believe what God says He can do, we shall see it with our eyes, but we shall not eat thereof. "They could *not* enter in because of unbelief."

> Peace, peace!
> To him that is far away.
> Turn, O wanderer! why wilt thou die,
> When the peace is made that shall bring thee nigh?
> Listen, O rebel! the heralds proclaim
> The King's own peace through a Saviour's name;
> Then yield thee today.

July 29

GOD'S DOING AND NOT OURS

Thou shalt come into the ark. Genesis 6:18

You would like to take this great step out of danger into safety; but you find it very hard, though it sounds very easy. You feel as if you had a spiritual nightmare — seeing the danger, and not able to stir hand or foot to escape it. Perhaps every one who comes to Christ has this sense of utter helplessness about it. This is because the Holy Spirit must convince us that the whole thing is God's doing, and not ours, so that He may have *all* the glory of saving us from beginning to end. It is not at all because He is not willing to save us, but just because He *is* willing, that He lets us find out for ourselves that our own will is so numb that it cannot rouse and move without the fire of His love and grace. Now just trust His promise, "Thou shalt come into the Ark"; in other words, believe that His power and love are even now being exerted upon you, and that your sense of helplessness is only part of His wonderful way of drawing you to Jesus.

> Now trust the one provided rope, now quit the broken mast,
> Before the hope of safety be for ever past.
> Fear not to trust His simple word, so sweet, so tried, so true,
> And you are safe for evermore, yes — even you!

July 30

WHO IS YOUR MASTER?

Behold, Satan hath desired to have you. Luke 22:31
No man can serve two masters. Matthew 6:24

Shall the devil have the use of our members? Oh, no, of course not! We start back at this, as a highly unnecessary question. Yet if Jesus has not, Satan has. For as all are serving either the Prince of Life or the prince of this world, and as no man can serve two masters, it follows that if we are not serving the one, we are serving the other. And Satan is only too glad to disguise this service under the less startling form of the world, or the still less startling one of self. All that is not "kept for Jesus," is left for self or the world, and therefore for Satan.

> Jesus, Thy life is mine! Dwell evermore in me;
> And let me see
> That nothing can untwine my life from Thine.
> Thy life in me be shown! Lord, I would henceforth seek
> To think and speak
> Thy thoughts, Thy words alone, no more my own.

July 31

ROYAL GRACE

I said, Behold me, behold me. Isaiah 65:1

Look at the central theme of the universe — the central moment not of a world's history only, but of eternity — look at the Saviour, "who His own self bare our sins in His own body on the tree," bowing His bleeding head under that awful burden, because His faithfulness was unto the death, and His love was strong as death! Then seek out all the exquisitely winning ways of Him who went about doing good, till you have heard Him and observed Him all through those years of patient and perfect ministry, and recollect all the time that it is He who says to you, "Come unto Me!" Unto Him, the man Christ Jesus, full of compassion, and tender yet royal grace.

> Behold your King, with His sorrow crowned,
> Alone, alone in the valley is He!
> The shadows of death are gathering round,
> And the Cross must follow Gethsemane.
> Darker and darker the gloom must fall,
> Filled is the Cup, He must drink it all!
> Oh, think of His sorrow! that we may know
> His wondrous love in His wondrous woe.

August 1

Then believed they his words; they sang his praise. Psalm 106:12
**Take heed . . . lest there be in any of you an evil heart of un-
belief.** Hebrews 3:12
What is the cause that the former days were better than these?
Ecclesiastes 7:10

Many a heart has echoed the little song:

> *Take my life, and let it be*
> *Consecrated, Lord, to Thee!*

And yet those echoes have not been, in every case and at all
times, so clear, and full, and firm, so continuously glad as we
would wish, and perhaps expected. Some of us have said:

> *I launch me forth upon a sea*
> *Of boundless love and tenderness;*

and after a little we have found, or fancied, that there is a
hidden leak in our bark, and though we are doubtless still
afloat, yet we are not sailing with the same free, exultant confidence as at first. What is it that has dulled and weakened
the echo of our consecration song? What is the little leak that
hinders the swift and buoyant course of our consecrated life?
It may have arisen from want of the simplest belief in the
simplest fact, as well as want of trust in one of the simplest
and plainest words our gracious Master ever uttered! The un-
believed fact being simply that He hears us; the untrusted
word being one of those plain, broad foundation-stones on which
we rested our whole weight, it may be many years ago, and
which we had no idea we ever doubted, or were in any danger
of doubting now — "Him that cometh to Me I will in no wise
cast out."

> Is this the peace of God, this strange, sweet calm?
> The weary day is at its zenith still,
> Yet 'tis as if beside some cool, clear rill,
> Through shadowy stillness rose an evening psalm,
> And all the noise of life were hushed away,
> And tranquil gladness reigned with gently soothing sway.
>
> It was not so just now. I turned aside
> With aching head, and heart most sorely bowed;
> Around me cares and griefs in crushing crowd,
> While inly rose the sense, in swelling tide,
> Of weakness, insufficiency, and sin,
> And fear, and gloom, and doubt, in mighty flood rolled in.
>
> It is not that I feel less weak, but Thou
> Wilt be my strength; it is not that I see
> Less sin, but more of pardoning love with Thee,
> And all-sufficient grace. Enough! And now
> All fluttering thought is stilled, I only rest,
> And feel that Thou art near, and know that I am blest.

August 2

TRANSCENDENT SATISFACTION

And ye shall know that I have not done without cause all that I have done.   Ezekiel 14:23

One revels in the thought of this great and eternal vindication of Him whom we love; His ways, His works, His word all justified, and Himself revealed to the silenced universe, henceforth only to receive honor and glory and blessing! It seems as if we should almost forget our own share in the glory and joy of His coming in this transcendent satisfaction.

> Our Father, we long for the glorious day
> When all shall adore Thee, and all shall obey.
> Oh hasten Thy kingdom, oh show forth Thy might,
> And wave o'er the nations Thy sceptre of right.
> Oh make up Thy jewels, the crown of Thy love,
> And reign in our hearts as Thou reignest above,
> For Thine is the power!

August 3

FOR OUR SAKES

Aaron and his sons laid their hands upon the head of the bullock for the sin offering.   Leviticus 8:14

Before the hands of the priests could be filled with the emblems of consecration, they had to be laid upon the emblem of atonement (Leviticus 8:14, etc.). That came first. So the transference of guilt to our Substitute, typified by that act, must precede the dedication of ourselves to God.

> *My faith would lay her hand*
> *On that dear head of Thine,*
> *While like a penitent I stand,*
> *And there confess my sin.*

The blood of that Holy Substitute was shed "to make reconciliation upon the altar." Without that reconciliation we cannot offer and present ourselves to God; but this being made, Christ Himself presents us. And you, that were sometime alienated, and enemies in your mind by wicked works, yet now hath He reconciled in the body of His flesh through death, to present you holy and unblamable and unreprovable in His sight.

Then Moses "brought the ram for the burnt offering; and Aaron and his sons laid their hands upon the head of the ram, and Moses burnt the whole ram upon the altar; it was a burnt-offering for a sweet savour, and an offering made by fire unto the Lord." Thus Christ's offering was indeed a whole one, body, soul, and spirit, each and all suffering even unto death. These atoning sufferings, accepted by God for us, are, by our own free act, accepted by us as the ground of our acceptance.

Then, reconciled and accepted, we are ready for consecration; for then "he brought the ram, the ram of consecration; and Aaron and his sons laid their hands upon the head of the ram." Here we see Christ, "who is consecrated for evermore." We enter by faith into union with Him who said, "For their sakes I sanctify Myself, that they also might be sanctified through the truth."

> Wounded for my transgression, stricken sore,
>   That I might "sin no more";
> Weak, that I might be always strong in Thee;
>   Bound, that I might be free;
> Acquainted with grief, that I might only know
> Fullness of joy in everlasting flow.
> Thy cross and passion, and Thy precious death,
>   While I have mortal breath,
> Shall be my spring of love and work and praise,
>   The life of all my days;
> Till all this mystery of love supreme
> Be solved in glory — glory's endless theme.

August 4

BY HIM — TO HIM — IN HIM . . . FOR HIM

Whether is greater, the gift, or the altar that sanctifieth the gift?
                                                    Matthew 23:19

Thanks be to God for the Altar that sanctifieth the gift, even our Lord Jesus Christ Himself! By Him we draw nigh unto God; to Him, as one with the Father, we offer our living sacrifice; in Him, as the Beloved of the Father, we know it is accepted. So, dear friends, when once He has wrought in us the desire to be altogether His own, and put into our hearts the prayer, "Take my life," let us go on our way rejoicing, believing that He has taken our lives, our hands, our feet, our voices, our intellects, our wills, our whole selves, to be ever, only, all for Him. Let us consider that a blessedly settled thing; not because of anything we have felt, or said, or done, but because we know that He heareth us, and because we know that He is true to His Word.

> Only a mortal's powers, weak at their fullest strength;
> Only a few swift-flashing hours, short at their fullest length.
> All! for far more I owe than all I have to bring;
> All! for my Saviour loves me so! All! for I love my King!

August 5

"COME" . . . "NOW"

Come now, and let us reason together, saith the Lord. Isaiah 1:18
The Holy Ghost saith, To day. Hebrews 3:7
And he [Pharaoh] said, To morrow. Exodus 8:10

"Come now!" Nothing can be plainer. Therefore, if you postpone coming, you are calmly disobeying God. When we bid a child to "come," we do not count it obedience unless he comes at once, then and there. It is not obedience if he stops to consider, and coolly tells you he is really thinking about coming, and waits to see how long you will choose to go on calling him. What right have we to treat our holy Lord as we would not think of letting a naughty child treat us? He says, "Come now." And "now" does not mean tomorrow. "Today if ye will hear His voice, harden not your hearts." Put it to yourself, what if this night God should require your soul of you, and you had not "come"? What if the summons find you still far off, when the precious blood was ready, by which you might have been brought nigh?

> Precious, precious blood of Jesus,
>   Shed on Calvary;
> Shed for rebels, shed for sinners,
>   Shed for me.
>
> Precious blood, whose full atonement
>   Makes us nigh to God!
> Precious blood, our song of glory,
>   Praise and laud.

August 6

JUSTICE AND MERCY FROM GOD'S LOVE

In this was manifested the love of God toward us, because that God sent his only begotten Son into the world, that we might live through him. 1 John 4:9
We love him, because he first loved us. 1 John 4:19

First, He loves us. Then the discovery of this leads us to love Him. Then, because He loves us, He claims us, and desires to have us wholly yielded to His will, so that the operations of love in and for us may find no hindrance. Then, because we love Him we recognize His claim and yield ourselves. Then, being thus yielded, He draws us nearer to Him and admits us, so to speak, into closer intimacy, so that we gain nearer and truer views of His perfections. Then the unity of these perfections becomes clearer to us. Now we not only see His justice and mercy flowing in an undivided stream from the cross of Christ, but we see that they never were divided, though the strange distortions of the dark, false glass of sin made them appear so, but that both are but emanations of God's holy love. Then having known and believed this holy love, we see further that His will is not a separate thing, but only love (and therefore all His attributes) in action; love being the primary essence of His being, and all the other attributes manifestations and combinations of that ineffable essence, for God *is* Love.

> He hath loved thee, and He knows
> All thy fears and all thy foes;
> Victor thou shalt surely be
> Ever through His love to thee.
> Rest in quiet joy on this —
> Greater love hath none than His:
> And may this thy life-song be,
> Love to Him that loveth thee!

August 7

PROMISES IN PRESENT EXPERIENCE

His heart is established, he shall not be afraid. Psalm 112:8

The Gracious One bears with us, and gives line upon line to His poor little children. And so He says, "The peace of God, which passeth all understanding, shall keep your hearts and minds, through Christ Jesus." And again, "Thy thoughts shall be established." And again, "Thou wilt keep him in perfect peace, whose mind is stayed on Thee, because he trusteth in Thee." And to prove to us that these promises can be realized in present experience He sends down to us through nearly three thousand years the words of the man who prayed, "Create in me a clean heart, O God," and lets us hear twice over the new song put by the same Holy Spirit into his mouth: "My heart is fixed, O God, my heart is fixed."

> That waiting One, who now is letting us try again;
> Watching us with the patient brow that bore the wreath of pain;
>   Thoroughly teaching what He would teach,
>   Line upon line,
>   Thoroughly doing His work in each.
> Then let our hearts be still, though our task is turned today,
> Oh let Him teach us what He will in His own gracious way.
>   Till, sitting only at Jesus' feet,
>   As we learn each line,
>   The hardest is found all clear and sweet!

August 8

BETTER FIRST THAN LAST

I will cry unto God most high; unto God that performeth all things for me.   Psalm 57:2

Does He mean as much as this? Well, He has caused it to be written for us "that we might have hope"; and what more do we want? Then let Him do it. Let Him perform all things for us. Not some things, but all things; or the very things which we think there is no particular need for Him to perform will be all failures — wood, hay and stubble to be burnt up. One by one let us claim this wonderful word; "the thing of a day in his day," "as the matter shall require," being always brought to Him with the God-given petition, "Do Thou for me." Do not wait to feel very much oppressed before you say, "O Lord, undertake for me." Far better say that at first than at last, as we have too often done! Bring the prayer in one hand, and clasp the promise in the other, joining them in the faith-clasp of "Do as Thou hast said!" And put both the hands into the hand of Him whom the Father heareth always, saying, "Do Thou for me, O Lord God, for Thy name's sake," for the sake of Jehovah-Jesus, the mighty God, the everlasting Father, yet the Saviour of sinners.

> And there was calm! O Saviour, I have proved
> That Thou to help and save art really near:
> How else this quiet rest from grief, and fear,
> And all distress? The cross is not removed,
> I must go forth to bear it as before,
> But, leaning on Thine arm, I dread its weight no more.

August 9

CHRIST MUST BE EVERYTHING

For it is God which worketh in you both to will and to do of his good pleasure.   Philippians 2:13

Does it not almost seem as if we were at times trusting to our trust, making everything hinge upon it, and thereby only removing a subtle dependence upon ourselves one step farther back, disguising instead of renouncing it? If Christ's keeping depends upon our trusting, and our continuing to trust depends upon ourselves, we are in no better or safer position than before, and shall only be landed in a fresh series of disappointments. The old story, something for the sinner to do, crops up again here, only with the ground shifted from works to trust. Said a friend to me, "I see now! I did trust Jesus to do everything else for me, but I thought that this trusting was something that I had to do." And so, of course, what she had to do had been a perpetual effort and frequent failure. We can no more trust and keep on trusting than we can do anything else of ourselves. Even in this it must be "Jesus only"; we are not to look to Him only to be the Author and Finisher of our faith, but we are to look to Him for all the intermediate fulfillment of the work of faith (2 Thessalonians 1:11); we must ask Him to go on fulfilling it in us, committing even this to His power.

> Distrust thyself, but trust His strength;
>   In Him thou shalt be strong:
> His weakest ones may learn at length
>   A daily triumph song.
>
> Distrust thyself, but trust alone
>   In Him, for all — for ever!
> And joyously thy heart shall own
>   That Jesus faileth never.

August 10

DO YOU WANT THE BLESSING?

Upon the first day of the week let every one of you lay by him in store, as God hath prospered him. 1 Corinthians 16:2

The very act of literally fulfilling this apostolic command seems to bring a blessing with it, as all simple obedience does. I wish, dear friends, you would try it! You will find it a sweet reminder on His own day of this part of your consecration. You will find it an immense help in making the most of your little charities. The regular inflow will guide the outflow, and insure your always having something for any sudden call for your Master's cause. Do not say you are afraid you could not keep to it. What has a consecrated life to do with being afraid? Some of us could tell of such sweet and singular lessons of trust in this matter, that they are written in golden letters of love on our memories. Of course, there will be trials of our faith in this, as well as in everything else. But every trial of our faith is but a trial of His faithfulness, and is "much more precious than gold which perisheth."

> Called to suffer with our Master, patiently to run His race;
> Called a blessing to inherit, called to holiness and grace;
> Called to fellowship with Jesus, by the Ever-faithful One;
> Called to His eternal glory, to the kingdom of His Son.

August 11

Come unto me. Matthew 11:28

This is the royal invitation. For it is given by the King of kings. We are so familiar with the words that we fail to realize them. May the Holy Spirit open our ear that we may hear the voice of our King in them, and that they may reach our souls with imperative power. Then "they shall know in that day that I am He that doth speak." Think of the day when the Great White Throne is set, and when the Son of man shall come in His glory; . . . and know that it is "this same Jesus" who now says to you, "Come unto Me!"

> Is it for me to listen to Thy beloved voice
> And hear its sweetest music bid even me rejoice?
> Is it for me, Thy welcome, Thy gracious "Enter in"?
> For me, Thy "Come, ye blessed!" for me, so full of sin?

August 12

AGED THROUGH SUFFERING

The things which he suffered. Hebrews 5:8

If we have some dear one gone before, who "suffered many things," there is neither comfort nor help to be had by dwelling on them. He would be a poor comforter who reminded you of them, and brought them back in detail to your scarred memory. One would rather do one's utmost to turn your thoughts away from them, leading you to dwell only on the present bliss, and one would fain blot out your painful remembrance of a past which it does no good to recall. Not so does our Divine Comforter work. When He takes of the things of Christ and shows them to us, we feel that the things which He suffered are precious exceedingly, and the Spirit-wrought remembrance of them powerful beyond all else.

This pathetic plural is full of suggestion. How much may be hidden under the supposition of the Jews that He was nearly fifty years of age, when so little beyond thirty! How sharp must have been the experiences which graved such lines upon the visage so marred more than any man! Think of all that must have gone on under the surface of His home life, where "neither did His brethren believe in Him." Consider Him that endured such contradiction of sinners against Himself. Think what temptation must have been to the Holy One, and what the concentration of malice and great rage when the prince of darkness went forth to do his worst against the lonely Son of Man, whom he knew to be the Son of God. Think of Jesus *alone* with Satan! Oh, what things He suffered *before* He came to the agony and bloody sweat, the cross and passion, which filled up the cup which His Father gave Him to drink for us men and for our salvation!

All this, that He might be made a perfect Saviour, having learnt by personal experience the suffering from which He saves as well as the suffering in which He supports and with which He sympathizes; having learnt by personal experience the obedience by which "many shall be made righteous," and which is at once our justification and our example. *All this*, that He might be a perfect Captain of our salvation, knowing all and far more than all the hardships of the rank and file. *All this*, that He might be the Author of eternal salvation to them that obey Him, to you and me!

> When thou passest through the waters,
>   I will be with thee!
> Sure and sweet and all-sufficient
>   Shall His presence be.
> All God's billows overwhelmed Him
>   In the great Atoning Day;
> Now He only leads thee through them,
>   With thee all the way.

August 13

A VISTA OF BRIGHTNESS

At evening time it shall be light. Zechariah 14:7

We should have said, "At evening time it shall be shadow";
God says, "At evening time it shall be light."

We are not to look for a very dismal afternoon of life with only some final sunset-glow, for He says it "shineth more and more unto the perfect day"; and "more and more" leaves no dark intervals; we are to expect a continual brightening path. "The future is one vista of brightness and blessedness" to those who are willing only "to walk in the light." Just think, when you are seven, or ten, or twenty years older, that will only mean seven or ten or twenty years' more experience of His love and faithfulness, more light of the knowledge of the glory of God in the face of Jesus Christ; and still the "more and more unto the perfect day," will be opening out before us! We are "confident of this very thing"!

> Fear not the westering shadows, O children of the day!
> For brighter still and brighter shall be your homeward way.
> Resplendent as the morning, with fuller glow and power,
> And clearer than the noonday, shall be your sunset hour.

August 14

I will be as the dew unto Israel: he shall grow as the lily, and cast forth his roots as Lebanon.   Hosea 14:5

You look out some dark night after a hot dusty day; there is no storm, no rain, there is not the least token to your senses of what is going on. You look out again in the morning, and you see every blade and leaf tipped with a dewdrop; everything is revived and freshened, prepared for the heat of the day, and smiling at the glow. Just so His words are silently falling on your souls in the darkness, and preparing them for the day. They do not come with any sensible power, nothing flashes out from the page as at other times, nothing shines so as to shed any pleasant light on your path, you do not hear any sound of abundance of rain. You seem as if you could not take the words in; and if you could, your mind is too weary to meditate on them. But they are distilling as the dew all the time!

> Springs of life in desert places
> Shall thy God unseal for thee;
> Quickening and reviving graces,
> Dew-like, healing, sweet and free.
> Springs of sweet refreshment flowing,
> When thy work is hard or long,
> Courage, hope, and power bestowing,
> Lightening labor with a song.

August 15

The water that I shall give him shall be in him a well of water springing up into everlasting life.   John 4:14

Did you ever think why it is so utterly hopeless and useless to try to quench that inner thirst with anything but the living water, "the supply of the Spirit of Jesus Christ"? He has said plainly and positively that you shall not succeed! He hath said "Whosoever drinketh of this water shall thirst again." You see there is no chance for you, for His Word cannot be broken, and He says you shall thirst again. There are only two issues of that perpetual thirst. One is the unanswered entreaty for a drop of water, only so much as a tip of the finger may bear, not to quench the unquenchable thirst, but only to cool a flame-tormented tongue. The only other, is "Whosoever drinketh of the water that I shall give him shall never thirst." And lest our slow perceptions should fail to grasp the fact in the figure, the Lord Jesus repeats the promise, and says, "He that believeth on Me shall never thirst." "Never"! for "He satisfieth the longing soul."

> To whom, O Saviour, shall we go
> For life, and joy, and light?
> No help, no comfort from below,
> No lasting gladness we may know,
> No hope may bless our sight.
> Our souls are weary and athirst,
> But earth is iron-bound and cursed,
> And nothing she may yield can stay
> The restless yearnings day by day;
> Yet, without **Thee**, Redeemer blest,
> We **would** not, if we **could**, find rest.

August 16

NOT A SHADOW — BUT HIMSELF

I will never leave thee, nor forsake thee. Hebrews 13:5

Are you a disciple of the Lord Jesus at all? If so, He says to you, "I am with you alway." That overflows all the regrets of the past and all the possibilities of the future, and most certainly includes the present. Therefore, at this present moment, as surely as your eyes rest on this page, so surely the Lord Jesus is with you. Is it not too bad to turn round upon that gracious presence, the Lord Jesus Christ's own personal presence here and now, and without one note of faith or whisper of thanksgiving, say, "Yes, but I don't realize it!" Then it is, after all, not the presence but the realization that you are seeking — the shadow, not the substance! Honestly, it is so! For you have such absolute assurance of the reality put into the very plainest words of promise that divine love could devise, that you dare not make Him a liar and say, "No! He is not with me!" All you can say is, "I don't feel a sense of His presence." Well, then, be ashamed of doubting your beloved Master's faithfulness, and "never open thy mouth any more" in His presence about it. For those doubting, desponding words were said in His presence. He was there with you while you said or thought them. What must He have thought of them?

> He will never fail us, He will not forsake;
> His eternal covenant He will never break!
> Onward, then, and fear not, children of the day!
> For His word shall never, never pass away!

August 17

WHY NOT YIELD TO IT?

**And we have known and believed the love that God hath
to us.** 1 John 4:16

Do not wrong, and wound, and insult that tremendous love by
refusing to believe it. He is at this moment giving you the
personal proof of it, by drawing you even for these few minutes.
Do not resist the half-formed wish to come to Jesus. It is very
solemn to realize that this is no less than the Father's own
drawing of you to His dear Son. Without it you could not come,
because you know you would have refused to come; but with
it, if only you yield to it, you shall come.

> Holy brethren, called and chosen by the sovereign Voice of Might,
> See your high and holy calling out of darkness into light!
> Called according to His purpose and the riches of His love;
> Won to listen by the leading of the gentle heavenly Dove!

August 18

WHAT SHALL THE HARVEST BE?

**Surely every man walketh in a vain shew: surely they are
disquieted in vain: . . . And now, Lord, what wait I for? my
hope is in thee.** Psalm 39:6, 7

"Yes, this is all very well for some people, or for older people,
but I am not ready for it; I can't say I see my way to this sort
of thing." I am going to take the lowest ground for a minute,
and appeal to *your* "past experience." Are you satisfied with
your experience of the other "sort of thing"? Your pleasant
pursuits, your harmless recreations, your nice occupations,
even your improving ones, what fruit are you having from
them? Your social intercourse, your daily talks and walks,
your investments of all the time that remains to you over and
above the absolute duties God may have given you, what fruit
that shall remain have you from all this? Day after day passes
on, and year after year, and what shall the harvest be? What
is even the present return? Are you getting any real and
lasting satisfaction out of it all? Are you not finding that
things lose their flavor, and that you are spending your
strength day after day for nought; that you are no more satisfied than you were a year ago — rather less so, if anything?
Does not a sense of hollowness and weariness come over you
as you go on in the same round, perpetually getting through
things only to begin again? It cannot be otherwise. Over
even the freshest and purest earthly fountains the Hand that

never makes a mistake has written, "He that drinketh of this water shall thirst again." Look into your own heart and you will find a copy of that inscription already traced, *"Shall thirst again."* And the characters are being deepened with every attempt to quench the inevitable thirst and weariness in life, which can only be satisfied and rested in full consecration to God. For "Thou hast made us *for Thyself,* and the heart never resteth till it findeth rest in Thee." Today I tell you of a brighter and happier life, whose inscription is, *"Shall never thirst,"* a life that is no dull round-and-round in a circle of unsatisfactorinesses, but a life that has found its true and entirely satisfactory center, and set itself towards a shining and entirely satisfactory goal, whose brightness is cast over every step of the way. Will you not seek it?

Springs of peace, when conflict heightens, thine uplifted eye shall see;
Peace that strengthens, calms, and brightens, peace, itself a victory.
Springs of comfort, strangely springing, thro' the bitter wells of woe;
Founts of hidden gladness, bringing joy that earth can ne'er bestow.

August 19

WITHOUT EXCUSE

The king said unto him, Wherefore wentest not thou with me?
2 Samuel 19:25

"With me!" To be with our King will be our highest bliss for eternity; and surely it is the position of highest honor and gladness now. But if we would always *be* with Him, we must sometimes be ready to *go* with Him. "The Son of God goes forth to war" nowadays. Do we go with Him? His cross is "without the gate." Do we go "forth unto Him without the camp, bearing His reproach"? Do we really go with Him every day and all day long, following "the Lamb whithersoever He goeth"? What about this week — this day? Have we loyally gone with our King wherever His footsteps go before? If the voice of our King is heard in our hearts, "Wherefore wentest *thou* not with me?" — *thou* who hast eaten "continually at the King's table," — thou who hast had a place among "the King's sons," — thou unto whom the King has shown "the kindness of God," we have no "because" to offer. He would have healed the spiritual lameness that hindered, and we might have run after Him. We are without excuse.

The Lord of Hosts, in whom alone our weakness shall be strong,
Shall lead us on to conquest with a mighty battle song;
And soon the warfare shall be past, the glorious triumph won,
The kingdoms of this world shall be the kingdoms of His Son.

August 20

LIFE — OR DEATH?

Ye will not come to me, that ye might have life. John 5:40

So long as you are not willing, i.e., not actually and actively willing to come (for that is the meaning of the original), of course you cannot come. And without coming to Jesus you cannot have life. And if you do not have life, there is nothing but death for you — the second death with all its unknown terrors, into the realities of which any moment may plunge you. Your not believing this makes no difference as to the fact. Your doubting it makes no difference to its certainty. I assert it on the authority of the Word of God. "I call heaven and earth to record this day against you, that I have set before you life and death . . . therefore choose life" (Deuteronomy 30:19). For in not willing life, you are willing death, and "why will ye die?"

> You could not do without Him, if once He made you see
> The fetters that enchain you, till He hath set you free.
> If once you saw the fearful load of sin upon your soul—
> The hidden plague that ends in death, unless He makes you whole!

> What will you do without Him, when death is drawing near?
> Without His love — the only love that casts out every fear;
> When the shadow-valley opens, unlighted and unknown,
> And the terrors of its darkness must be all passed alone!

August 21

WHEN SILENCE IS NEGATIVE

David the king also rejoiced with great joy. 1 Chronicles 29:9

Do not let us think of the joy of our King over His people as only future. While we cannot look forward too much to the day when He shall present us "faultless before the presence of His glory with exceeding joy," let us not overlook the present gladness which we, even we, who have so often grieved Him, may give to our King. Elsewhere we hear of the joy of angels over repenting sinners; here we have a glimpse of the joy of the King of angels over His consecrated ones. Look at the whole passage—it is full of typical light—and let us take it for our learning. "Who then is willing to consecrate his service this day unto the Lord?" Silence is negative here; there must be a definite heart response if we are willing. Are you? If so, when? The king's question says nothing of some day, but of "this day." And the question is put to you: if never before, it is sounding in your ears now. Shall your service be His "this day," and henceforth, or not? Shall not "this day" be "the day of the gladness of His heart"? Will you not consecrate your service today unto Him? For then, "He will save, He will rejoice over thee with joy; He will rest in His love; He will joy over thee with singing." As our own hearts are filled with the intense joy of consecration to our Lord, a yet intenser glow will come as we remember that His joy is greater than ours, for He is anointed with the oil of gladness above His fellows.

O the gladness of the spirit, when the true and only Light
Pours in radiant resplendence, making all things new and bright!
When the love of Jesus shineth in its overcoming power,
When the secret sweet communion hallows every passing hour.

August 22

IMPUTED BEAUTY

So shall the king greatly desire thy beauty. Psalm 45:11

Can this be? What beauty have we that the King can desire? For the more we have seen of His beauty, the more we have seen of our own ugliness. What, then, can He see? "My comeliness which I had put upon thee." "The beauty of the Lord our God be upon us." For "He will beautify the meek with salvation." And so the desire of the King is set upon us. Perhaps it is upon the emphatic *"so,"* as pointing to the context, that the intensity of the emphatic *"greatly"* hinges. It is when the bride forgets her own people and her father's house—that is, when her life and love are altogether given to her Royal Bridegroom—that He shall greatly desire her beauty. When His glorious beauty has so filled our eyes, and His incomprehensible love has so filled our hearts, that He is first, and most, and dearest of all — when we can say not merely, "The desire of our souls is to Thy name," but "There is none upon earth that I desire beside Thee"—when thus we are, to the very depth of our being, really and entirely our Beloved's, then we may add, in solemn, wondering gladness, "And His desire is toward me."

O love surpassing thought
So bright, so grand, so clear, so true, so glorious;
Love infinite, love tender, love unsought,
Love changeless, love rejoicing, love victorious!
And this great love for us in boundless store;
Christ's everlasting love! What wouldst thou more?

August 23

Shew us thy mercy, O Lord, and grant us thy salvation.
Psalm 85:7
Return unto the Lord, and he will have mercy. Isaiah 55:7

People do not come for what they do not want. Until the Holy Spirit shows us our need of mercy, and puts reality into the prayer, "Have mercy upon us miserable sinners," we shall never come to the throne of grace to obtain mercy.

He that into God's kingdom comes,
Must enter by this door.

So, if you have never yet felt that you could sincerely say, "God be merciful *to me* a sinner" and therefore have never yet felt particularly anxious to come to the throne of grace to obtain it, I would urgently entreat you to pray, "Lord, show me myself!" When the Holy Spirit answers that prayer, you will be eager enough to come and obtain mercy! It will be the one thing then that you will be particularly anxious about.

Return!
O wanderer from My side!
Soon droops each blossom of the darkening wild,
Soon melts each meteor which thy steps beguiled,
Soon is the cistern dry which thou hast hewn,
And thou wilt weep in bitterness full soon.
Return! ere gathering night shall shroud the way
Thy footsteps yet may tread, in this accepted day.

August 24

CONTINUAL AND CONSISTENT CARE

He careth for you. 1 Peter 5:7

It is so pleasant to be cared for; to have some kind relatives and friends who show that they love you by their care for you. But all earthly care for you comes because "He careth for you." He planned and arranged everything, without your having anything to do with it, so that you shall be cared for. And He did not arrange it once for all, and then leave things to go on as might happen. No! Every day, every moment, He careth, *goes on* caring, for you. Not only thinking of you and watching you, but working for you; making things come right, so that everything should be just the best that could happen to you. Not managing the great things, and leaving the little things to arrange themselves; but giving loving care to the least, the very least that concerns you. Even in small troubles which no one else seems to care about, "He careth"; or when every one else is too much taken up with other things to attend to you, "He careth for you." You can never get beyond God's care, for it always reaches you; you can never be outside of it, for it is always enfolding you.

Who will take care of me? darling, you say!
Lovingly, tenderly watched as you are!
Listen! I give you the answer today,
One who is never forgetful or far.
He will take care of you! all through the year,
Crowning each day with His kindness and love,
Sending you blessing and shielding from fear,
Leading you on to the bright home above.

August 25

CHRIST FIRST; OTHERS SECOND; ME LAST

I have given you an example, that ye should do as I have done.
John 13:15

Do you really wish to follow the footsteps of the Lord Jesus? Have you asked God to make you more like Him? Are you ready to begin today? Then here is a motto for today, "Even Christ pleased not Himself." Will you take it, and try to imitate Him? You are sure to have plenty of opportunities of acting upon it, and thus proving not only to others, but to the Saviour Himself that you mean what you say, and mean what you pray. You cannot tell, till you have fairly tried, how happy you can feel when you have cheerfully given up to another, for Jesus' sake, something which you would have liked for yourself, nor how happy you can be, when of your own free will, and by God's grace, you have chosen to do what your conscience tells you would please the Lord Jesus instead of what would have pleased yourself. If you have never tried it yet, begin today, and you will find it is quite a new happiness. What would have become of us if Christ had only pleased Himself, and stayed in His glorious home instead of coming down to save us? Think of that when you are tempted to please yourself instead of pleasing Him, and the remembrance that even He pleased not Himself, because He so loved you, will help you to try and please Him, and to please others for His sake.

If washed in Jesus' blood, then bear His likeness too!
And as you onward press, ask, "What would Jesus do?"
Give with a full, free hand; God freely gives to you!
And check each selfish tho't with, "What would Jesus do?"

August 26

CLAIM THE PROMISES

There hath not failed one word of all his good promise.
1 Kings 8:56
Whereby are given unto us exceeding great and precious promises.
2 Peter 1:4

Unclaimed promises are like uncashed checks; they will keep us from bankruptcy, but not from want. But if not, why not? What right have we to pick out one of His faithful sayings, and say we don't expect Him to fulfill that? What defense can we bring, what excuse can we invent, for so doing? If you appeal to experience against His faithfulness to His word, I will appeal to experience too, and ask you, Did you ever *really trust* Jesus to fulfill any word of His to you, and find your trust deceived? Whatever you did really trust Him to keep, He has kept; and the unkept things were never really entrusted. Scrutinize this past experience as you will, and it will only bear witness against your unfaithfulness, never against His absolute faithfulness.

> Master, I set my seal that Thou art true,
> Of Thy good promise not one thing hath failed!
> And I would send a ringing challenge forth,
> To all who know Thy name, to tell it out,
> Thy faithfulness to every written word,
> Thy lovingkindness crowning all the days—
> To say and sing with me: "The Lord is good,
> His mercy is forever, and His truth
> Is written on each page of all my life!"

August 27

TONGUES — A MIGHTY INFLUENCE

Talk ye of all his wondrous works. Psalm 105:2

Just consider what a power in the world talking is! Words dropped, caught up, repeated, then ventilated, combined, developed, set brains and pens to work; these again set the tongues to work; the talking spreads, becomes general, public opinion is formed and inflamed, and the results are engraved in the world's history. This is what talking can do when exercised about the affairs of "the kingdoms of the world and the glory of them." And we, who have been translated into the kingdom of God's dear Son — we have tongues too, and what have we been talking about? How have we used this same far-spreading power? Only suppose that for every time each English-speaking Christian had talked about the day's news of the kingdoms of this world, he had spent the same breath in telling the last news of the kingdom of Jesus Christ to his friends and casual acquaintances!

God intends and commands us to do this. We often quote "All Thy works shall praise Thee, O Lord, and Thy saints shall bless Thee." That sounds tolerably easy; but what next? "They shall speak of the glory of Thy kingdom, and talk of Thy power." Is this among the things that we ought to have done and have left undone? Are we not verily guilty as to this command? "Lord, have mercy upon us, and incline our hearts to keep this law!"

Are you shining for Jesus, dear one, so that the holy light
May enter the hearts of others, and make them glad and bright?
Have you spoken a word for Jesus, and told to some around,
Who do not care about Him, what a Saviour you have found?
Have you lifted the lamp for others, that has guided your own glad feet?
Have you echoed the loving message, that seemed to you so sweet?

August 28

HANDS — A MIGHTY MECHANISM

Whatsoever thy hand findeth to do, do it with thy might.
Ecclesiastes 9:10
Let us lift up our . . . hands unto God in the heavens.
Lamentations 3:41

Stay a minute, and look at your hand, the hand that holds this little book as you read it. See how wonderfully it is made; how perfectly fitted for what it has to do; how ingeniously connected with the brain, so as to yield that instantaneous and instinctive obedience without which its beautiful mechanism would be very little good to us! *Your* hand, do you say? Whether it is soft and fair with an easy life, or rough and strong with a working one, or white and weak with illness, it is the Lord Jesus Christ's. It is not your own at all; it belongs to Him. He made it, for without Him was not anything made that was made, not even your hand. And He has the added right of purchase—He has bought it that it might be one of His own instruments. We know this very well, but have we realized it? Have we really let Him have the use of these hands of ours? and have we ever simply and sincerely asked Him to keep them for His own use?

Jesus, Master, whom I serve, though so feebly and so ill,
Strengthen hand and heart and nerve all Thy bidding to fulfill;
Open Thou mine eyes to see all the work Thou hast for me.

August 29

Surely he hath borne our griefs, and carried our sorrows.
Isaiah 53:4

The sorrows of the past, the very sorrow that may be pressing heavily at this moment; all yours, all mine; all the sorrows of all His children all through the groaning generations; all that were "too heavy" for them—Jesus bore them all. "Is it nothing to you?" It is when the Lord says, "Now will I gather them" (the rebels and wanderers), that He adds, "And they shall sorrow a little for the burden of the King of princes." Have we this proof that He has indeed gathered us? But look forward! Because He has drunk "of the brook in the way, therefore shall He lift up the head." Already the "exceeding sorrowful" is exchanged for "Thou hast made Him [the King] exceeding glad"; and when the ransomed and gathered of the Lord shall return with everlasting joy, "their King also shall pass before them."

> "He suffered!" Was it, Lord, indeed for me,
> The Just One for the unjust; Thou didst bear
> The weight of sorrow that I hardly dare
> To look upon, in dark Gethsemane?
> "He suffered!" Thou, my near and gracious Friend,
> And yet my Lord, my God! Thou didst not shrink.

August 30

Behold, thy King cometh unto thee. Zechariah 9:9

That our King should let us come to Him is condescension indeed. But have we praised Him for His still more wonderful condescension: "Thy King *cometh unto thee*"? "Unto *thee*," rebel, traitor, faithless subject, coward, and coldhearted follower; for where is the life that has not fallen under these charges, when seen in the double light of the King's perfect law and the King's great love? Yes, He cometh unto thee, and it is enough to break our hearts when we get one contrasted glimpse of this undeserved grace and unparalleled condescension. His great promise has had its first fulfillment "unto thee." Thy King has come, and His own voice has given the objects of His coming. But you want a further fulfillment — you want a present coming of your King. You have His most sweet word, "I will come to you"; and you respond, "Oh, *when* wilt Thou come unto me?" Are you ready to receive the King's own answer now? Do you so desire His coming, that you do not want it postponed at all? Can you defer all other comers, and say in reality, "*Let* my Beloved come"?

Is it for me, dear Saviour, Thy glory and Thy rest?
For me, so weak and sinful, oh shall I thus be blessed?
Is it for me to see Thee in all Thy glorious grace,
And gaze in endless rapture on Thy beloved face?
Behold Thee in Thy beauty, behold Thee face to face;
Behold Thee in Thy glory, and reap Thy smile of grace;
And be with Thee forever, and never grieve Thee more!
Dear Saviour, I must praise Thee, and lovingly adore.

August 31

A GOOD ARGUMENT

He hath given you the former rain moderately, and he will cause to come down for you the rain, the former rain, and the latter rain in the first month.   Joel 2:23

This principle (and it is a very delightful one) of arguing from what God has done for us to what He will do for us, comes up perpetually in all parts of His Word. If He *hath* given us the former rain, it is the pledge and proof that "He *will* cause to come down for us the rain, the former rain, *and* the latter rain"; the blessing already given shall be continued or repeated, and a fuller future one shall be certainly added. Manoah's wife argued well: "If the Lord were pleased to kill us, He would not . . . have showed us all these things, nor told us such things as these." Oh, consider *what* things the Lord has shown and told you and me! Are they not abounding proofs of His purposes towards us? David made frequent use of the thought, arguing from the less to the greater: "The Lord that delivered me out of the paw of the lion and out of the paw of the bear, He will deliver me out of the hand of the Philistine." Paul gives a close parallel, rising from temporal to spiritual deliverance: "I was delivered out of the mouth of the lion. And the Lord shall deliver me from *every* evil work."

He, who hath won thy heart, will keep it true and free;
He, who hath shown thee what thou art, will show Himself to thee.
He, who hath bid thee live, and made thy life His own,
Life more abundantly will give, and keep it His alone.
He loveth always, faileth never; so rest on Him, today, forever!

He, who hath made thee nigh, will draw thee nearer still;
He, who hath given the first supply, will satisfy and fill.
He, who hath given thee grace, yet more and more will send;
He, who hath set thee in the race, will speed thee to the end.
He loveth always, faileth never; so rest on Him, today, forever.

September 1

MUTUAL ACCEPTANCE

As the servants of Christ, doing the will of God. Ephesians 6:6

Not until we have presented our bodies a living sacrifice can we prove what is that good, and perfect, and acceptable will of God. But in thus proving it, this continual presentation will be more and more seen to be our reasonable service, and becomes more and more a joyful sacrifice of praise.

The connection in Romans 12:1, 2 between our sacrifice which He so graciously calls acceptable to Himself and our finding out that His will is acceptable to ourselves, is very striking. One reason for this connection may be that only love can really understand love, and love on both sides is at the bottom of the whole transaction and its results.

> And if it seemeth good to Thee, my Father,
> Shall it seem aught but good to me?
> Thy will be done! Thou knowest I would rather
> Leave all with Thee.

September 2

HANDS REVEAL THE HEART

**Is thine heart right, as my heart is with thy heart? . . .
If it be, give me thine hand.** 2 Kings 10:15

What a call to confidence, and love, and free, loyal, happy service is this! and how different will the result of its acceptance be from the old lamentation: "We labour and have no rest; we have given the hand to the Egyptians and to the Assyrians." In the service of these other lords, under whatever shape they have presented themselves, we shall have known something of the meaning of having "both the hands full with travail and vexation of spirit." How many a thing have we taken in hand, as we say, which we expected to find an agreeable task, an interest in life, a something towards filling up that unconfessed aching void which is often most real when least acknowledged; and after a while we have found it change under our hands into irksome travail, involving perpetual vexation of spirit! The thing may have been of the earth and for the world, and then no wonder it failed to satisfy even the instinct of work, which comes natural to many of us. Or it may have been right enough in itself, something for the good of others so far as we understood their good, and unselfish in all but unraveled motive, and yet we found it full of tangled vexations, because the hands that held it were not simply consecrated to God. Well, if so, let us bring these soiled and tangle-making hands to the Lord, "Let us lift up our heart with our hands" to Him, asking Him to clear and cleanse them, "Forasmuch as ye are manifestly declared to be the epistles of Christ . . . written . . . in fleshly tables of the heart."

Let Him write what He will upon our hearts
With His unerring pen. They are His own,
Hewn from the rock by His selecting grace,
Prepared for His own glory. Let Him write!
Be sure He will not cross out one sweet word
But to inscribe a sweeter — but to grave
One that shall shine forever to His praise,
And thus fulfill our deepest heart-desire.
The tearful eye at first may read the line
"Bondage to grief!" but He shall wipe away
The tears, and clear the vision, till it read
In ever-brightening letters "Free to serve!"
For whom the Son makes free is free indeed.

September 3

JOY INWARD AND UPWARD

I have willingly offered all these things: and now have I seen with joy thy people, which are present here, to offer willingly unto thee. 1 Chronicles 29:17

The result of willing consecration of ourselves and our service is always joy. But was it not far more, far sweeter, that their king "also rejoiced with great joy"? For when a heart and life are willingly offered and fully surrendered to Him, He sees of "the travail of His soul" in it; it is a new accomplishment of the work which He came to do; and what then? He "is satisfied." If motive were wanting to yield ourselves unto Him, would it not be more than supplied by the thought that it will be satisfaction and joy to Him "who loved us and washed us from our sins in His own blood"? It seems just the one blessed opportunity given to us of being His true cupbearers, of bringing the wine of joy to our King; and in so doing He will make our cups to run over.

Our Father, we pray that Thy will may be done,
For full acquiescence is Heaven begun—
Both in us and by us Thy purpose be wrought,
In word and in action, in spirit and thought;
And Thou canst enable us thus to fulfill,
With holy rejoicing, Thy glorious will,
    For Thine is the Power!

September 4

A FIRM GRASP AND A FULL RECEPTION

Rejoice in the Lord, O ye righteous. Psalm 33:1
Serve the Lord with gladness. Psalm 100:2

Let us not, either for ourselves or others, acquiesce in disobedience to any of His commandments. See how absolute
they are! Think of the terribly distinct condemnation, "Because thou servedst not the Lord thy God with joyfulness,
and with gladness of heart . . . therefore shalt thou serve
thine enemies . . . and He shall put a yoke of iron upon thy
neck, until He have destroyed thee." Thank God, our experience is not the measure of His promises; they are all yea
and Amen in Christ Jesus and our varying, short-falling experience touches neither their faithfulness nor their fullness.
Forget the things which are behind, and press on to firmer
grasp and fuller reception of Christ and His joy. Then it
shall be always "praise . . . more and more," "more grace,"
"grace for grace," "from strength to strength" — yes, even
"from glory to glory."

"From glory unto glory!" Thank God, that even here
The starry words are shining out, our heavenward way to cheer!
That e'en among the shadows the conquering brightness glows,
As ever from the nearing Light intenser radiance flows.

September 5

OUR LIPS FOR FRUITFUL PRAISE

**With men of other tongues and other lips will I speak
unto this people.** 1 Corinthians 14:21

There seems a sevenfold sequence in His filling the lips of His
messengers. First, they must be purified. The live coal from
off the altar must be laid upon them, and He must say, "Lo,
this hath touched thy lips, and thine iniquity is taken away,
and thy sin is purged." Then He will create the fruit of them,
and this seems to be the great message of peace, "Peace to
him that is far off, and to him that is near, saith the Lord;
and I will heal him" (see Isaiah 57:19). Then comes the
prayer, "O Lord, open Thou my lips," and its sure fulfillment.
For then come in the promises, "Behold, I have put my words
in thy mouth," and, "They shall withal be fitted in thy lips."
Then, of course, "the lips of the righteous feed many," for

the food is the Lord's own giving. Everything leads up to praise, and so we come next to "My mouth shall praise Thee with joyful lips, when I remember Thee." And lest we should fancy that *"when"* rather implies that it is not, or cannot be, exactly *always*, we find that the meditation of Jesus throws this added light upon it, "By *Him*, therefore, let us offer the sacrifice of praise to God *continually*, that is, the fruit of our lips, giving thanks to" (margin, confessing) "His name."

Have you not a word for Jesus? Will the world His praise proclaim?
Who shall speak if ye are silent? ye who know and love His name.
You, whom He hath called and chosen His own witnesses to be,
Will you tell your gracious Master, "Lord, we cannot speak for Thee!"

September 6

SANCTIFIED—ENERGIZED—STRENGTHENED

A new commandment I give unto you, That ye love one another.
                                                    John 13:34

The love of Christ is not an absorbing, but a radiating love. The more we love Him, the more we shall most certainly love others. Some have not much natural power of loving, but the love of Christ will strengthen it. Some have had the springs of love dried up by some terrible earthquake. They will find "fresh springs" in Jesus, and the gentle flow will be purer and deeper than the old torrent could ever be. Some have been satisfied that it should rush in a narrow channel, but He will cause it to overflow into many another, and widen its course of blessing. Some have spent it all on their God-given dear ones. Now He is come whose right it is; and yet in the fullest resumption of that right, He is so gracious that He puts back an even larger measure of the old love into our hand, sanctified with His own love, and energized with His blessing, and strengthened with His new commandment.

But He had need of her. Not one new gem
But many, for His crown — not one fair sheaf,
But many she should bring. And she should have
A richer, happier harvest-home at last . . .
               *   *   *   *   *   *
Then through the darkness and the chill He sent
A heat-ray of His love, developing
The mystic writing, till it glowed and shone
And lit up all her life with radiance new—
The happy service of a yielded heart,
With comfort that He never ceased to give
(Because her need could never cease) she filled
The empty chalices of other lives,
And time and tho't were thenceforth spent for Him
Who loved her with His everlasting love.

September 7

CLEAN HANDS AT THE TABLE

Behold, the hand of him that betrayeth me is with me on the table. Luke 22:21
He that dippeth his hand with me in the dish, the same shall betray me. Matthew 26:23

It was a literal hand that our Lord Jesus spoke of; a hand so near to Jesus, with Him on the table, touching His own hand in the dish at that hour of sweetest, and closest, and most solemn intercourse, and yet betraying Him! That same hand taking the thirty pieces of silver! What a tremendous lesson of the need of keeping for our hands! Oh, that every hand that is with Him at His table, and that takes the memorial bread, may be kept from any faithless and loveless motion! And again, it was by literal "wicked hands" that our Lord Jesus was crucified and slain. Does not the thought that human hands have been so treacherous and cruel to our beloved Lord make us wish the more fervently that our hands may be totally faithful and devoted to Him? Danger and temptation to let the hands move at other impulses is every bit as great to those who have nothing else to do but to render direct service, and who think they are doing nothing else.

He will sanctify thee wholly; body, spirit, soul shall be
Blameless till thy Saviour's coming in His glorious majesty!
He hath perfected forever those whom He hath sanctified;
Spotless, glorious, and holy is the Church, His chosen Bride.

September 8

ROYAL SERVANTS

Choose you this day whom ye will serve. Joshua 24:15
What doth the Lord thy God require of thee, but to fear the Lord thy God, to walk in all his ways, and to love him, and to serve the Lord thy God with all thy heart and with all thy soul. Deuteronomy 10:12
Let us have grace, whereby we may serve God acceptably with reverence and godly fear. Hebrews 12:28

Choose this day whom you will serve with real, thoroughgoing, wholehearted service, and He will receive you; and you will find, as we have found, that He is such a good Master that you are satisfied with His goodness, and that you will never want to go out free. Nay, rather take His own word for it; see what He says: "If they obey and serve Him, they shall spend their days in prosperity, and their years in pleasures." You cannot possibly understand that till you are really in His service! For He does not give, nor even show, His wages before you enter it. And He says, "My servants shall sing for joy of heart." But you cannot try over that song to see what it is like, you cannot even read one bar of it, till your nominal or even promised service is exchanged for real and undivided consecration. But when He can call you, "My servant," then you will find yourself singing for joy of heart, because He says you shall.

"My Lord!" My heart hath said it joyfully.
Nay, could it be my own cold, treacherous heart?
'Tis comfort to remember that we have
No will or power to think one holy thought,
And thereby estimate His power in us—
"No man can say that Jesus is the Lord.
But by the Holy Ghost." Then it must be
That all the sweetness of the word, "Thy Lord,"
And all the long glad echoes that it woke,
Are whispers of the Spirit, and a seal
Upon His work, as yet so faintly seen.

September 9

RETREAT MEANS DEFEAT

Without me ye can do nothing.   John 15:5
I can do all things through Christ which strengtheneth me.
                                        Philippians 4:13

We had such a nice little quiet, shady corner in the vineyard, down among the tender grapes, with such easy little weedings and waterings to attend to. And then the Master comes and draws us out into the thick of the work, and puts us into a part of the field where we never should have thought of going, and puts larger tools in our hands, that we may do more at a stroke. And we know we are not sufficient for these things, and the very tools seem too heavy for us, and the glare too dazzling, and the vines too tall. Ah! but would we really go back? He would not be in the old shady corner with us now; for when He put us forth He went before us, and it is only by close following that we can abide with Him. Without Him we could do nothing if we perversely and fearfully ran back to our old work. With Him, "through Christ which strengtheneth" us, we "can do all things" in the new work. Not our power, but His presence will carry us through.

I could not do without Thee! No other friend can read
The Spirit's deepest longings, interpreting its need.
No human heart could enter each dim recess of mine,
And soothe and hush and calm it, O blessed Lord, but Thine!

September 10

To day thy servant knoweth that I have found grace in thy sight, my lord, O king, in that the king hath fulfilled the request of his servant. 2 Samuel 14:22

An answered prayer makes us glad for its own sake. But there is grace behind the gift which is better and more gladdening than the gift itself. For which is most valued, the engagement ring, or the favor of which it is the token? Setting aside judicial answers to unspiritual prayers, which an honest conscience will have no difficulty in distinguishing, the servants of the King may take it that His answers to their requests are proofs and tokens of His grace and favor — of His real, and present, and personal love to themselves individually. When they are receiving few or none, they should search for the cause, lest it should be some hidden or unrecognized sin. For "if I regard iniquity in my heart, the Lord will not hear me"; so never let us go on comfortably and easily when He is silent to us. And instead of envying others who get such wonderful answers, "Let us search and try our ways."

> And evermore the Father sends radiantly down
> All-marvelous responses, His ministers to crown;
> The incense-cloud returning as golden blessing-showers,
> We in each drop discerning some feeble prayer of ours,
> Transmuted into wealth unpriced, by Him who giveth thus
> The glory all to Jesus Christ, the gladness all to us!

September 11

Thou understandest my thought. Psalm 139:2

Who does not know what it is to be misunderstood? Perhaps no one ever is always and perfectly understood, because so few Christians are like their Master in having the spirit of quick understanding. But this does not make it the less trying to you; and you do not feel able to say with Paul, "With me it is a very small thing." But this precious Word which meets every need, gives you a steppingstone which is quite enough to enable you to reach that brave position, if you will only stand on it. "Thou understandest my thought." Even if others "daily mistake" your words, He understands your thought, and is not this infinitely better? He Himself, your ever-loving, ever-present Father, understands. He understands perfectly just what and just when others do not. Not your actions merely, but your thought — the central self which no words can reveal to others. "All my desire is before Thee." He understands how you desired to do the right thing when others thought you did the wrong thing. He understands how His poor, weak child wants to please Him, and secretly mourns over grieving Him. "Thou understandest" seems to go even a step further than the great comfort of "Thou knowest." "His understanding is infinite."

> She could not have put it in words,
>   But the Teacher understood,
> As God understands the chirp of the birds
>   In the depths of an autumn wood.
> And a quiet touch on a reddening cheek
>   Was quite enough;
> No need to question, no need to speak.

September 12

THE EARNEST OF THINGS TO COME

Who delivered us from so great a death, and doth deliver: in whom we trust that he will yet deliver us. 2 Corinthians 1:10

"The Lord hath heard the voice of my supplication; the Lord will receive my prayer." "The Lord hath dealt bountifully with me," comes first; then follows, "Deal bountifully with Thy servant"; and then, "Thou shalt deal bountifully with me." "The Lord hath done great things for us, whereof we are glad," leads us on to the prophecy, "Be glad and rejoice, for the Lord will do great things." The same argument is used in prayer. "Pardon, I beseech Thee, the iniquity of Thy people . . . as Thou hast forgiven this people, from Egypt even until now." "Thou hast delivered my soul from death; wilt Thou not deliver my feet from falling?" So in the lovely typical request of Achsah to her father, "Give me a blessing; for thou hast given me a south land; give me also springs of water." The basis for such expressions of trust and petition are found in Romans 8:32, "He that spared not His own Son"—there is the entirely incontrovertible fact of what He hath done — "shall He not with Him also freely give us all things" — there is the inspired conclusion of what He will do.

> All my desire Thou grantest, whatsoe'er
> I ask! Was ever mythic tale or dream
> So bold as this reality — this stream
> Of boundless blessings flowing full and free?
> Yet more than I have thought or asked of Thee,
> Out of Thy royal bounty still Thou givest me.

September 13

TRUSTING

When we were yet without strength, in due time Christ died for the ungodly. Romans 5:6
Lord, thou wilt ordain peace for us; for thou also hast wrought all our works in us. Isaiah 26:12

What a long time it takes to come down to the conviction, and still more to the realization of the fact that without Him we can do *nothing*, but that He must work *all* our works in us! This is the work of God, that ye believe in Him whom He has sent. And no less must it be the work of God that we go on believing, and that we go on trusting. Then, dear friends who are longing to trust Him with unbroken and unwavering trust, cease the effort and drop the burden, and now entrust your trust to Him! He is just as well able to keep that as any other part of the complex lives which we want Him to take and keep for Himself. And oh, do not pass on content with the thought, "Yes, that is a good idea; perhaps I should find that a great help!" But, "Now, then, *do it.*" It is no help to the sailor to see a flash of light across a dark sea, if he does not instantly steer accordingly.

> I am trusting Thee, Lord Jesus, trusting only Thee;
> Trusting Thee for full salvation, great and free.
> I am trusting Thee, Lord Jesus; never let me fall!
> I am trusting Thee forever, and for all.

September 14

WHO CAN BE AGAINST US?

The Lord shall fight for you. Exodus 14:14

How glad the children of Israel must have been when Moses said these words to them on the shores of the Red Sea! For when they "lifted up their eyes, behold, the Egyptians marched after them; and they were sore afraid." The Egyptians had been cruel masters to them; and they had horses and chariots to pursue them with; and there was the sea close before them, and no boats! Perhaps some of the Israelites thought it was no use trying to escape; they would only be overtaken and conquered, and be worse off than before. And so, left to themselves, they would have been; but God fought for them in a way they never thought of, for "the Lord saved Israel that day out of the hand of the Egyptians, and Israel saw the

Egyptians dead upon the seashore." What about your Egyptians?—the angry tempers, the impatient words, the vain and foolish thoughts, the besetting sins that master you so often. Have you tried so often to fight against them, and failed, that it seems almost no use, and you do not see how to conquer them or to escape them? Are you very tired of fighting, and "sore afraid" of being always overcome just the same as ever? Now hear God's true, strong promise to you, "The Lord shall fight for you!" Will He really? Yes, really, and He will conquer for you too, if you will only believe His Word and trust the battle to Him, and *let* Him fight for you.

> So, when you meet with trials, and know not what to do,
> Just cast the care on Jesus, and He will fight for you.
> Gird on the heavenly armor of faith, and hope, and love;
> And when the conflict's ended, you'll reign with Him above.

September 15

ROYAL PARTNERSHIP

Labourers together with God.	1 Corinthians 3:9
Workers together with him.	2 Corinthians 6:1
The Lord working with them.	Mark 16:20

Divine fellowship of work! Will not this thought ennoble everything He gives us to do today, even if it is among plants and hedges! Even the pottery will be grand! But dwelling and working must go together. If we are indeed dwelling with the King, we shall be working for Him, too, "as we have opportunity." The working will be as the dwelling—a settled, regular thing, whatever form it may take at His appointment. Nor will His work ever be done when we are not dwelling with Him. It will be our own work then, not His, and it will not "abide." We shall come under the condemnation of the vine which was pronounced "empty," because "he bringeth forth fruit unto himself." We are, like the potters of old, to dwell with the King "for His work"; but He will see to it that it shall be for a great deal besides—for a great continual reward according to His own heart and out of His royal bounty—for peace, for power, for love, for gladness, for likeness to Himself. "Be strong, all ye people of the land, saith the Lord, and work, for I am with you, saith the Lord of hosts."

> Lord! to Thy command we bow, touch our lips with altar fire;
> Let Thy Spirit kindle now, faith and zeal and strong desire;
> So that henceforth we may be fellow-workers, Lord, with Thee.

September 16

ENTHRONE HIM WHOSE RIGHT IT IS

In time past, when Saul was king over us, thou wast he that leddest out and broughtest in Israel. 2 Samuel 5:2

Chosen, anointed, given by God, continually leading and caring for us, yet not accepted, not crowned, not enthroned by us; our real allegiance, our actual service, given to another! Self has been our Saul, our central tyranny; and many have been its officers domineering in every department. But "the time past of our life may suffice us to have wrought the will" of self — Satan — the world. We do not want "to live the rest of our time" to any but One Will. Let us with full purpose of heart, dethrone the usurper and give the diadem to Him "whose right it is," a blood-bought and death-sealed right.

> I spent long years for thee, in weariness and woe,
> That an eternity of joy thou mightest know.
> I spent long years for thee;
> Hast thou spent one for Me?
>
> Oh, let thy life be given, thy years for Him be spent,
> World-fetters all be riven, and joy with suffering blent;
> I gave Myself for thee:
> Give thou thyself to Me!

September 17

"WHATSOEVER YE DO"

And whatsoever ye do in word or deed, do all in the name of the Lord Jesus. Colossians 3:17

A Christian school-girl loves Jesus; she wants to please Him all day long, and so she practices her scales carefully and conscientiously. It is at the impulse of His love that her fingers move so steadily through the otherwise tiresome exercises. Some day her Master will find a use for her music; but meanwhile it may be just as really done unto Him as if it were Mr. Sankey at his organ, swaying the hearts of thousands. The hand of a Christian lad traces his Latin verses, or his figures, or his copying. He is doing his best, because a banner has been given him that it may be displayed, not so much by talk as by continuance in well-doing. And so, for Jesus' sake, his hand moves accurately and perseveringly.

A busy wife, or daughter, or servant has a number of little manual duties to perform. If these are done slowly and leisurely, they may be got through, but there will not be time left for some little service to the poor, or some little kindness to a suffering or troubled neighbor, or for a little quiet time alone with God and His Word. And so the hands move quickly, impelled by the loving desire for service or communion, kept in busy motion for Jesus' sake. Or it may be that the special aim is to give no occasion of reproach to some who are watching, but so to adorn the doctrine that those may be won by the life who will not be won by the Word. Then the hands will have their share to do; they will move carefully, neatly, perhaps even elegantly, making everything around as nice as possible, letting their intelligent touch be seen in the details of the home, and even of the dress, doing or arranging all the little things decently and in order for Jesus' sake. And so on with every duty in every position.

The morning light flingeth its wakening ray,
And as the day bringeth the work of the day,
The happy heart singeth; Awake and away!
No life can be dreary when work is delight;
Though evening be weary, rest cometh at night;
And all will be cheery, if faithful and right.

September 18

STRONG CONSOLATION

The Lord shall preserve thee from all evil. Psalm 121:7

Do you believe that? But He who knows our little faith never gives an isolated promise. He leaves us no chance of overlooking or misunderstanding anyone except by willful neglect because it is always confirmed in other parts of the Word. So He has given the same strong consolation in other terms. "There shall no evil happen to the just." "In seven [troubles] there shall no evil touch thee." He is the "wall of fire round about" us; and what fortification so impenetrable—nay, so unapproachable! And "He that toucheth you toucheth the apple of His eye"—the very least touch is felt by the Lord, who loves us and is mighty to save! Well may He say, "And who is he that will harm you?"

Thy power, Thy love, Thy faithfulness,
With lip and life I long to bless.
Thy faithfulness shall be my tower,
My sun Thy love, my shield Thy power,
In darkest night,
In fiercest fight,
With lip and life I long to bless
Thy power, Thy love, Thy faithfulness.

September 19

OUR ROYAL HIGH PRIEST

Let us therefore come boldly unto the throne of grace, that we may obtain mercy, and find grace to help in time of need.
Hebrews 4:16

"Therefore!" because we have "such an High Priest," touched with the feeling of our infirmities, and in all points tempted like as we are; because He is "a Priest upon His throne," ever living, with His royal power to save to the uttermost, and His priestly power to make intercession; "let us *therefore* come boldly unto the throne of grace." Boldness and faith go together; fear and unbelief go together. "If ye will not believe, surely ye shall not be established." It is always want of faith that is at the bottom of all fear. "Why are ye fearful?" is the question for those "of little faith." So, in order to come boldly, and therefore joyfully, all we need is more faith in the Great High Priest who sits upon the throne of grace.

Yet there are some who see not their calling high and grand,
Who seldom pass the portals, and never boldly stand
Before the golden altar on the crimson-stained floor,
Who wait afar and falter, and dare not hope for more.
Will ye not join the blessed ranks in their beautiful array?
Let intercession blend with thanks as ye minister today!

So the incense-cloud ascendeth as through calm, crystal air,
A pillar reaching unto Heaven of wreathed faith and prayer.
For evermore the Angel of Intercession stands
In His Divine High Priesthood, with fragrance-filled hands,
To wave the golden censer before His Father's throne,
With Spirit-fire intenser, and incense all His own.

September 20

SHIELDED FROM THE ENEMY

Thou hast also given me the shield of thy salvation.
2 Samuel 22:36

The salvation which the Lord Jesus came to bring is not only salvation at last, just escaping hell, but it is salvation now, and salvation in everything. Salvation does not only mean victory at last, but it is like a broad shining shield, given to us in the midst of the battle, coming between us and the poisoned arrows and sharp sword-thrusts of the enemy. It is a shield not only to keep us from death, but to keep us from being hurt and wounded. It is the shield which the Captain has given us to use now, as well as the crown which He will give when the warfare is ended. If you have come to the Lord Jesus to be saved, He does not merely say He *will* save you, but that you *are* saved. This is how you are to use the shield—believe it, and be sure of it, because you have His word for it; and then, when a temptation comes, tell the enemy that he has nothing to do with you, for you are saved; that you belong to Jesus, and not to him. Did He ever let any find themselves deceived and mistaken who looked up in faith and confidence to Him, trusting in His great salvation? Never! and never will you find this shield of His salvation fail to cover you completely. Satan himself cannot touch you when you are behind this shield!

> He is with thee! — in thy dwelling,
> Shielding thee from fear of ill;
> All thy burdens kindly bearing;
> For thy dear ones gently caring,
> Guarding, keeping, blessing still.

September 21

USELESS OR USEFUL OCCUPATION

Let the words of my mouth, and the meditation of my heart, be acceptable in thy sight, O Lord, my strength, and my redeemer.
Psalm 19:14

What about our letter-writing? Have we not been tempted (and fallen before the temptation), according to our various dispositions, to let the hand that holds the pen move at the impulse to write an unkind thought of another; or to say a clever and sarcastic thing, or a slightly colored and exaggerated thing, which will make our point more telling; or to let out a grumble or a suspicion; or to let the pen run away with us into flippant and trifling words, unworthy of our high and holy calling? Have we not drifted away from the golden reminder, "Should he reason with unprofitable talk, and with speeches wherewith he can do no good?" Why has this been, perhaps again and again? Is it not for want of putting our hands into our dear Master's hand, and asking and trusting Him to keep them? He *could* have kept; He *would* have kept! Whatever our work or our special temptations may be, the principle remains the same, only let us apply it for ourselves.

> I look up to my Father, and know that I am heard,
> And ask Him for the glowing thought, and for the fitting word;
> I look up to my Father, for I cannot write alone,
> 'Tis sweeter far to seek His strength than lean upon my own.

September 22

ALL THINGS NOW READY

It is finished. John 19:30

Even if you did not heed nor believe any other words of Jesus, could you—*can* you—doubt His dying words? Surely they are worthy of all acceptation! What are they? "It is finished!" *What* is finished? "I have finished the work that Thou gavest me to do." And what is that work? Simply the work of our salvation. That is the reason why all things are now ready, because Jesus has finished that all-inclusive work. When a thing is finished, how much is there left to do? The question sounds too absurd with respect to ordinary things. We hardly take the trouble to answer, "Why nothing, of course!" When Jesus has finished the work, how much is there left for you to do? Do you not see? *Nothing,* of course! You have only to accept that work as really finished, and accept His dying declaration that it is so. What further assurance would you have? Is not this enough? Does your heart say Yes, or No?

> Oh believe the Lord hath done it!
> Wherefore linger? Wherefore doubt?
> All the clouds of black transgression
> He Himself hath blotted out.
> He hath done it! Come and bless Him,
> Swell the grand thanksgiving shout
> Evermore and evermore.

September 23

TESTED TRUST

Do thou for me. Psalm 109:21

The Psalmist does not say what he wanted God to do for him. He leaves it open. So this most restful prayer is left open for all perplexed hearts to appropriate "according to their several necessities." And so we leave it open for God to fill up in His own way. Only a trusting heart can pray this prayer at all; the very utterance of it is an act of faith. We could not ask anyone whom we did not know intimately and trust implicitly to "do" for us, without even suggesting what. Only a self-emptied heart can pray it. It is when we have come to the end of our own resources, or rather, come to see that we never had any at all, that we are willing to accept the fact that we can "do nothing," and to let God do everything for us. Only a loving heart can pray it, for nobody likes another to take him and his affairs in hand and "do" for him, unless that other is cordially loved. We might submit to it, but we should not like it, and certainly should not seek it. So, if we have caught at this little prayer as being just what we want, just what it seems a real test to say, I think it shows that we do trust in Him and not in ourselves, and that we do love Him really and truly.

> He heard the prayer, and gave the will and strength to touch the hem;
> And gave the faith, and virtue flowed from Him, and healed them:
> For every one whose feeblest touch thus met the Saviour's power,
> Rose up in perfect health and strength in that accepted hour.

September 24

A PROMISE TO MEET EVERY FEAR

No weapon that is formed against thee shall prosper. Isaiah 54:17

Man's curse shall be turned into God's blessing: Jehovah Himself, watering His vineyard every moment, says: "Lest any hurt it, I will keep it night and day." Again, the promise, with a solemn condition, takes an even stronger form: "Whoso keepeth the commandment shall feel no evil thing." Is not all this enough? It might well be, but His wonderful love has yet more to say—not only that nothing shall hurt us, but that all things work together for our good; not merely shall work, but actually are working. All things, if it means all things, must include exactly those very things, whatever they may be, which you and I are tempted to think will hurt us, or, at least, *may* hurt us. Now will we today trust our own ideas, or God's Word? One or the other must be mistaken. Which is it? Christ, my own Master, my Lord, my God, has given a promise which meets every fear; therefore, "I will both lay me down in peace, and sleep: for Thou, Lord, only makest me to dwell in safety."

> But Faith and Love with angel-might, break up life's dismal tomb,
> Transmuting into golden light the words of leaden gloom.
> No shadow, but its sister light not far away must burn!
> No weary night, but morning bright shall follow in its turn.
> No chilly snow, but safe below a million buds are sleeping;
> No wintry days, but fair spring rays are swiftly onward sweeping.
> With fiercest glare of summer air comes fullest leafy shade;
> And ruddy fruit bends every shoot, because the blossoms fade.
> No note of sorrow but shall melt in sweetest chord unguessed;
> No labor all too pressing felt, but ends in quiet rest.
> No sigh but from the harps above, soft echoing tones shall win;
> No heart-wound but the Lord of Love shall pour His comfort in.
> No withered hope, while loving best thy Father's chosen way;
> No anxious care, for He will bear thy burdens every day.

September 25

REST ASSURED

**For he that is entered into his rest, he also hath ceased from
his own works, as God did from his.** Hebrews 4:10

After forgiveness there comes a thought of great comfort in
our freshly felt helplessness, rising out of the very thing that
makes us realize this helplessness. Just because our influence
is to such a great extent involuntary and unconscious, we may
rest assured that if we ourselves are truly kept for Jesus, this
will be, as a quite natural result, kept for Him also. It cannot
be otherwise, for as is the fountain, so will be the flow; as the
spring, so the action; as the impulse, so the communicated motion. Thus there may be, and in simple trust there will be, a
quiet rest about it, a relief from all sense of strain and effort,
a fulfilling of the words, "For he that is entered into his rest,
he also hath ceased from his own works, as God did from His."
It will not be a matter of trying to have good influence, but
just of having it, as naturally and constantly as the magnetized
bar.

> Resting on the faithfulness of Christ our Lord.
> Resting on the fullness of His own sure word;
> Resting on His power, on His love untold;
> Resting on His covenant secured of old.
> Resting and believing, let us onward press,
> Resting in Himself, the Lord our Righteousness;
> Resting and rejoicing, let His saved ones sing,
> Glory, glory, glory be to Christ our King!

September 26

WAIT FOR HIS ROYAL RESPONSE

Let my lord the king now speak. 2 Samuel 14:18
**Lest, if thou be silent to me, I become like them that go
down into the pit.** Psalm 28:1

Are we not apt to think more of speaking to the King than of
the King speaking to us? We come to the throne of grace
with the glad and solemn purpose, "I will now speak unto the
King." And we pour out our hearts before Him, and tell Him
all the sins and all the needs, all the joys and all the sorrows,
till the very telling seems almost an answer, because it brings
such a sense of relief. It is very sweet, very comforting to do
this. But this is only half-communion; and we miss, perhaps,
a great deal of unknown blessing by being content with this
one-sided audience. We should use another *"now,"* and say,

"Let my Lord the King now speak." We expect Him to speak some time, but not actually and literally "now," while we kneel before Him. And therefore we do not listen, and therefore we do not hear what He has to say to us. What about the last time we knelt in prayer? Surely He had more to say to us than we had to say to Him, and yet we never waited a minute to see! We did not give Him opportunity for His gracious response. We rushed away from our King's presence as soon as we had said our say, and vaguely expected Him to send His answers after us somehow and some time, but not there and then. What wonder if they have not yet reached us! The only wonder is that He ever speaks at all when we act thus.

Master, speak! Thy servant heareth, waiting for Thy gracious word,
Longing for Thy voice that cheereth; Master! let it now be heard.
I am listening, Lord, for Thee; what hast Thou to say to me?
Often through my heart is pealing many another voice than Thine,
Many an unwilled echo stealing from the walls of this Thy shrine:
Let Thy longed-for accents fall; Master, speak! and silence all.

September 27

YOU COULD BE MISTAKEN

How can a man then understand his own way? Proverbs 20:24

Even this difficulty He meets, for "He declareth unto man what is His thought." But are you willing to let Him do this? He may show you that those who have, as you suppose, misunderstood you, may have guessed right after all. He may show you that your desire was not so honest, your motives not so single as you fancied; that there was self-will where you only recognized resolution, sin where you only recognized infirmity or mistake. Let Him search, let Him declare it unto you. For then He will declare another message to you: "The blood of Jesus Christ His Son cleanseth us from all sin." Then, when all is clear between Him and you, "nothing between" (and let that "when" be "now"), how sweet you will find it in the light of His forgiveness, and the new strength of His cleansing, to look up and say, "Thou understandest!" and wait patiently for Him to let you be understood or misunderstood, just as He will, even as Jesus did. For who was ever so misunderstood as He?

Even our present way is known to ourselves alone,
Height and abyss and torrent, flower and thorn and stone;
But we gaze on another's path as a far-off mountain scene,
Scanning the outlined hills, but never the vales between.

September 28

A SAFE WAY ON THE PATHLESS SEA

Bid me come unto thee on the water. Matthew 14:28

Perhaps it is night in your soul—as dark as ever it can be. It would not be so bad if you could even distinctly see the waves of the troubled sea on which you are tossing. You do not know where you are. All seems vague and uncertain and wretched and confused. And though the Lord Jesus is very near you, though He has come to you, walking on the water, and has said, "It is I, be not afraid," you cannot see Him, and you are not at all sure it is His voice; or if it is, that He is speaking to you. So, of course, you are "troubled." And if, in this trouble, you go on trying to steer and row for yourself, these same waves will prove themselves to be awful realities, and you will be lost in the storm. Do not venture that; but venture out, through the darkness and upon the waves at the bare word of Jesus.

> She had spoken of Jesus' wondrous call,
>   As He trod the waves of Galilee.
> They asked, as she gazed from the sunset shore,
> "If He walked that water, what would you do?"
> Then fell the answer, glad and true,
>   "If He beckoned me,
> I would go to Him on the pathless sea."

September 29

WHAT'S HIS IS OURS

A king shall reign . . . and this is his name whereby he shall be called, THE LORD OUR RIGHTEOUSNESS.
Jeremiah 23:5, 6

We cannot do without this most wonderful name. It can never be an old story to us. It is always a "new name" in freshness and beauty and power. It is our daily need and our daily joy. For strength it is indeed "a strong tower; the righteous runneth into it, and is safe." For sweetness it is "as ointment poured forth." In it we see at once the highest height and the deepest depth; Jehovah, God of God, Light of Light, and our need of a righteousness which is not our own at all, because we have none. We stand as upon an Alpine slope, face to face with the highest, grandest, purest summit above, and the darkest, deepest valley below, seeing more of the height because of the depth, and more of the depth because of the height. Jesus our King "hath by inheritance obtained a more excellent name" than angels, for His Father has given Him His own name—"He shall be called Jehovah." But this alone would be too great, too far off for us; it might find echoes among the harpings of sinless angels, but not among the sighings of sinful souls. And so the name was completed for us, by the very word that expresses our truest, deepest, widest, most perpetual need, and the Holy Ghost revealed the Son of God to us as "Jehovah our Righteousness."

Therefore, justified forever by the faith which He hath given,
Peace, and joy, and hope abounding, smooth thy trial path to Heaven:
Unto Him betrothed forever, who thy life shall crown and bless,
By His name thou shalt be called, Christ, "The Lord our Righteousness!"

September 30

THE "LEAST" IS NOT FORGOTTEN

I will sift the house of Israel among all nations, like as corn is sifted in a sieve, yet shall not the least grain fall upon the earth.   Amos 9:9

Satan has desired to have us, that he might sift us as wheat; but the Lord Himself holds the sieve in His own hand, and pledges His word that not the least grain shall fall on the earth. We are so glad of that word, "not the least"; not even I, though less than the least of all saints, though feeling as if my only claim upon Christ Jesus is that I am the chief of sinners. "Not the least grain"; for He says, "Ye shall be gathered one by one." Think of His hand gathering you separately and individually out of His million-sheaved harvest; gathering you, one by one always, into His garner, even in that tremendous day of sifting, when He shall thoroughly purge His floor. You may feel a little overlooked sometimes now; only one among so very many, and perhaps not first, nor even second in anybody's love, or care, or interest, but He is watching His "least grains" all the time. A flock of sheep look most uninterestingly alike and hopelessly indistinguishable to us, but a good shepherd knows every one quite well. Yes, the Good Shepherd calleth His own sheep by name here, and "in Zion every one of them appeareth before God."

Our Saviour and our King, enthroned and crowned above,
Shall with exceeding gladness bring the children of His love.
All that the Father gave, His glory shall behold;
Not one whom Jesus came to save is missing from His fold.

October 1

He is able even to subdue all things unto himself. Philippians 3:21

We talk sometimes as if, whatever else could be subdued unto Him, self could never be. Did Paul forget to mention this important exception to the "all things" in Philippians 3:21? David said, "Bless the Lord, O my soul, *and all that is within me*, bless His Holy Name." Did he, too, unaccountably forget to mention that he only meant all that was within him, *except* self? If not, then self must be among the "all things" which the Lord Jesus Christ is able to subdue unto Himself, and which are to "bless His Holy Name." It is self which, once His most treacherous foe, is now, by full and glad surrender, His own soldier—coming over from the rebel camp into the royal army. It is not someone else, some temporarily possessing spirit, which says within us, "Lord, Thou knowest that I love Thee," but our true and very self, only changed and renewed by the power of the Holy Ghost. And when we do that we would not, we know that "it is no more I that do it, but sin that dwelleth in me." Our true self is the new self, taken and won by the love of God, and kept by the power of God.

> Thanks, more than thanks, to Him ascend,
> Who died to win
> Our life, and every trophy rend
> From Death and Sin;
> Till, when the thanks of Earth shall end,
> The thanks of Heaven begin.

October 2

Blessed are the dead which die in the Lord. Revelation 14:13
Thou hast made him most blessed for ever: thou hast made him exceeding glad with thy countenance. Psalm 21:6

Probably every one who reads this has at least one of those golden links to Heaven which God's own hand has forged from our earthly treasures. It may be that the very nearest and dearest that had been given are now taken away. And how often "no relation, only a dear friend" is an "only" of heart-crushing emphasis! Human comfort goes for very little in this; but let us lay our hearts open to the comfort wherewith we are comforted of God Himself about it. There is not much directly to ourselves; He knew that the truest and sweetest comfort would come by looking not at our loss, but at their gain. Whatever this gain is, it is all His own actual and immediate doing. *"Thou* hast made him" (read here the name of the very one for whom we are mourning) "most blessed." "Most!" How shall we reach that thought? Make a shining stairway of every bright beatitude in the Bible, blessed upon blessed, within and also far beyond our own experience. And when we have built them up till they reach unto Heaven, still this *"most* blessed" is beyond, out of our sight, in the unapproachable glory of God Himself. It will always be "most," for it is "for ever" — everlasting light without a shadow, everlasting songs without a minor.

The prayer of many a day is all fulfilled,
Only by full fruition stayed and stilled;
You asked for blessing as your Father willed,
Now He hath answered: "Most blessed forever."
From the great anthems of the Crystal Sea,
Through the far vistas of eternity,
Grand echoes of the word peal on for thee,
Sweetest and fullest: "Most blessed forever."

October 3

"COME" MEANS COME

And he said, Come. Matthew 14:29

But what is "coming"? One's very familiarity with the terms used to express spiritual things, seems to have a tendency to make one feel mystified about them. And their very simplicity makes one suspicious, as it were, that there must be some mysterious and mystical meaning behind them, because they sound *too* easy and plain to have such great import. "Come" means "come"—just that! and not some occult process of mental effort. What would you understand by it, if you heard it today for the first time, never having had any doubts or suppositions or previous notions whatever about it? What does a little child understand by it? It is positively too simple to be made plainer by any amount of explanation.

Here, it is "calling apart," and the place may be desert indeed,
Leaving and losing the blessings linked with our busy need;
There!—why should I say it? hath not the heart leapt up,
Swift and glad, to the contrast, filling the full, full cup?
Still shall the key-word, ringing, echo the same sweet "Come!"
"Come" with the blessed myriads safe in the Father's home;
"Come"—for the work is over; "come"—for the feast is spread;
"Come"—for the crown of glory waits for the weary head.

October 4

SPECIALLY TENDER — SPECIALLY PRECIOUS

He himself hath suffered being tempted. Hebrews 2:18

Sometimes the Lord leads His people into rough places of suffering, whether from temptation, pain, or any adversity. Not one step here but Jesus has gone before us; and He still goeth before us, often so very close before us, that even by the still waters we never seemed so near Him. "The things which He suffered" include and cover, and stretch wide on every side beyond, all possible "sufferings of this present time." It is in patient suffering, rather than in doing, that we are specially called "to follow His steps." "The footsteps of Thine anointed have lain through reproach," and "the reproach of Thy servants" is no light part of "the fellowship of His sufferings." How specially tender the Master's hand is when it is laid upon us to put us forth into any path of suffering! How specially precious, then, to know that it is indeed His own doing!

> E'en in our hearts is evil bound,
> And, lurking stealthily around,
>   Still for our souls doth wait.
> Thou tempted One, whose suffering heart
> In all our sorrows bore a part,
> Whose life-blood only could atone,
> Too weak are we to stand alone;
> And nothing but Thy shield of light
> Can guard us in the dreaded fight.

October 5

KEPT CONTINUALLY

I am with thee, and will keep thee. Genesis 28:15
I also will keep thee from the hour of temptation.
Revelation 3:10

Kept for Him! Why should it be thought a thing incredible with you, when it is only the fulfilling of His own eternal purpose in creating us? "This people have I formed *for Myself.*" Not ultimately only, but presently and continually; for He says, "Thou shalt abide *for Me*"; and, "He that remaineth, even he shall be *for our God.*" Are you one of His people by faith in Jesus Christ? Then see what you are to Him. You, personally and individually, are part of the Lord's portion (Deuteronomy 32:9) and of His inheritance (1 Kings 8:53 and Ephesians 1:18). His portion and inheritance would not be complete without you; you are His peculiar treasure (Exodus

19:5) ; "a *special* people" (how warm, and loving, and natural that expression is!) *"unto Himself"* (Deuteronomy 7:6). Would you call it "keeping," if you had a "special" treasure, a darling little child, for instance, and let it run wild into all sorts of dangers all day long, sometimes at your side, and sometimes out in the street, with only the intention of fetching it safe home at night? If ye then, being evil, would know better, and do better than that, how much more shall our Lord's keeping be true, and tender, and continual, and effectual, when He declares us to be His peculiar treasure, purchased (see 1 Peter 2:9, margin) for Himself at such unknown cost!

> Everlasting life Thou givest,
> Everlasting love to see;
> They shall live because Thou livest,
> And their life is hid with Thee.
> Safe Thy members shall be found,
> When their glorious Head is crowned!

October 6

PROMISED — THEREFORE SURE

Whom he did predestinate, them he also called: and whom he called, them he also justified: and whom he justified, them he also glorified.
Romans 8:30

If some of us were asked, "How do you know you have everlasting life?" we might say, "Because God has promised it." But how do you know He has promised it to you? And then if we answered, not conventionally, nor what we think we ought to say, but honestly what we think, we might say, "Because I have believed and have come to Jesus." And this looks like resting our hope of salvation upon something that we have done, upon the fact of our having consciously believed and consciously come. And then, of course, any whirlwind of doubt will raise the dust enough to obscure that fact and all the comfort of it. Yet there is grand comfort not in it, but in the glorious chain of which even this little human link is first forged and then held by Jehovah's own hand. Apart from this, it is worth nothing at all.

> In those heavenly constellations,
> Lo! what differing glories meet;
> Stars of radiance soft and tender,
> Stars of full and dazzling splendor,
> All in God's own light complete;
> Brightest they whose holy feet,
> Faithful to His service sweet,
> Nearest to their Master trod,
> Winning wandering souls to God.

October 7

A VOICE CONTINUALLY CALLING

And the Spirit and the bride say, Come. Revelation 22:17

Every "come" in the Bible is the call of the Spirit. For "all
Scripture is given by inspiration of God," and the "holy men
of God spake as they were moved by the Holy Ghost." And
every time that a still small voice in your heart says "Come,"
it is the call of the Spirit. Every time the remembrance of the
Saviour's sweetest spoken word floats across your mind, it is
the Holy Spirit's fulfillment of our Lord's promise that "He
shall bring all things to your remembrance, whatsoever I have
said unto you." The last time those words, "Come unto Me,"
came into your mind, whether in some wakeful night hour,
or suddenly and unaccountably amid the stir of the day, did
you think that it was the very voice of the Holy Spirit speaking in your heart? Or did you let other voices drown it, not
knowing that the goodness of God was leading you by it?

> The seed of a single word
>   Fell among the furrows deep,
>   In their silent, wintry sleep,
> And the sower never an echo heard.
> But the "Come!" was not in vain,
>   For that germ of Life and Love,
> And the blessed Spirit's quickening rain,
> Made a golden sheaf of precious grain
>   For the Harvest Home above.

October 8

LET HIM USE WHAT YOU HAVE

**He is the Rock, his work is perfect: for all his ways are
judgment: a God of truth and without iniquity, just and
right is he.** Deuteronomy 32:4
He that is perfect in knowledge is with thee. Job 36:4

He who made every power can use every power — memory,
judgment, imagination, quickness of apprehension or insight;
specialties of musical, poetical, oratorical, or artistic faculty;
special tastes for reasoning, philosophy, history, natural science,
or natural history—all these may be dedicated to Him, sanctified by Him, and used by Him. Whatever He has given, He
will use if we will let Him. Often, in the most unexpected ways.
and at the most unexpected turns, something read or acquired
long ago suddenly comes into use. We cannot foresee what will
thus "come in useful"; but He knew, when He guided us to

learn it, what it would be wanted for in His service. So may we not ask Him to bring His perfect foreknowledge to bear on all our mental training and storing; to guide us to read or study exactly what He knows there will be use for in the work to which He has called or will call us?

He traineth thus
That we may teach the lessons we are taught;
That younger learners may be further brought,
Led on by us:
Well may we wait, or toil, or suffer long,
For His dear service so to be made fit and strong.

He traineth so
That we may shine for Him in this dark world,
And bear His standard dauntlessly unfurled:
That we may show
His praise, by lives that mirror back His love—
His witnesses on earth, as He is ours above.

October 9

GOD TRUSTED HIM! CAN YOU DO LESS?

Trust in him at all times. Psalm 62:8

"All times" includes the time when we almost fancy the salvation of a dear one depends on our little bits of prayers and efforts. Not that this trust will lead to an easy-going idleness. It never does this when it is real. The deepest trust leads to the most powerful action. It is the silencing oil that makes the machine obey the motive power with greatest readiness and result. It may seem a great trial of trust very often, but who is it that we have to trust thus unquestioningly and quietly? Jesus Christ! Cannot we trust Him whom the Father trusted with the tremendous work of redemption? Shall He not do right? Cannot we trust the Good Shepherd about His own sheep? Why should it actually seem harder to trust Him about His own affairs than about our own?

Oh make us fervent in the quest, that we may bring them in,
The weary and the wounded, and the sufferers from sin;
The stricken and the dying, let us seek them out for Thee,
And lay them at Thy glorious feet, that healed they may be.

Oh pour upon our waiting hearts the Spirit of Thy grace,
That we may plead with Thee to show the brightness of Thy face,
Beseeching Thee to grant the will and strength and faith to such
As lie in helpless misery, Thy garment's hem to touch.

And then, Lord Jesus, make them whole, that they may rise and bring
New praise and glory unto Thee, our Healer and our King;
Yea, let Thy saving health be known through all the earth abroad,
So shall the people praise Thy Name, our Saviour and our God.

October 10

Thou hast in love to my soul delivered it. Isaiah 38:17
Therefore we will sing my songs. Isaiah 38:20

When the dove found no rest for the soul of her foot, and returned to Noah because the waters were on the face of the whole earth, "then he put forth his hand, and took her, and pulled her in" (margin, "caused her to come") "unto him in the Ark." What a beautiful picture is this little helpless, tired dove of our helplessness and weariness, and the kind hand, strong and tender, which does not leave us to flutter and beat against a closed window, but takes us, and pulls us "unto Him, into the Ark!" So we have the willingness of the Father in one part of the type, and the willingness of the Son in another part — willingness to receive you into safety and rest.

> O ye who seek the Saviour, look up in faith and love,
> Come up into the sunshine, so bright and warm above!
> No longer tread the valley, but, clinging to His hand,
> Ascend the shining summits and view the glorious land.
> Our harp-notes should be sweeter, our trumpet-tones more clear,
> Our anthems ring so grandly, that all the world must hear!
> Oh, royal be our music, for who hath cause to sing
> Like the chorus of redeemed ones, the children of the King.

October 11

THE SAVIOUR-KING HOLDS THE SCEPTRE

The king held out . . . the golden sceptre. Esther 5:2

Jesus is He "that holdeth the sceptre" — the symbol first of kingly right and authority, and next of righteousness and justice. "A sceptre of righteousness is the sceptre of Thy kingdom"—"a right sceptre." And yet the golden sceptre was held out as the sign of sovereign mercy to one who, by "one law of his to put him to death," must otherwise have perished, "that he may live." Thus, by the combination of direct statement and type, we are shown in this figure the beautiful, perfect meeting of the "mercy and truth" of our King, the "righteousness and peace" of His kingdom. To "the King's enemies" the sceptre is a "rod of iron" (for the word is the same in Hebrew). They cannot rejoice in the justice which they defy. To the King's willing subjects it is indeed golden, a beautiful thing. We admire and glory in His absolute justice and righteousness; it satisfies the depths of our moral being—it is so strong, so perfect. And oh, how "sweet is thy mercy"! and just because of the justice, how "sure"! Esther said, "If I perish, I perish." So need not we, "for His mercy endureth for ever." And so, every time we come into the audience chamber of our King, we know that the golden sceptre will be held out to us: first, "that we may live," and then for favor after favor. "Let us therefore come boldly unto the throne of grace, that we may obtain mercy, and find grace to help in time of need." Not stand afar off and think about it, and keep our King waiting; but, like Esther, "let us draw near," and "touch the top of the sceptre."

If Thou hast said it, I must believe,
It is only "ask" and I shall receive;
If Thou hast said it, it must be true,
And there's nothing else for me to do!
    For Christ's sake, give it to me.

So I come and ask, because my need
Is very great and real indeed.
On the strength of Thy word I come and say,
Oh, let Thy word come true today!
    For Christ's sake, give it to me.

October 12

HIS HEART SET ON US

What is man . . . that thou shouldest set thine heart upon him? and that thou shouldest visit him every morning, and try him every moment?   Job 7:17-18

Terribly solemn and awful would be the thought that He has been trying us every moment, were it not for the yearning gentleness and love of the Father revealed in that wonderful expression of wonder, "What is man, that Thou shouldest set Thine heart upon him?" Think of that ceaseless setting of His heart upon us, careless and forgetful children as we have been! And then think of those other words, nonetheless literally true because given under a figure: "I, the Lord, do keep it; I will water it every moment."

Look on to this
Through all perplexities of grief and strife—
To this, thy true maturity of life,
        Thy coming bliss;
That such high gifts thy future dower may be,
And for such service high thy God prepareth thee.
        What though today
Thou canst not trace at all the hidden reason
For His strange dealings through the trial-season—
        Trust and obey.

October 13

They came to him from every quarter. Mark 1:45

Begin with the eighth chapter of Matthew, and trace out all through the Gospels how others came to Jesus with all sorts of different needs, and trace in these your own spiritual needs of cleansing, healing, salvation, guidance, sight, teaching. They knew what they wanted, and they knew Whom they wanted. And consequently they just *came*. Ask the Lord to show you what you want and Whom you want, and you will talk no more about what it means, you will just *come!* And then you will say, "Now, we believe, not because of thy saying; for we have heard Him ourselves, and know that this is indeed the Christ, the Saviour of the world"; and you will say, *"My* Lord and *my* God."

> Will you not come to Him for peace?
> Peace through His cross alone.
> He shed His precious blood for you;
> The gift is free, the word is true:
> He is our peace—oh, is He your own?
>
> Will you not come to Him for rest?
> All that are weary, come!
> The rest He gives is deep and true,
> 'Tis offered now, 'tis offered you!
> Rest in His love, and rest in His home.

October 14

A PLANNED AND PURPOSED SALVATION

Which were born, not . . . of the will of the flesh, nor of the will of man, but of God. John 1:13

Have not some of us had a scarcely detected notion, as if to some extent the salvation of others depended upon our efforts? Of course, we never put it in so many words; but has there not been something of a feeling that if we tried very hard to win a soul we should succeed and if we did not try quite enough it would get lost? And this has made our service anxious and burdensome. But what says Christ? "All that the Father giveth Me shall come to Me." They shall come, for the Father will draw them, and Jesus will attract them, and the Holy Spirit will lead them. And the purpose precedes the promise, even as the promise precedes the call, and the call precedes the coming. Thus God first planned and proposed the ark for the salvation of Noah from the flood. Then He said, "Thou shalt come into the ark." Long after that, when all things were ready, He said, "Come thou and all thy house into the ark." And then Noah went in; and then "the Lord shut him in." Now let us, in our work, practically trust our Lord as to His purposes, promises, and calls; quite satisfied that He "will work, and who shall let it?" that He will not accidentally miss anybody, or lose anything of all that the Father hath given Him, for this is the Father's will.

> He shall confess His own from every clime and coast,
> Before His Father's glorious throne, before the angel host,
> By new creation Thine, by purpose and by grace,
> By right of full redemption Mine, faultless before Thy face.

October 15

DOUBLY SEALED

The writing which is written in the king's name, and sealed with the king's ring, may no man reverse. Esther 8:8

Such is the writing which by God's great goodness is the glory of our land and the treasure of our hearts, full of exceeding great and precious promises, of commands not less great and not less precious, and of words of prophecy (which are only words of promise a little farther off) "more sure" than the testimony of an apostle's senses to the excellent glory and the heavenly voice. It is written in the King's name. The living Word of God, who came to declare, to manifest, and to glorify the Father, has imprinted His own name upon the same testimony as written by the Spirit, and has given it to us as the "Word of God." It is sealed with the King's ring. Sealing is a special work of the Holy Spirit, exercised in different ways; and how clearly has He sealed this great writing with the King's ring, engraved with His own image and superscription, the convincing token of its being indeed from Himself, and sent forth in unchangeable authority and power! It is a double sealing, without and within—first, the external and distinctly visible declaration that the writing is "by the Holy Ghost"; and then the all-convincing evidence that it is so by its effectual working in our own hearts with a power which, we know for ourselves, cannot be less than almighty and therefore divine.

> Oh, this is more than poem, and more than the highest song;
> A witness with our spirit, though hidden, full and strong.
> 'Tis no new revelation vouchsafed to saint or sage,
> But light from God cast bright and broad upon the sacred page.

October 16

This is not your rest. Micah 2:10

God says so, and therefore it is no use seeking or hoping or trying for it. You may as well give up first as last. The dove found no rest for the sole of her foot until she came to the ark; and neither will you. And the end of the dreary vista of unrest all through the years of a life without Christ, is, "They have no rest day nor night." "The people shall weary themselves for very vanity." Do you know anything about that? "They weary themselves to commit iniquity." "Thou art wearied with the greatness of thy way." Do these words come home to you? Or, "But now he hath made me weary; Thou hast made desolate all my company"? Whether it is the weariness of sin or of sorrow, of vanity or of desolation (and sooner or later the one must lead into the other), the gentle call floats over the troubled waters, "Come unto Me, all ye that labour and are heavy laden, and I will give you rest."

> And then, oh, then the wail is stilled, the wandering is o'er,
> The rest is gained, the certainty that never wavers more;
> And then the full, unquivering praise arises glad and strong,
> And life becomes the prelude of the everlasting song!

October 17

WORDS ARE LIMITLESS

They talked together of all these things which had happened.
Luke 24:14
They shall speak of the glory of thy kingdom, and talk of thy power.   Psalm 145:11

Not one sentence that passes these lips of ours but must be an invisibly prolonged influence, not dying away into silence, but living away into the words and deeds of others. The thought would not be quite so oppressive if we could know what we have done and shall be continuing to do by what we have said. But we never can, as a matter of fact. We may trace it a little way, and get a glimpse of some results for good or evil; but we never can see any more of it than we can see of a shooting star flashing through the night with a momentary revelation of one step of its strange path. Even if the next instant plunges it into apparent annihilation as it strikes the atmosphere of the earth, we know that it is not really so, but that its mysterious material and force must be added to the complicated materials and forces with which it has come in contact, with a modifying power nonetheless real because it is beyond our ken. And this is not comparing a great thing with a small, but a small thing with a great. For what is material force compared with moral force? What are gases, and vapors, and elements, compared with souls and the eternity for which they are preparing? We have no choice in the matter; we cannot evade or avoid it; and there is no more possibility of our limiting it, or even tracing its limits, than there is of setting a bound to the far-vibrating sound-waves, or watching their flow through the invisible air.

A look of great affliction, as you tell what one told you,
With a feeble contradiction, or a "hope it is not true!"
Only a low, "I wonder!" Nothing unfair at all;
But the whisper grows to thunder, and a scathing bolt may fall;
And a good ship is dismasted, and hearts are like to break,
And a Christian life is blasted, for a scarcely-guessed mistake!

October 18

THE ALARMING ALTERNATIVE

With me thou shalt be in safeguard.　　1 Samuel 22:23
Come thou and all thy house into the ark.　Genesis 7:1

No need to repeat the story! We knew it all at six years old. Today the words are sent to you, *"Come thou!"* We are either inside or outside the Ark. There is no half-way in this. Outside is death, inside is life. Outside is certain, inevitable, utter destruction. Inside is certain and complete safety. Where are you at this moment? Perhaps you dare not say confidently and happily, "I am inside"; and yet you do not like to look the alarming alternative in the face, and say, "I am outside!" And you prefer trying to persuade yourself that you do not exactly know, and can't be expected to answer such a question. And you say, perhaps with a shade of annoyance, "How *am* I to know?" God's infallible Word tells you very plainly, "If any man be in Christ, he is a new creature: old things are passed away; behold, all things are become new."

Ye who hear the blessed call of the Spirit and the Bride,
Hear the Master's word to all, your commission and your guide—
"And let him that heareth say, Come," to all yet far away.
"Come!" to those who, while they hear, linger, hardly knowing why·
Tell them that the Lord is near, tell them Jesus passes by.
Call them now; oh, do not wait, lest tomorrow be too late!

October 19

GOD ENGAGES THE HEART

All that the Father giveth me shall come to me.   John 6:37

Do not fear to take the *shall* to yourself. Remember the great "whosoever will," and look up at this star of promise in the dark. And the Father says, "I will cause him to draw near, and he shall approach unto Me; for who is this that engaged his heart to approach unto Me?" Whose heart? Is it not yours? And if it is so engaged, who engaged it? Who but the God from whom alone *all* holy desires do proceed?

> Behold the handmaid of the Lord!
> Thou callest, and I come to Thee:
> According to Thy faithful word,
> O Master, be it unto me!
>
> Thy love I cannot comprehend,
> I only know Thy word is true,
> And that Thou lovest to the end
> Each whom to Thee the Father drew.
>
> Oh! take the heart I could not give
> Without Thy strength-bestowing call;
> In Thee, and for Thee, let me live,
> For I am nothing, Thou art all.

October 20

KEPT FROM TO BE KEPT FOR

I the Lord do keep it . . . every moment: lest any hurt it.
Isaiah 27:3
For . . . suddenly are my tents spoiled, and my curtains in a moment.
Jeremiah 4:20

The sanctified and Christ-loving heart cannot be satisfied with only negative keeping. We do not want only to be kept from displeasing Him, but to be kept always pleasing Him. Every "kept *from*" should have its corresponding and still more blessed "kept for." We do not want our moments to be simply kept from Satan's use, but kept for His use; we want them to be not only kept from sin, but kept for His praise. Do you ask, "But what use can He make of mere moments?" I will not stay to prove or illustrate the obvious truth that, as are the moments so will be the hours and the days which they build. You understand that well enough. I will answer your question as it stands.

Look back through the history of the Church in all ages,

and mark how often a great work and mighty influence grew out of a mere moment in the life of one of God's servants; a mere moment, but overshadowed and filled with the fruitful power of the Spirit of God. The moment may have been spent in uttering five words, but they have fed five thousand, or even five hundred thousand. Or it may have been lit by the flash of a thought that has shone into hearts and homes throughout the land, and kindled torches that have been borne into earth's darkest corners. The rapid speaker or the lonely thinker little guessed what use his Lord was making of that single moment. There was no room in it for even a thought of that. If that moment had not been, though perhaps unconsciously, "kept for Jesus." but had been otherwise occupied, what a harvest to His praise would have been missed!

O precious blood! Lord, let it rest on me!
I ask not only pardon from my King,
But cleansing from my Priest. I come to Thee
Just as I came at first — a sinful, helpless thing.

O Saviour, bid me "go and sin no more,"
And keep me always 'neath the mighty flow
Of Thy perpetual fountain; I implore
That Thy perpetual cleansing I may fully know.

October 21

UNBELIEF OPENS THE WAY TO DARKNESS

They tempted the Lord, saying, Is the Lord among us, or not?
Exodus 17:7

Unbelief and forgetfulness are the only shadows which can come between us and the Lord's presence, though, when they have once made the separation, there is room for all others. Otherwise, though all the shadows of earth fell around, none could fall between; and their very darkness could only intensify the brightness of the pavilion in which we dwell, the secret of His presence. They could not touch what one has called "the unutterable joy of shadowless communion." What shall we say to our Lord tonight? He says, "I am with you alway." Shall we not put away all the captious contradictoriness of quotations of our imperfect and double-fettered experience, and say to Him, lovingly, confidingly, gratefully, "Thou art with me!"

He is with thee! With thee always,
All the nights and all the days;
Never failing, never frowning,
With His loving-kindness crowning,
Tuning all thy life to praise.

October 22

**Mine iniquities are gone over mine head: as an heavy burden
they are too heavy for me.** Psalm 38:4

So much too heavy for you, that if you do not accept Christ's
offer of rest from that burden, you will never be able to find
or follow the path of life. But why bear it one minute longer
when Jesus says, "Come unto Me, all ye that labour and are
heavy laden, and I will give you rest"? But stay; you may,
or rather you must, put in a double claim to the promise. You
may not be consciously, particularly weary or labouring; but
whether conscious of it or not, you *are* heavy laden, unless
the one great burden of sin is taken away from you. It is a
fact, whether the Holy Spirit has convinced you of it or not
as yet, that unless your iniquity is taken away by personal
washing in the only Fountain, you are in the position described
by the Psalmist.

Bring every weary burden,
Thy sin, thy fear, thy grief;
He calls the heavy laden,
And gives them kind relief.

October 23

OUR FEET FOR HIM

How beautiful are thy feet with shoes, O prince's daughter!
Song of Solomon 7:1

The figurative keeping of the feet of His saints, with the promise that when they run they shall not stumble, is a most beautiful and helpful subject. But it is quite distinct from the
literal keeping for Jesus of our literal feet.

There is a certain homeliness about the idea which helps to
make it very real. These very feet of ours are purchased for
Christ's service by the precious drops which fell from His own
torn and pierced feet upon the cross. They are to be His errand-
runners. How can we let the world, the flesh, and the devil
have the use of what has been purchased with such payment?

Shall the world have the use of them? Shall they carry us
where the world is paramount, and the Master cannot be even
named, because the mention of His Name would be so obviously
out of place? I know the apparent difficulties of a subject which
will at once occur in connection with this, but they all vanish

when our bright banner is loyally unfurled, with its motto, "*All* for Jesus!" Do you honestly want your very feet to be "kept for Jesus"? Let these simple words, "Kept for Jesus," ring out next time the dancing difficulty or any other difficulty of the same kind comes up, and I know what the result will be! Shall "the flesh" have the use of them? Shall they carry us hither and thither merely because we like to go, merely because it pleases ourselves to take this walk or pay this visit? And after all, what a failure it is!

And Thou hast left a solemn word behind Thee,
Solemn, yet fraught with blessing — would we learn
How we may gain Thy dwelling, and there find Thee?
Thou sayest, "Follow Me." Be this our great concern
And oh! how blessed thus to mark each hour
The footsteps of our Saviour, and to know
That in them we are treading — then each flower
Of hope seems fairer, and each joy doth yet more brightly glow.
Oh that I always followed Him alone!
I know that I am His, for I have bowed
In peaceful faith before my Saviour's throne,
And gladly there to Him my life, my all, have vowed,
And He hath pardoned me, and washed away
Each stain of guilt, and bade me quickly rise
And follow Him each moment of each day;
And He hath set a crown of life and joy before mine eyes.

October 24

HASTE IS NOT WASTE

The king's business required haste.   1 Samuel 21:8
And see that ye hasten the matter. Howbeit the Levites
hastened it not.   2 Chronicles 24:5

And yet there is no other business about which the average Christians take it so easy. They "must" go their usual round, they "must" write their letters, they "must" pay off their visits and other social claims, they "must" do all that is expected of them; and then, after this and that and the other thing is cleared off, they will do what they can of the King's business. They do not say "must" about that, unless it is some part of His business which is undertaken at second-hand, and with more sense of responsibility to one's "clergyman" than to one's King. Is this being faithful and loyal and single hearted? If it has been so, oh, let it be so no more! How can "Jesus Only" be our motto, when we have not even said, "Jesus First"?

But if ye dare not hold it fast, yours only is the loss,
For it shall be victorious, this Standard of the Cross!
It shall not suffer, though ye rest beneath your sheltering trees,
And cast away the Victor's crown for love of timid ease.

October 25

HEART-ASSENT MEANS LIFE

Do ye now believe? John 16:31

Settle that; and then what follows? Hear another word of the Faithful Witness. Remember, it is no less true than His other words. The holy lips that said on the cross, "It is finished," spoke nothing that could deceive or mislead. "Verily, verily, I say unto you, He that heareth My word and believeth on Him that sent Me hath everlasting life." What does this mean? Just what it says, and nothing less! It means that even if you never believed before — even if you never had a spark of faith or glimmer of hope before—yet if you have now given your heart-assent to Jesus and His finished work, you have now everlasting life! That heart-assent is believing; and "He that believeth on the Son hath everlasting life." And this "believing" is "coming"; and thus coming, you shall find for yourself that all things are indeed ready.

> Reality! Reality!
> Such let our adoration be!
> Father, we bless Thee with heart and voice,
> For the wondrous grace of Thy sovereign choice,
> That patiently, gently, sought us out.
>
> In the far-off land of death and doubt,
> That drew us to Christ by the Spirit's might,
> That opened our eyes to see the light
> That arose in strange reality,
> From the darkness falling on Calvary.

October 26

INFINITE GOD . . . AND YET MINE

But I trusted in thee, O Lord: I said, Thou art my God. Psalm 31:14

Some of us may have an unexpressed notion that, after all, God being our God does not come so near to us as the thought of "Jesus, my Saviour." We almost feel dazzled at the vastness of the idea of "God." And we take refuge, mentally, in what seems more within reach. This is almost always the case in the earlier stages of our Christian life. Having been drawn by the Father to the Lord Jesus Christ, we almost lose sight of the Father in the Son, instead of beholding the glory of God in the face of Jesus Christ as He intends us to do. Practically, some of us know consciously only one Person in the Blessed Trinity, and do not honor the Father as we honor the Son.

We shall not love Jesus less, but more, as we learn to love God, who was in Christ reconciling us to Himself. We shall not be less tenderly grateful for His coming to die for us, but more as we rise to adore the mystery of love which alone illumines the inconceivable eternity of the past when the Word was with God and the Word was God. We shall find, too, that, while there is more than scope enough in the thought and revelation of God *as* God for the strongest hour, the very zenith of our intellect, there is rest in it for the weariest hour of the weakest frame. For when my heart and my flesh faileth, God is the strength of my heart and my portion for ever.

> By change untouched, by thought untraced,
>   And by created eye unseen,
> In Thy great Present is embraced
>   All that shall be, all that hath been.
> O Father of our spirits, now
>   We seek Thee in our Saviour's face;
> In truth and spirit we would bow,
>   And worship where we cannot trace.

October 27

UNQUENCHABLE LOVE

Love is strong as death.   Song of Solomon 8:6
Many waters cannot quench love. Song of Solomon 8:7

He proved His love to you and me to be strong as death, and when all God's waves and billows went over Him, the many waters could not quench it. In His love and in His pity He redeemed us; in the same love He bears us and carries us all the day long. He "loveth at all times," and that includes this present moment; now, while your eye is on this page, His eye of love is looking on you, and the folds of His banner of love are overshadowing you. Is there even a feeble pulse of love to Him? He meets it with, "I love them that love Me." "I will love him, and will manifest Myself to him." And so surely as the bride says, "Thy love is better than wine," so surely does the heavenly Bridegroom respond with incomprehensible condescension: "How fair is thy love, my sister, my spouse! how much better is thy love than wine!" May this love of Christ constrain us to live unto Him "who loved me and gave Himself for me."

> Sit down beneath His shadow, and rest with great delight;
> The faith that now beholds Him is pledge of future sight.
> Our Master's love remember, exceeding great and free;
> Lift up thy heart in gladness, for He remembers thee.

October 28

REDEEM THE TIME

O that thou hadst hearkened . . . then had thy peace been as a river, and thy righteousness as the waves of the sea.   Isaiah 48:18

Oh, how much we have missed by not placing all at His disposal! What might He not have done with the moments freighted with self or loaded with emptiness, which we have carelessly let drift by! Oh, what might have been if they had all been kept for Jesus! How He might have filled them with His light and life, enriching our own lives that have been impoverished by the waste, and using them in far-spreading blessing and power!

> Take us, Lord, oh, take us truly, mind and soul and heart and will;
> Empty us and cleanse us throughly, then with all Thy fullness fill.
> Make us in Thy royal palace, vessels worthy for the King;
> From Thy fullness fill our chalice, from Thy never-failing spring.
> Father, by this blessed filling, dwell Thyself in us, we pray;
> We are waiting, Thou art willing, fill us with Thyself today!

October 29

"ONLY" AND "EVER" HIS

A garden inclosed is my sister, my spouse; a spring shut up, a fountain sealed.   Song of Solomon 4:12
This people have I formed for myself.   Isaiah 43:21

You have not given "all" to Jesus while you are not quite ready to be "only" for Him. And it is no use to talk about "ever" while we have not settled the "only" and the "all." You cannot be "for Him" in the full and blessed sense, while you are partly "for" anything or anyone else. For "the Lord hath *set apart* him that is godly for Himself." You see, the "for Himself" hinges upon the "set apart." There is no consecration without separation. If you are mourning over want of realized consecration, will you look humbly and sincerely into *this* point? "A garden *inclosed* is my sister, my spouse," saith the Heavenly Bridegroom.

> Set apart for Jesus! Is not this enough,
> Though the desert prospect open wild and rough?
> Set apart for His delight,
> Chosen for His holy pleasure,
> Sealed to be His special treasure!
> Could we choose a nobler joy?—
> And would we if we might?

October 30

The Lord is . . . not willing that any should perish, but that all should come to repentance.　　　　2 Peter 3:9

Then why do any perish? Simply because they *won't* come; because they will not yield to the winning love and the drawing power which is now being put forth to save you, if, as you read this, you *want* to be saved. There is no sadder word in the Bible than "Ye *will* not come to Me, that ye might have life." But if you are saying, ever so feebly and faintly, "I will," God meets it with His strong and gracious "Thou *shalt*."

> What will you do without Him,
> When He hath shut the door,
> And you are left outside, because
> You would not come before?
> When it is no use knocking,
> No use to stand and wait,
> For the word of doom tolls thro' your heart,
> That terrible "Too late!"

October 31

For he that cometh to God must believe that he is. Hebrews 11:6

The coming so hinges on that, as to be really the same thing. The moment you really believed, you would really come; and the moment you really come, you really believe. Now the Lord Jesus is as truly and actually "nigh thee" as if you could see Him. And He as truly and actually says "Come" to you as if you heard Him. Fear not, believe only, and *let* yourself come to Him straight away! "Take with you words, and turn to the Lord: say unto Him, Take away all iniquity, and receive us graciously." And know that His answer is, "Him that cometh to Me I will in no wise cast out."

> Reality in greatest need,
> Lord Jesus Christ, Thou art indeed!
> Is the pilot real, who alone can guide
> The drifting ship through the midnight tide?
> Is the lifeboat real, as it nears the wreck,
> And the saved ones leap from the parting deck?
> Is the haven real, where the barque may flee
> From the autumn gales of the wild North Sea?
> Reality indeed art Thou,
> My Pilot, Lifeboat, Haven now.

November 1

ALL THINGS NOT EXPEDIENT

Whether therefore ye eat, or drink, or whatsoever ye do, do all to the glory of God. 1 Corinthians 10:31

This is not fully obeyed when we drink, merely because we like it, what is the very greatest obstacle to that glory in this world of ours. What matter that we prefer taking it in a more refined form, if the thing itself is daily and actively and mightily working misery, and crime, and death, and destruction to thousands, till the cry thereof seems as if it must pierce the very heavens! And so it does — sooner, a great deal, than it pierces the walls of our comfortable dining room! I only say here, you who have said, "Take my lips," stop and repeat that prayer next time you put that to your lips which is binding men and women hand and foot, and delivering them over, helpless to Satan! Let those words pass once more from your heart *out* through your lips, and I do not think you will feel comfortable in letting the means of such infernal work pass *in* through them.

> Church of God, beloved and chosen,
> Church of Christ for whom He died,
> Claim thy gifts and praise thy Giver!—
> "Ye are washed and sanctified."
> Sanctified by God the Father, and by Jesus Christ His Son,
> And by God the Holy Spirit, Holy, Holy Three in One.

November 2

NO WANTING IN HEAVEN

The righteous hath hope in his death. Proverbs 14:32
Let me die the death of the righteous. Numbers 23:10

What will the harps of Heaven be to the thrill of the one Voice, saying, "Come, ye blessed of my Father!" and, "Well done, good and faithful servant, enter thou into the joy of thy Lord." Our dear departed ones have heard that! and that one word of the King must have made them most blessed forever. At this moment they are exceeding glad, and the certainty of it stills every quiver of our selfish love. The glory and joy of our Lord Jesus Christ are revealed to them, and they are "glad also with exceeding joy," rejoicing together with Jesus. How can they help reflecting His divine joy when they see it no longer by faith and afar off, but visibly, actually face to face!

nay, more, eye to eye, that very closest approach of tenderest intercourse too deep for words. They see Him as He is; in all His beauty and love and glory; through no veil, no glass, no tear-mist. The prayer for them, "The Lord lift up His countenance upon thee," is altogether fulfilled, and they are "full of joy with Thy countenance." And every other prayer we ever prayed for them is fulfilled exceeding abundantly above all we asked or thought. We may not pray any more for them, because God has not left one possibility of blessedness unbestowed.

> For I know
> That they who are not lost, but gone before,
> Are only waiting till I come; for death
> Has only parted us a little while,
> And has not severed e'en the finest strand
> In the eternal cable of our love:
> The very strain has twined it closer still,
> And added strength. The music of these lives
> Is nowise stilled, but blended so with songs
> Around the throne of God, that our poor ears
> No longer hear it.

November 3

KING OF YOUR LIFE

Because the Lord hath loved his people, he hath made thee king over them. 2 Chronicles 2:11

God has appointed His King to be ruler over Israel and over Judah. Thus He gives His children a great bond of union. For "one King shall be king to them all," and He shall "gather together in one the children of God which were scattered abroad." "Satan scatters, but Jesus gathers." Shall we then let the enemy have his way, and induce us to keep apart and aloof from those over whom our beloved King reigns also? Let us try this day to recollect this, and make it practical in all our contact with His other subjects. Why has God made Jesus King? Who would have guessed the right answer? "Because the Lord loved His people." So the very thought of the kingship of Christ sprang from the everlasting love of God to His people. Bring that wonderful statement down to personal reality — "His people" — that is, you and me. God made Jesus King over you because He loved you, and that with nothing less than the love wherewith He loved Him.

> And closer yet, and closer the golden bonds shall be,
> Enlinking all who love our Lord in pure sincerity;
> And wider yet, and wider shall the circling glory glow,
> As more and more are taught of God that mighty love to know.

November 4

Having loved his own which were in the world, he loved them unto the end. John 13:1

"He which hath begun a good work in you will perform it until the day of Jesus Christ." How true is the type, both as to each individual temple of the Holy Ghost, and "all the building that groweth unto an holy temple in the Lord"; "The hands of Zerubbabel have laid the foundation of this house, his hands shall also finish it" — "His own house, whose house are we." Our Lord Jesus Christ endorses it in the very amen of His great prayer, "I have declared unto them Thy name, and will declare it." Only let us simply receive and believe what He shows us and tells us, and then to every Nathanael who comes to Him, He will say, "Because I said unto thee, I saw thee under the fig-tree, believest thou? thou shalt see greater things than these." Then we shall have, personally and indeed, "showers of blessing."

> Unto him that hath, Thou givest
> Ever "more abundantly."
> Lord, I live because Thou livest,
>   Therefore give more life to me;
> Therefore speed me in the race;
> Therefore let me grow in grace.

November 5

ENLARGED CAPABILITIES

And his servants shall serve him. Revelation 22:3

What will it be to be able at last to express not only all the love we now feel, but all the perfected love of infinitely enlarged capability of loving in the equally perfected service of equally enlarged capability of serving? — able to show Jesus a love which would burst our hearts if poured into them now! Able to put all the new rapture of praise into living action for Him! Able to go on serving Him day and night without any weariness in it, and never a hateful shadow of weariness of it; without any interruptions; without any mistakes at all; without any thinking how much better someone else could have done it, or how much better we ought to have done it; above all, without the least mixture of sin in motive or deed—pure, perfect service of Him whom we love and see face to face! What can be more joyful? We are not told much about it, we could not understand it now! the secrets of this wonderful service will only be told when we are brought to His house above, and see what are the heavenly "good works which God hath before ordained" (margin, *prepared*) for us. How full of surprises the new service will be!—new powers, new and entirely congenial fellow-workers, new spheres, new ministries; only two things not new, if our earthly service has been true—no new power, and no new end and aim, but the same, even His power and His glory! Then shall come the full accomplishment of the Messianic prophecy: "A seed *shall* serve Him"; and still we shall say (only I think we shall sing it), "Thine is the kingdom, and the power, and the glory, for ever. Amen." "Whose I am and whom I serve" for ever!

Lord, Thou needest not, I know, service such as I can bring;
Yet I long to prove and show full allegiance to my King.
Thou an honor art to me, let me be a praise to Thee.

November 6

A LIVING COMMENTARY

Remember the word unto thy servant, upon which thou hast caused me to hope.   Psalm 119:49

God keeps writing a commentary on His Word in the volume of our own experience. That is, insofar as we put that volume into His hands, and do not think to fill it with our own scribble. We are not to undervalue or neglect this commentary, but to use it as John Newton did, when he wrote,

His love in times past forbids me to think
He'll leave me at last in trouble to sink;
Each sweet Ebenezer I have in review
Confirms His good pleasure to help me quite through.

Every record of love bears the great signature, "I am the Lord, I change not"; "Jesus Christ, the same yesterday, and today, and for ever." Every "hitherto" of grace and help is a "henceforth" of more grace and more help. Every experience of the realities of faith widens the horizon of the possibilities of faith. Every realized promise is the steppingstone to one yet unrealized.

Hitherto the Lord hath helped us, guiding all the way;
Henceforth let us trust Him fully, trust Him all the day.
Hitherto the Lord hath loved us, caring for His own;
Henceforth let us love Him better, live for Him alone.

November 7

**With desire I have desired to eat this passover with you
before I suffer.** Luke 22:15

With Gethsemane and Calvary in fullest view, His heart's desire was to spend those few last hours in closest intercourse
with His disciples. Now, if we take the King at His word, and
really believe that He thus desires us, can we possibly remain
coldhearted and indifferent to Him? Can we bear the idea of
disappointing His love — *such* love — and meeting it with any
such pale, cool response as would wound any human heart, "I
do not know whether I love you or not!" Oh, do let us leave
off morbidly looking to see exactly how much we love (which
is just like trying to warm ourselves with a thermometer, and
perhaps only ends in doubting whether we love at all), and
look straight away at His love and His desire! Think of Jesus
actually wanting you, really desiring your love, not satisfied
with all the love of all the angels and saints unless you love
Him too—needing that little drop to fill His cup of joy! Is
there no answering throb, no responsive glow?

> Within an "upper room" are met a small, yet faithful band,
> On whom a deep yet chastened grief hath laid its softening hand.
> Among them there is One who wears a more than mortal mien,
> 'Tis He on whom in all distress the weary one may lean.

November 8

MY LORD AND I

Come with me. Song of Solomon 4:8

It is a very common experience in great things and small, that
the person or thing we most want is not there just when we
most want him or it. Never shall we have to complain of this
as to the promised perpetual presence of our Lord; for He says,
"I will be with him in trouble." "When thou passest through
the waters, I will be with thee." And in the deepest need of
all, in the valley of the shadow of death, the soul that has
yielded to the present call will be able to say, "Thou art with
me!" I do not think we consider enough how we disappoint the
love of Jesus when we refuse to come with Him. For He does
truly and literally desire us to be with Him. Would He have
made it the very climax of His great prayer, representing it

as the very culmination of His own rest and glory that His people should be with Him, if He did not so very much care about it, and was only seeking and saving us out of bare pity? No, it was in His love as well as in His pity that He redeemed us! And love craves nearness. This is the very thing that differences love from the lesser glow of mere pity, or kindness, whatever their degrees or combinations. The Lord Jesus would not say, "Come with Me," if He did not feel towards us something far beyond any degree of pity and kindness.

"Certainly I will be with thee!" Starry promise in the night!
All uncertainties, like shadows, flee away before its light.
"Certainly I will be with thee!" He hath spoken: I have heard!
True of old, and true this moment, I will trust Jehovah's word.

November 9

FORMED FOR HIS GLORY FOREVER

I know that, whatsoever God doeth, it shall be for ever.
Ecclesiastes 3:14

Therefore, we may rejoicingly say "ever" as well as "only" and "all for Thee!" For the Lord is our Keeper, and He is the Almighty and the Everlasting God, with whom is no variableness, neither shadow of turning. He will never change His mind about keeping us, and no man is able to pluck us out of His hand. Neither will Christ let us pluck ourselves out of His hand, for He says, "Thou *shalt* abide for Me many days." And He that keepeth us will not slumber. Once having undertaken His vineyard, He will keep it night and day, till all the days and nights are over, and we know the full meaning of the salvation ready to be revealed in the last time, unto which we are kept by His power. And then, for ever for Him! — passing from the gracious keeping by faith for this little while, to the glorious keeping in His presence for all eternity! For ever fulfilling the object for which He formed us and chose us, we showing forth His praise, and He showing the exceeding riches of His grace in His kindness towards us in the ages to come! *He for us, and we for Him for ever!* Oh, how little we can grasp this! Yet this is the fruition of being "kept for Jesus!"

Set apart forever for Himself alone!
Now we see our calling gloriously shown!
Owning, with no secret dread,
    This our holy separation,
    Now the crown of consecration
Of the Lord our God shall rest upon our willing head!

November 10

LIFTED BY WAY OF REMEMBRANCE

O my God, my soul is cast down within me. Psalm 42:6

Whenever you say this, add at once, "Therefore will I remember Thee." And what then? What comes of thus remembering Him? "My soul shall be satisfied as with marrow and fatness, and my mouth shall praise Thee with joyful lips." What can be a sweeter, fuller promise than this! Our heart's desire fulfilled in abundant satisfaction and joyful power of praise! Yet there is a promise sweeter and more thrilling still to the loving, longing heart. And so, this very night, as you put away the profitless musings and memories, and remember Him upon your bed, He will keep His word and meet you, for has He not said, "Thou meetest . . . those that remember Thee in Thy ways"? The darkness shall be verily the shadow of His wing, for your feeble, yet Spirit-given remembrance, shall be met by His real and actual presence, for "hath He said and shall He not do it?" Let us pray that this night the desire of our soul may be "to Thy name, and to *the remembrance of Thee.*"

> O sunlight of thanksgiving! Who that knows
> Its bright forth-breaking after dreariest days,
> Would change the after-thought of woes
> For memory's loveliest light that glows,
> If so he must forego one note of that sweet praise?

November 11

A MIND AT PERFECT PEACE

Bringing into captivity every thought to the obedience of Christ. 2 Corinthians 10:5

Are there any tyrants more harassing than our own thoughts? Control of deeds and words seems a small thing in comparison; but have we not been apt to fancy that we really cannot help our thoughts? Instead of our dominating them, they have dominated us; and we have not expected nor even thought it possible, to be set free from the manifold tyranny of vain thoughts, and still less of wandering thoughts. Yet, all the time, *here* has been God's Word about this hopeless, helpless matter, only *where* has been our faith? It is very strong language that the inspiring Spirit uses here—not "thoughts" in general, but definitely, and with no room for distressing exceptions, *"every* thought." Must it not be glorious rest to have *every* thought of day and night brought into sweet, quiet, complete captivity to Jesus, entirely "obedient to the faith," to His holy and loving influence, to His beautiful and perfect law? We should not have dared to hope or dream of such a rest to our souls; we should not have guessed it included in that promise to those who take the yoke of Christ upon them; and if we could find one text stating that it was not any part of God's infinitely gracious purpose for us, we should only say, "Of course, for it stands to reason it could not be!"

> Not yet thou knowest what I do within thine own weak breast
> To mold thee to My image true, and fit thee for My rest.
> But yield thee to My loving skill; the veiled work of grace,
> From day to day progressing still, it is not thine to trace.

November 12

SPEAK JUST A WORD

As we have therefore opportunity, let us do good unto all men, especially unto them who are of the household of faith. Galatians 6:10
He giveth goodly words. Genesis 49:21

Satan even perverts humility into a hindrance, and persuades us that of course our friend knows as much or more of the things of God than we do, and that telling of what we have found in Jesus, may seem like or lead to talking about ourselves. Yet perhaps all the while, that friend is hungering and feeling besieged, while we are withholding good tidings of plenty and deliverance. Have there not been days when the brightest of us would have been most thankful for the simplest word about Jesus, from the humblest Christian? — days when even "the mention of His name" might have been food and freedom! It does not in the least follow that members of Christian families need no such "good tidings" because of their favored position. They may need it all the more, because no one thinks it necessary to try and help them. And when? The constantly recurring word meets us here again, *"Now!"*

> The memory of a kindly word for long gone by,
> The fragrance of a fading flower sent lovingly,
> The gleaming of a sudden smile or sudden tear,
> The warmer pressure of the hand, the tone of cheer,
> The hush that means "I cannot speak, but I have heard!"
> The note that only bears a verse from God's own Word—
> Such tiny things we hardly count as ministry;
> The givers deeming they have shown scant sympathy;
> But, when the heart is overwrought, oh who can tell
> The power of such tiny things to make it well!

November 13

THE LAMB THE KING

God will provide himself a lamb. Genesis 22:8
I have provided me a king. 1 Samuel 16:1

So the source of the kingship of Christ is God Himself, in the eternal counsels of His love. It is one of the grand thoughts of God. Christ said to His Father, "Thou lovedst Me before the foundation of the world." At that mysterious date, not of time, but of everlasting love, God "chose us in Him." Before the world began, God, that cannot lie, gave the promise of eternal life to Him for us, and made with Him for us "a covenant ordered in all things, and sure." The leading provisions of that covenant were, a Lamb for our atonement, and a King for our government — a dying and a living Saviour. Having provided, He appointed and anointed His King: "Yet have I set [margin, anointed] My King upon My holy hill of Zion." What a marvelous meeting-place is thus found in the Kingship of Jesus for God's heart and ours! He says in His majestic sovereignty, "I have set my King"; and we say in lowly and loving loyalty, "Thou art my King."

True the report that reached my far-off land
Of all His wisdom and transcendent fame;
Yet I believed not until I came—
Bowed to the dust till raised by royal hand.
The half was never told by mortal word;
My King exceeded all the fame that I had heard!

November 14

CLEAVING WITH PURPOSE

He . . . exhorted them all, that with purpose of heart they would cleave unto the Lord. Acts 11:23

Cleaving to the Lord is not a mere terrified clinging for safety —it is the bright, brave resolution, strengthened, not weakened, by the sight of waverers or renegades, to be on His side, come what may, because He is our King, because we love Him, because His cause and His kingdom are so very dear to us. We cannot thus cleave, without loosening from other interests. But what matter! Let us be noble for Jesus, like the men of might who "separated themselves unto David," and who "held strongly with him in his kingdom." Shall we be mean enough to aim at less, when it is our Lord Jesus who would have us entirely "with Him"? It is, after all, the easiest and safest course. The especial friends and "the mighty men which belonged to David," not only did not follow the usurping Adonijah, but they were never tempted to do so. "But me, even me thy servant . . . hath he not called." There is many a temptation, very powerful and dangerous to a camp-follower, which the enemy knows it is simply useless to present to one of the bodyguard. Our Father leads us "not into temptation," when He leads us closer to Jesus.

> Unfurl the Christian standard, and follow through the strife
> The noble army who have won the martyr's crown of life;
> Our ancestors could die for Truth, could brave the deadly glow,
> And shall we let the standard fall, and yield it to the foe?

November 15

WORDS THAT PAY

Jephthah uttered all his words before the Lord. Judges 11:11
The Lord . . . did let none of his words fall to the ground.
1 Samuel 3:19

A cottager of no more than average sense and intelligence remarked, "It was all so trifling at the reading; I wish gentle folks would believe that poor people like something better than what's just to make them laugh." After all, nothing really pays like direct, straightforward, uncompromising words about God and His works and word. Nothing else ever made a man say, as a poor Irishman did when he heard the Good News for the first time, "Thank ye, sir; you've taken the hunger off us today!" What about our words? They are all uttered before the Lord in one sense, whether we will or no; for there is not a word in my tongue, but lo, Thou, O Lord, knowest it altogether! How solemn is this thought, but how sweet does it become when our words are uttered consciously before the Lord as we walk in the light of His perpetual presence! Oh, that we may so walk, that we may so speak, with kept feet and kept lips, trustfully praying, "Let the meditation of my heart and the words of my mouth be alway acceptable in Thy sight, O Lord, my Strength and my Redeemer!"

> Yes, we have a word for Jesus! Living echoes we will be
> Of Thine own sweet words of blessing, of Thy gracious "Come to Me."
> Jesus, Master! yes, we love Thee, and to prove our love, would lay
> Fruit of lips which Thou wilt open, at Thy blessed feet today.
> Many an effort it may cost us, many a heart-beat, many a fear,
> But Thou knowest, and wilt strengthen, and Thy help is always near.
> Give us grace to follow fully, vanquishing our faithless shame,
> Feebly it may be, but truly, witnessing for Thy dear Name.

November 16

NO CLEANSING WITHOUT CONFESSION

Give, I pray thee, glory to the Lord God of Israel, and make confession unto him. Joshua 7:19

Why transgress ye the commandments of the Lord, that ye cannot prosper? 2 Chronicles 24:20

We must not forget the things that are behind till they are confessed and forgiven. Let us now bring all this unsatisfactory past experience, and, most of all, the want of trust which has been the poison-spring of its course, to the precious blood of Christ, which cleanseth us, even us, from all sin, even this sin. . . . And, oh, let us wonderingly love Him the more that He has been so patient and gentle with us, upbraiding not, though in our slow-hearted foolishness we have been grieving Him by this subtle unbelief; and then, by His grace may we enter upon a new era of experience, our lives kept for Him more fully than ever before, because we trust Him more simply and unreservedly to keep them!

> Oh, cleanse me now! My Lord, I cannot stay
> For evening shadows and a silent hour:
> Now I have sinned, and now, with no delay,
> I claim Thy promise and its total power.

November 17

INFINITE MIND THINKING ON US

He telleth the number of the stars; he calleth them all by their names. Great is our Lord, and of great power: his understanding is infinite. Psalm 147:4-5

He healeth the broken in heart, and bindeth up their wounds. Psalm 147:3

Why did He expend such immeasurable might of mind upon a world which is to be burnt up, but that He would fit it perfectly to be, not the home, but the school of His children? The infinity of His skill is such that the most powerful intellects find a lifetime too short to penetrate a little way into a few secrets of some one small department of His working. If we turn to Providence, it is quite enough to take only one's own life, and look at it microscopically and telescopically, and marvel at the treasures of wisdom lavished upon its details, ordering and shaping and fitting the tiny confused bits into the true mosaic which He means it to be. Many a little thing in our lives reveals the same Mind which, according to a well-known and very beautiful illustration, adjusted a perfect proportion in the delicate hinges of the snowdrop and the droop of its bell with the mass of the globe and the force of gravitation. How kind we think it if a very talented friend spends a little of his thought and power of mind in teaching us or planning for us! Have we been grateful for the infinite thought and wisdom which our Lord has expended upon us and our creation, preservation, and redemption?

> . . . . There we see
> His thoughts to usward, thoughts of peace
> That stoop to tenderest love; that still increase
> With increase of our need; that never change,
> That never fail, or falter, or forget.
>   O pity infinite!
>   O royal mercy free!
> O gentle climax of depth and height
> Of God's most precious tho'ts, most wonderful, most strange!
> "For I am poor and needy, yet
> The Lord Himself, Jehovah, thinketh upon me!"

November 18

FIRST OF ALL

For thy servant doth know that I have sinned: therefore, behold, I am come the first this day of all the house of Joseph to go down to meet my lord the king.   2 Samuel 19:20

Yes, I have sinned. I *know* that I have sinned. Whether I feel it more or less does not touch the fact: I *know* it. And what then? "Therefore, behold, I am come the first this day of all . . . to meet my Lord the King." Just because I *know* I have sinned, I come to Jesus. He came to call sinners, He came to save sinners, so He came to call and to save me. "This is all my desire." Just because I know that I have sinned, I may and must come "the first of all." Thousands are coming, but the heart knoweth its own bitterness. So, not waiting for others, not coming in order, but "first of all," by the pressure of my sore need of pardon, I come. There is no waiting for one's turn in coming to Jesus. "The first of all," because it is against *"my* Lord the King" that I have sinned. I am His servant, so I have the greater sin. The first of all, because I have so much to be forgiven, and have already been forgiven so much, that I must, I do, love much; and love, even of a sorrowing sinner, seeks nearness, and cannot rest in distance. "Therefore," also, "I am come *this day*." I dare not and could not wait till tomorrow. No need to wait, even till tonight!

> I bring my sins to Thee, the sins I cannot count,
> That all may cleansed be in Thy once-opened Fount.
> I bring them, Saviour, all to Thee.
> The burden is too great for me.

November 19

BEYOND OUR KEN BUT NOT OUR SPIRIT

And who then is willing to consecrate his service
this day unto the Lord?   1 Chronicles 29:5

Do not startle at the term, or think, because you do not understand all it may include, you are therefore not qualified for it. I dare say it comprehends a great deal more than either you or I understand, but we can both enter into the spirit of it, and the detail will unfold itself as long as our probation shall last. Christ demands a hearty consecration in *will*, and He will teach us what that involves in act. This explains the paradox that full consecration may be in one sense the act of a moment, and in another the work of a lifetime.

> Who is on the Lord's side? Who will serve the King?
> Who will be His helpers, other lives to bring?
> Who will leave the world's side? Who will face the foe?
> Who is on the Lord's side? Who for Him will go?
> By Thy call of mercy, by Thy grace divine,
> We are on the Lord's side; Saviour, we are Thine.

November 20

POOR WITHIN REACH OF TREASURES

We do not well: this day is a day of good tidings, and we hold
our peace: if we tarry till the morning light, some mischief
will come upon us: now therefore come, that we may go and
tell the king's household.   2 Kings 7:9

Just the last persons who would seem to need the good tidings, and the last, too, who would seem likely to have them to convey! But, oh, how true the figure is! How many among the King's own household need the good tidings which these lepers brought! For they are starving so near to plenty, and poor within reach of treasure, and thinking themselves besieged when the Lord has dispersed the foe for them. Is it not often the spiritual leper, the conscious outcast, the famine-stricken, possession-less soul, who takes the boldest step into the fullest salvation, and finds deliverance and abundance and riches beyond what the more favored and older inmate of the King's household knows anything about? It may be one of the enemy's devices, that we sometimes hold back good tidings, just because we shrink from telling them to the King's household. How many who do not hesitate to speak of Jesus to little children or poor people, or even to persons who openly say, "We will not have this man to reign over us," never say one word to their fellow-subjects about the blessed discoveries that the Holy Spirit has made to them of the fullness of His salvation, and the reality of His power, and the treasures of His Word, and the satisfaction of His love, and the far-reaching fulfillments of His promises, and the real, actual deliverance, and freedom, and victory, which He gives, and the strength and the healing that flow through faith in His name!

Tell it out among the nations that the Saviour reigns!
Tell it out among the heathen, bid them burst their chains!
Tell it out among the weeping ones that Jesus lives;
Tell it out among the weary ones what rest He gives;
Tell it out among the sinners that He came to save;
Tell it out among the dying that He triumphed o'er the grave.

November 21

HUMBLING BLESSEDNESS

Blessed is the man whom thou chastenest, O Lord, and teachest him out of thy law.   Psalm 94:12

Perhaps we have gone through all this, and known the humbling blessedness of being searched and "told," and then pardoned and cleansed; and now again there is something not right. We hardly know what, only there is a misgiving, a dim, vague uneasiness; we "really don't know of anything in particular," and yet there is something unsatisfied and unsatisfactory. There is nothing for it but to come to our Saviour afresh, and ask Him to tell us what we have done, or are doing, which is not in accordance with His will. It will be useless coming if we are not sincerely purposed to let Him tell us what He will, and not merely what we expect; or if we hush up the first word of an unwelcome whisper, and say, "Oh, that can't have anything to do with it!" or, "I am all right there, at any rate!" We must simply say, "Master, say on"; and perhaps He will then show us, as He did Simon, that we have not done Him the true and loving service which some poor, despised one has rendered.

Oh, never shrink from the probings of our beloved Physician. Dearer and dearer will the hand become as we yield to it. Sweeter and sweeter will be the proofs that He is our own faithful Friend, who only wounds that He may perfectly heal.

Is it not often so,
That we only learn in part,
And the Master's testing time may show
That it was not quite "by heart"?
Then He gives, in His wise and patient grace,
    That lesson again
With the mark still set in the self-same place.

November 22

Come, ye blessed of my Father, inherit the kingdom prepared for you from the foundation of the world. Matthew 25:34

The call will be no longer, Come unto Me, all ye that are weary and heavy laden; for the weariness and the burdens that have been cast upon Jesus will be at an end for ever. It will be, "Come, ye blessed!" Not "blessed" then for the first time, but "ye" whose position already is that of "the blessed of the Lord." Every one who comes to Jesus takes that glorious position, and possesses all its manifold privileges. If you are only come today for the first time, "thou art now the blessed of the Lord." You are now made kings and priests unto God by Him who loved you and washed you from your sins in His own blood. By faith in Christ Jesus you are the children of God. "And if children, then heirs; heirs of God, and joint-heirs with Christ." He will make you inherit the throne of His glory. He has prepared not only a place, and a city, but a kingdom for you.

> What then? eye hath not seen, ear hath not heard!
> Wait till thou too hast fought the noble strife,
> And won, through Jesus Christ, the crown of life!
> Then shalt thou know the glory of the word,
> Then as the stars for ever — ever shine.
> Beneath the King's own smile — perpetual Zenith thine!

November 23

GRADUALLY OR DECISIVELY?

If any man be in Christ, he is a new creature: old things are passed away; behold, all things are become new.
2 Corinthians 5:17

"A very severe test!" you say. I cannot help that; I can only tell you exactly what God says. I cannot reverse it, and you cannot alter it. So then, if old things have *not* passed away in your life, and if you are *not* a new creature, "born again," altogether different in heart and life and love and aim, you are not "in Christ." And if you are not *in* Christ, you are *out* of Christ, outside the only place of safety. "Come thou *into* the Ark!" It is one of the devices of the destroyer to delude you into fancying that no very decided step is necessary. He is very fond of the word "gradually." You are to become more earnest — gradually. You are to find salvation — gradually.

You are to turn your mind to God — gradually. Did you ever think that God never used this word nor anything like it? Neither the word nor the sense of it occurs anywhere in the whole Bible with reference to salvation. You might have been gradually approaching the Ark, and gradually making up your mind to enter; but unless you took the one step *into* the Ark, the one step from outside to inside, what would have been your fate when the door was shut?

Complete in Him, our glorious Head,
With Jesus raised from the dead,
And by His mighty Spirit led!
O blessed Lord, is this for me?
Then let my whole life henceforth be
One Allelujah-song to Thee.

November 24

HIS PERSONAL POSSESSION OURS

My peace I give unto you. John 14:27

"Peace I leave with you" is much; "*My* peace I give unto you" is more. The added word tells the fathomless marvel of the gift—"My peace." Not merely "peace with God"; Christ has made that by the blood of His cross, and being justified by faith we have it through Him. But after we are thus reconciled, the enmity and the separation being ended, Jesus has a gift for us from His own treasures; and this is its special and wonderful value, that it is His very own. How we value a gift which was the giver's own possession! What a special token of intimate friendship we feel it to be! To others we give what we have made or purchased; it is only to very near and dear ones that we give what has been our own personal enjoyment or use. And so Jesus gives us not only peace made and peace purchased, but a share in His very own peace — divine, eternal, incomprehensible peace — which dwells in His own heart as God, and which shone in splendor of calmness through His life as man. No wonder that it "passeth all understanding."

Thy reign is perfect peace;
    Not mine, but Thine!—
A stream that cannot cease.
For its fountain is Thy heart. O depth unknown!
    Thou givest of Thine own,
Pouring from Thine and filling mine.
The "noise of war" hath passed away;
    God's peace is on the throne,
Ruling with undisputed sway.

November 25

FULLNESS OF PLEASURE

Let every one of us please his neighbour for his good to edification. For even Christ pleased not himself.   Romans 15:2-3

If people only would believe it, self-pleasing is always a failure in the end. Our good Master gives us a reality and fullness of pleasure in pleasing Him which we never get out of pleasing ourselves.

> Dialects of love are many, though the language be but one;
> Study all you can, or any, while life's precious school-hours run.
> Silence is no certain token that no secret grief is there;
> Sorrow which is never spoken is the heaviest load to bear.
> Seldom can the heart be lonely, if it seek a lonelier still,
> Self-forgetting, seeking only emptier cups of love to fill.

November 26

THE POWER OF GOD'S WILL

[God] worketh all things after the counsel of his own will.
Ephesians 1:11
He doeth according to his will in the army of heaven, and among the inhabitants of the earth.   Daniel 4:35

Think of the *infinite mysteries* of that will! For ages and generations the hosts of Heaven have wonderingly watched its vouchsafed unveilings and its sublime developments, and still they are waiting, watching, and wondering.

Creation and Providence are but the whisper of its power, but Redemption is its music, and praise is the echo which shall yet fill His temple. The whisper and the music, yes, and "the thunder of His power," are all for thee. For what is "the good pleasure of His will" (Ephesians 1:5)? Oh, what a grand list of blessings purposed, provided, purchased, and possessed, all flowing to us out of it! And nothing but blessings, nothing but privileges, which we never should have imagined, and which even when revealed, we are "slow of heart to believe"; nothing but what should even now fill us "with joy unspeakable and full of glory!"

Think of this will as always and altogether on our side—always working for us, and in us, and with us, if we will only let it. Think of it as always and only synonymous with infinitely wise and almighty love. Think of it as undertaking all for us, from the great work of our eternal salvation down to the momentary details of guidance and supply, and do we not feel utter shame and self-abhorrence at ever having hesitated for an instant to give up our tiny, feeble, blind will, to be—not crushed, not even bent, but bent with His glorious and perfect will?

> Blest will of God! most glorious, the very fount of grace,
> Whence all the goodness floweth that heart can ever trace—
> Temple whose pinnacles are love, and faithfulness its base.
>
> Blest will of God! whose splendor is dawning on the world,
> On hearts in which Christ's banner is manfully unfurled,
> On hearts of childlike meekness, with dew of youth impearled.

November 27

THE POWER OF THE KING'S WORD

Where the word of a king is, there is power. Ecclesiastes 8:4

Then the question is "Where is it?" "Let the word of Christ dwell in you richly," and there, even in you, will be power. The Crowned One, who is now "upholding all things by the word of His power," hath said, "I have given them Thy word." And those who have received this great gift, "not as the word of men, but, as it is in truth, the word of God," know that there is power with it, because it effectually worketh also in them. They know its life-giving power, for they can say, "Thy word hath quickened me"; and its life-sustaining power, for they live "by every word that proceedeth out of the mouth of God." They can say, "Thy word have I hid in my heart, that I might not sin against Thee"; for in proportion as the word of the King is present in the heart, "there is power" against sin. Then let us use this means of absolute power more, and more life and more holiness will be ours. "His word was with power" in Capernaum of old, and it will be with the same power in any place nowadays. His word cannot fail; it "shall not return void"; it "shall prosper." Therefore, when our "words fall to the ground," it only proves that they were not His words. So what we want is not merely that His power may accompany our word, but that we may not speak our own at all, but simply and only the very word of the King. Then there will be power in and with it. Bows drawn at a venture hit in a way that astonishes ourselves, when God puts His own arrows on the string.

> Upon the Word I rest, so strong, so sure,
> So full of comfort blest, so sweet, so pure!
> The charter of salvation, faith's broad foundation.

November 28

Philip findeth Nathanael, and saith unto him, We have found him. John 1:45

When Jesus had found Philip, Philip *knew* that he had found Him. And the next thing to knowing that we have found Him is to find someone else, and say, "Come and see! . . . We have found Him . . . We see Jesus!" If you only knew the irresistible longing, the very heart's desire that you should find, and see Him too, you would pardon all the pertinacity, all the insistence, with which again and again we say, "Come and see!" The woman of Samaria left her waterpot, and went her way into the city with the same message: "Come, see a man which told me all things that ever I did." And we to whom Jesus has said, "I that speak unto thee am He," cannot do otherwise or less.

> "Come!" to those who never heard
> Why the Saviour's blood was shed;
> Bear to them the message-word
> That can quicken from the dead;
> Tell them Jesus "died for all,"
> Tell them of His loving call.

November 29

UNLIMITED GRACE

And unto one he gave five talents, to another two, and to another one; to every man according to his several ability. Matthew 25:15
But unto every one of us is given grace according to the measure of the gift of Christ. Ephesians 4:7

Which is greatest, gifts or grace? *Gifts* are given "to every man according to his several ability." That is, we have just as much given as God knows we are able to use, and what He knows we can best use for Him. "But unto every one of us is given grace according to the measure of the gift of Christ." Claiming and using that royal measure of grace, you may, and can, and will do more for God than the mightiest intellect in the world without it. For which, in the clear light of His Word, is likely to be most effectual, the natural ability which at its best and fullest, without Christ, "can do *nothing*" (observe and believe that word!), or the grace of our Almighty God and the power of the Holy Ghost, which is as

free to you as it ever was to any one? If you are responsible
for making use of your limited gift, are you not equally responsible for making use of the grace and power which are
to be had for the asking, which are already yours in Christ,
and which are not limited?

In God's great field of labor all work is not the same,
He hath a service for each one who loves His holy Name.
And you, to whom the secrets of all sweet sounds are known,
Rise up! for He hath called you to a mission of your own.
And, rightly to fulfill it, His grace can make you strong,
Who to your charge hath given the ministry of song.

November 30

THE MOUTH BETRAYS THE HEART

**He that loveth pureness of heart, for the grace of his lips
the king shall be his friend.** Proverbs 22:11

Who can say, "I have made my heart clean, I am pure"? Who
must not despair of the friendship of the King if this were
the condition? But His wonderful condescension in promising
His friendship bends yet lower in its tenderly devised condition. Not to the absolutely pure in heart, but to the perhaps
very sorrowfully longing lover of that pureness, comes the
gracious words, "The King shall be his Friend." Yet there
must be some proof of this love; and it is found in "the grace
of His lips." "For out of the abundance of the heart the mouth
speaketh." Here, again, we stop and question our claim; for
our speech has not always been "with grace"; and the memory
of many a graceless and idle word rises to bar it. How, then,
shall the King be our Friend? Another word comes to our
help: "Grace is poured into thy lips"—grace that overflowed
in gracious words, such as never man spake, perfectly holy and
beautiful; and we look up to our King and plead that He has
Himself fulfilled the condition in which we have failed—that
this is part of the righteousness which He wrought for us, and
which is really unto us and upon us, because we believe in Him;
and so, for the grace of His own lips, the King shall be our
Friend.

Just to let Him speak to thee through His Word,
Watching, that His voice may be clearly heard.
Just to tell Him everything as it rises,
And at once to Him to bring all surprises.
Just to listen, and to stay
Where you cannot miss His voice.
This is all! And thus today,
Communing, you shall rejoice.

December 1

I know whom I have believed, and am persuaded that he is able to keep that which I have committed unto him against that day. 2 Timothy 1:12

Having already said, "Take my life, for I cannot give it to Thee," let us now say, with deepened conviction, that without Christ we really can do nothing—"Keep my life, for I cannot keep it for Thee." Yes! He who is able and willing to take unto Himself, is no less able and willing to keep for Himself. Our willing offering has been made by His enabling grace, and this our King has seen with joy. Let us ask this with the same simple trust to which, in so many other things, He has so liberally and graciously responded. For this is the confidence that we have in Him, that if we ask anything according to His will, He heareth us; and if we know that He hears us, whatsoever we ask, we know that we have the petitions that we desired of Him. There can be no doubt that this petition is according to His will, because it is based upon many a promise.

And now I find Thy promise true, of perfect peace and rest;
I cannot sigh — I can but sing while leaning on Thy breast,
And leaving everything to Thee, whose ways are always best.

December 2

TOO FEEBLE TO GROPE

Who is among you that feareth the Lord . . . that walketh in darkness and hath no light? let him trust in the name of the Lord, and stay upon his God. Isaiah 50:10

There are times when we simply cannot see anything, when there is nothing to do, but to hold on and trust in the dark; times when we do not seem even to be walking in the dark, but when, like Micah, we "sit in darkness," too feeble even to grope. Such darkness often comes in a time of reaction and weariness after special work and exertion, very often indeed after great or exciting success, sometimes even after unusually vivid spiritual blessing. An interval of convalescence after acute illness, when the overtaxed nervous energy has more than it can do in slowly refilling the chalice of life that had been so nearly "spilled on the ground," is peculiarly liable to it. And the sufferers who never pass beyond that stage, who are never any more than "a little better," know its shadow perhaps best of all. It does not say so, but I think the Lord Jesus must have known it, because He was made like unto us in all things, and submitted not only to the causes but to the effects of all the natural experiences of the nature which He took on Him.

I cannot hear Thy voice, Lord! dost Thou still hear my cry?
I cling to Thine assurance that Thou art ever nigh;
I know that Thou art faithful; I trust, but cannot see
That it is still the right way by which Thou leadest me.
I think I could go forward with brave and joyful heart,
Though every step should pierce me with unknown fiery smart,
If only I might see Thee, if I might gaze above
On all the cloudless glory of the sunshine of Thy love.

December 3

ALL FOR ME

Blessed be the Lord, who daily loadeth us with benefits.
Psalm 68:19

Just think of them deliberately (they are far too many to think of all in a flash) ; and how many did we actually ask for? Even that poor little claim was never brought to bear on thousands of them. To begin at the beginning, we certainly did not ask Him to choose us in Christ Jesus before the world began, and to predestinate us to be conformed to the image of His Son. Then, we certainly did not ask Him to call us by His grace; for before that call, we could not have wished, much less asked, for it. Then, who taught us to pray, and put into our entirely corrupt and sinful hearts any thought of asking Him for anything at all? Look back at our early prayers. Has He not more than granted them? Did we even know how much He could do for us? Did He not answer prayer by opening out new vistas of prayer before us, giving us grace to ask for more grace, faith to plead for more faith? And this is going on now, and will go on forever, when He has brought us with gladness and rejoicing into His own palace. Not till then shall we understand about those riches of glory in Christ Jesus, out of which He is even now pouring the supply of all our need.

Thanks be to God!
The thirsty land He laveth,
The perishing He saveth;
The floods lift up their voices,
The answering earth rejoices.
Thanks be to Him, and never-ending laud,
For this new token of His bounteous love,
Who reigns in might the water floods above:
The gathering waters rush along;
And leaps the exultant shout, one cataract of song,
Thanks be to God!

December 4

Thy love to me was wonderful.   2 Samuel 1:26
As the Father hath loved me, so have I loved you:
continue ye in my love.   John 15:9

His love! What manner of love is it? What should be quoted to prove or describe it? First the whole Bible with its mysteries and marvels of redemption, then the whole book of Providence and the whole volume of Creation. Then add to these the unknown records of eternity past and the unknown glories of eternity to come, and then let the immeasurable quotation be sung by "angels and archangels, and all the company of Heaven," with all the harps of God, and still that love will be untold, still it will be "the love of Christ that passeth knowledge."

His love "for thee." Not a passive, possible love, but outflowing, yes, *outpouring* of the real, glowing, personal love of His mighty and tender heart. Love not as an attribute, a quality, a latent force, but an acting, moving, reaching, touching, and grasping power. Love, not a cold, beautiful, far-off star, but a sunshine that comes and enfolds us, making us warm and glad, and strong and bright and fruitful.

O Master, at Thy feet I bow in rapture sweet!
Before me, as in darkening glass, some glorious outlines pass,
Of love, and truth, and holiness, and power;
I own them Thine, O Christ, and bless Thee for this hour.
O full of truth and grace, smile of Jehovah's face,
O tenderest heart of love untold! Who may Thy praise unfold?
Thee, Saviour, Lord of lords and King of kings,
Well may adoring seraphs hymn with veiling wings.

December 5

The love of the Lord toward the children of Israel, who look
to other gods, and love flagons of wine.   Hosea 3:1

Put that into the personal application which no doubt underlies it, and say, "The love of the Lord towards me, who have looked away from Him, with wandering, faithless eyes, to other helps and hopes, and have loved earthly joys and sought earthly gratifications—the love of the Lord toward even me!" And then hear Him saying in the next verse, "So I bought her to Me"; stooping to do *that* in His unspeakable condescension of love, not with the typical silver and barley, but with the precious blood of Christ. Then, having thus loved us, and rescued us, and bought us with a price indeed, He says, still under the same figure, "Thou shalt abide for Me many days." This is both a command and a pledge. But the very pledge implies our past unfaithfulness, and the proved need of even our own part being undertaken by the ever patient Lord. He Himself has to guarantee our faithfulness, because there is no other hope of our continuing faithful. Well may such love win our full and glad surrender, and such a promise win our happy and confident trust! But He says more. He says, "So will I also be for thee!" And this seems an even greater marvel of love, as we observe how He meets every detail of our consecration with this wonderful word.

> Made for Thyself, O God!
> Made for Thy love, Thy service, Thy delight;
> Made to show forth Thy wisdom, grace, and might;
> Made for Thy praise, whom veiled archangels laud;
> Oh strange and glorious thought, that we may be
> A joy to Thee!
>
> Yet the heart turns away
> From this grand destiny of bliss, and deems
> 'Twas made for its poor self, for passing dreams,
> Chasing illusions melting day by day;
> Till for ourselves we read on this world's best,
> "This is not rest!"

December 6

NOW IS THE ONLY TIME TO SUFFER

If so be that we suffer with him, that we may be also glorified together.   Romans 8:17

It is only now that we can go with Jesus into conflict, suffering, loneliness, weariness. It is only now that we can come to the help of the Lord against the mighty in this great battlefield. Shall we shrink from opportunities which are not given to angels? Surely, even with Him in glory, the disciples must remember the words of the Lord Jesus, how He said to them, "Ye are they which have continued with Me in My temptations," with a thrill of rapturous thanksgiving that such a privilege was theirs.

> He knelt and prayed, and kissed the stake,
> And blessed his Master's name
> That he was called his cross to take,
> And counted worthy for His sake
> To suffer death and shame.

December 7

Thou meetest . . . those that remember thee in thy ways.
Isaiah 64:5

The holy remembrance, wrought by the Spirit, widens. For "we will remember the name of the Lord our God" in its sweet and manifold revelations. "I will remember the years" and "the works of the Lord." "Surely I will remember Thy wonders of old." Most of all "we will remember Thy love," the everlasting love of our Father, the "exceeding great love of our Master and only Saviour," the gracious, touching love of our Comforter. And the remembrance of all this love will include that of its grand act and proof, "Thou shalt remember that . . . Jehovah thy God redeemed thee."

> O Love that chose, O Love that died,
> O Love that sealed and sanctified,
> All glory, glory, glory be,
> O covenant, Triune God, to Thee!

December 8

DELIGHT OF SELF-DENIAL

Then said Jesus unto his disciples, If any man will come after me, let him deny himself. Matthew 16:24
I count all things but loss for the excellency of the knowledge of Christ Jesus my Lord: for whom I have suffered the loss of all things. Philippians 3:8

"What about self-denial?" some reader will ask. Consecration does not supersede this, but transfigures it. Literally, a consecrated life is and must be a life of denial of self. But all the effort and pain of it is changed into very delight. We love our Master; we know, surely and absolutely, that He is listening and watching our every word and way, and that He has called us to the privilege of walking "worthy of the Lord unto all pleasing." And in so far as this is a reality to us, the identical things which are still self-denial in one sense, become actual self-delight in another. It may be self-denial to us to turn away from something within reach of our purse which it would be very convenient or pleasant to possess. But if the Master lifted the veil, and revealed Himself standing at our side, and let us hear His audible voice asking us to reserve the price of it for His treasury, should we talk about self-denial then? Should we not be utterly ashamed to think of it? or rather, should we, for one instant, think about self or self-denial at all? Would it not be an unimaginable joy to do what He asked us to do with that money? But as long as His own unchangeable promise stands written in His Word for us, "Lo, I am with you alway," we may be sure that He is with us, and that His eye is as certainly on our opened or half-opened purse as it was on the treasury, when He sat over against it and saw the two mites cast in. So let us do our shopping "as seeing Him who is invisible."

> Only one heart to give, only one voice to use;
> Only one little life to live, and only one to lose.
> Poor is my best, and small; how could I dare divide?
> Surely my Lord shall have it all, He shall not be denied!

December 9

DWELLING AND WORKING

There they dwelt with the king for his work. 1 Chronicles 4:23

"There!" Not in any likely place at all, not in the palace, not in the city of the great king, but in about the last place one would have expected, "among plants and hedges." It does not even seem clear why they were there at all, for they were potters, not gardeners—thus giving us the combination of simple labor of the hands, carried on in out-of-the-way places; and yet they were dwellers with the king, and workers with the king. Anywhere and everywhere we, too, may dwell with the King for His work. We may be in a very unlikely or unfavorable place for this — it may be in a literal country life, with little enough to be seen of the goings of the King around us; it may be among hedges of all sorts, hindrances in all directions; it may be, furthermore, with our hands full of all manner of pottery for our daily task. No matter! The King who placed us there will come and dwell there with us; the hedges are all right, or He would soon do away with them, and it does not follow that what seems to hinder our way may not be for its very protection; and as for the pottery, why, that is just exactly what He has seen fit to put into our hands, and therefore it is, for the present, "His work."

> Now I will turn to my own land, and tell
> What I myself have seen and heard of Thee,
> And give Thine own sweet message, "Come and see!"
> And yet in heart and mind forever dwell
> With Thee, my King of Peace, in loyal rest,
> Within the fair pavilion of Thy presence blest.

December 10

IGNORANCE AND KNOWLEDGE

**These things will they do . . . because they have not
known the Father.** John 16:3
Ye have known the Father. 1 John 2:13

"If they only knew!" How often we say or think this when
they misunderstand and misjudge a person, a position, or an
action just because they do not know what we know! How we
chafe against their speaking evil of things which they know
not, and most of all when they speak wrongly or unworthily
of a person whom we know much better than they do! Ah,
if they only knew! This grieving sense of the injustice of ig-
norance rises to a feeling which needs much tempering of faith
and patience when we see our God Himself misunderstood
and misjudged. Oh, how they daily mistake His words and
His character, and how it does pain us! How we do want
them to know what He is, even so far as we are privileged to
know Him! . . . What added grandeur it gives to our anticipations of the day when every eye shall see Him, that He,
our Father, will be known at last to be what He is, and that
Jesus, our Lord and Master, will be seen in His own glory,
and can never, never be misunderstood any more!

> Oh, the joy to see Thee reigning,
> Thee, my own beloved Lord!
> Every tongue Thy name confessing,
>   Brought to Thee with glad accord!
> Thee, my Master and my Friend,
>   Vindicated and enthroned,
> Unto earth's remotest end
>   Glorified, adored, and owned!

December 11

DRAWN BY LOVE

**I have loved thee with an everlasting love: therefore with
lovingkindness have I drawn thee.** Jeremiah 31:3

Just examine now—was it not so? Was it with anything but
lovingkindness that He drew you? Remember the way by
which He led you; it may have been hedged with thorns, but
was it not paved with love? Were not the very stones laid with
fair colors? Can you help seeing the lovingkindness of the
Lord all along? And what were they lavished for, but to draw
you? That being acknowledged, what next? Lovingkindness is

the fruit and expression and absolute proof of everlasting love. There is no escape from this magnificent conclusion—"Yea, I have loved thee [personally *thee*] . . . therefore . . . have I drawn thee [personally *thee*]." The coming was personal and individual. It may have been "in the press," but we had nothing to do with the rest of the throng. We know in ourselves that we, you and I, individually, have come. That personal coming was because of God the Father's personal drawing. I do not know how He drew you, you do not know how He drew me, but without it most certainly neither you nor I ever could have come, because we never would have come.

> From no less fountain such a stream could flow,
> No other root could yield so fair a flower;
> Had He not loved, He had not drawn us so;
> Had He not drawn, we had nor will nor power
> To rise, to come — the Saviour had passed by
> Where we in blindness sat without one care or cry.

December 12

LASTING JOY

These things have I spoken unto you, that my joy might remain in you, and that your joy might be full.   John 15:11

Who that has known anything of joy in the Lord but has asked, "But will it last?" And why has the question been so often the very beginning of its not lasting? Because we have either asked it of ourselves or of others, and not of the Lord only. His own answers to this continually recurring question are so different from the cautious, chilling, saddening ones which His children so often give. They are absolute, full, reiterated. We little realize how unscriptural we are when we meet His good gift of joy to ourselves or to others with a doubtful, and therefore faithless, "If it lasts!" "To the law and to the testimony," O happy Christian! there you shall find true and abundant answer to our only shadow on the brightness of the joy. So long as you believe your Lord's word about it, so long it will last. So soon as you ask of other counselors, and believe their word instead, so soon it will fail. Jesus meets your difficulty explicitly. He has provided against it by giving the very reason why He spoke the gracious words of His last discourse. "That My joy might remain in you."

> O the freedom and the fervor after all the faithless days!
> O the ever-new thanksgiving and the ever-flowing praise!
> Shall we tempt the gaze from Jesus, and a doubting shadow cast,
> Satan's own dark word suggesting by the whisper "if it last"?

December 13

AS THE TREE FALLS, SO IT LIES

Thou art my hiding place; thou shalt preserve me from trouble.   Psalm 32:7

A man shall be as an hiding place from the wind, and a covert from the tempest.   Isaiah 32:2

Any hour may be the sunset of your day of grace, with no twilight of possibilities of salvation beyond. And then, as the tree falleth, so it lieth. As death finds you, so judgment will find you. Where it finds you . . . there the day of the Lord will find you, "in the which the heavens shall pass away with a great noise, and the elements shall melt with fervent heat; the earth also, and the works that are therein, shall be burned up." What will you do then, when neither heavens nor earth afford even a standing place for you? But come to Jesus. He is the hiding place from that fiery tempest. "I flee unto Thee to hide me" "from the wrath to come." "Thou art my Hiding-place."

> Thou hast the words of endless life;
> Thou givest victory in the strife;
> Thou only art the changeless Friend,
> On whom for aye we may depend:
> In life, in death, alike we flee,
> O Saviour of the world, to Thee.

December 14

OUR ROYAL SUBSTITUTE

I will smite the king only. 2 Samuel 17:2

It may be that this futile threat of a wicked man against the king was like the saying of Caiaphas — "not of himself," but written for our learning "more about Jesus." A deadly stroke was to be aimed at "the king only," for he was "worth ten thousand" of the people; if he were smitten, they should escape. Do the words of David in another place tell of his great Antitype's desire that it should be so? "Let Thine hand, I pray Thee, O Lord my God, be on me, . . . but *not* on Thy people." "For the transgression of my people was the stroke upon Him" (margin) ; therefore not upon us, never upon us. The lightning that strikes the conductor instead of the building to which it is joined, has spent its fiery force and strikes no more.

"The King *only*." For "by Himself He purged our sins."

Certainly we had nothing to do with it then! Certainly no other man or means had anything to do with it! and certainly nothing and no one now can touch that great fact, so far out of reach of human quibbling and meddling, that Jesus, "His own self, bare our sins in His own body on the tree." Is not the fact that He "with whom we have to do," *was smitten of God instead of us,* enough? What else can we want to guarantee our salvation?

"Now I see!" But not the parting of the melting earth and sky,
Not a vision dread and startling, forcing one despairing cry.
But I see the solemn saying, All have sinned, and all must die;
Holy precepts disobeying, guilty all the world must lie.
Bending, silenced, to the dust, now I see that God is just.

"Now I see!" But not the glory, not the face of Him I love,
Not the full and burning story of the mysteries above.
But I see what God hath spoken, how His well-beloved Son
Kept the laws which man hath broken, died for sins which man
       hath done;
Dying, rising, throned above! Now I see that God is love.

December 15

WORDS WITH WEIGHT

Grace is poured into thy lips: therefore God hath blessed thee for ever. .   Psalm 45:2
And all bare him witness, and wondered at the gracious words which proceeded out of his mouth.   Luke 4:22

It is often helpful to read straight through one or more of the Gospels with a special thought on our mind, and see how much bears upon it. When we read one through with this thought— "His lips for me"—wondering, verse by verse, at the grace which was poured into them and the gracious words which fell from them, wondering more and more at the cumulative force and infinite wealth of tenderness and power and wisdom and love flowing from them, we cannot but desire that our lips and all the fruit of them should be wholly for Him. "For thee" they were opened in blessing; "for thee" they were closed when He was led as a lamb to the slaughter. And whether teaching, warning, counsel, comfort, or encouragement, commandments in whose keeping there is a great reward, or promises which exceed all we ask or think—all the precious fruit of His lips is "for thee," really and truly meant "for thee."

Christ is precious, oh most precious, gift by God the Father sealed;
Pearl of greatest price and treasure, hidden, yet to us revealed;
His own people's crown of glory, and resplendent diadem;
More than thousand worlds, and dearer than all life and love to them.

December 16

JOE IN SERVING

JOY IN SERVING

He that waiteth on his master shall be honoured. Proverbs 27:18
And he shall serve him for ever.   Exodus 21:6

A promise only differs from a threat by one thing, love! But
that makes all the difference. To those who are still enemies
in their minds, the prospect of serving forever would be anything but pleasant. But when the enmity is slain by the cross
of Christ, and all things are become new, and the love of
Christ constraineth, then it is among the brightest of our
many bright anticipations, and everlasting joy and everlasting service become almost synonymous. Rest is sweet, but
service (in proportion to our love) is sweeter still. Those who
have served much here cannot but anticipate the fuller and
more perfect service above. Those who have to do little more
than stand and wait here, will perhaps revel even more than
others in the new experience of active service, coming at once,
as it were, into its full delight.

> "Shall serve Him" — and forever;
> Oh, hope most sure, most fair!
> The perfect love outpouring
> In perfect service there!

December 17

GIVING MUST COST

**The abundance of their joy and their deep poverty abounded
unto the riches of their liberality.**   2 Corinthians 8:2
**Neither will I offer . . . unto the Lord my God of that which
doth cost me nothing.**   2 Samuel 24:24

But I do not see at all how self-indulgence and needless extrava-
gance can possibly co-exist with true consecration. If we really
never do go without anything for the Lord's sake, but, just
because He has graciously given us means, always supply for
ourselves not only every need but every notion, I think it is
high time we looked into the matter before God. Why should
only those who have limited means have the privilege of offering to their Lord that which has really cost them something
to offer? Observe, it is not merely going without something
we would naturally like to have or do, but going without it
for Jesus' sake. Not, "I will go without it, because, after all,
I can't very well afford it"; or, "because I dare say I shall be
glad I have not spent the money"; but, "I will do without it,

because I do want to do a little more for Him who so loves me—just that much more than I could do if I did this other thing." I fancy this is more often the heart-language of those who have to cut and contrive, than of those who are able to give liberally without any cutting and contriving at all. The very abundance of God's good gifts too often hinders from the privilege and delight of really doing without something superfluous or comfortable or usual, that they may give just that much more to their Lord. What a pity!

> All! for the last and least
> He stoopeth to uplift:
> The altar of my great High Priest
> Shall sanctify my gift.

December 18

A SAFEGUARD FROM TEMPTATION

And the priest shall take some of the blood of the trespass offering, and the priest shall put it . . . upon the thumb of his right hand. Leviticus 14:14
We have given the hand to the Egyptians. Lamentations 5:6

It may seem an odd idea, but a simple glance at one's hand, with the recollection, "This hand is not mine; it has been given to Jesus, and it must be kept for Jesus," may sometimes turn the scale in a doubtful matter, and be a safeguard from certain temptations. With that thought fresh in your mind as you look at your hand, can you let it take up things which, to say the very least, are not for Jesus? things which evidently cannot be used, as they most certainly are not used, either for Him or by Him? Cards, for instance! Can you deliberately hold in it books of a kind which you know perfectly well, by sadly repeated experience, lead you farther from instead of nearer to Him? books which must and do fill your mind with those other things which, entering in, choke the Word? books which you would not care to read at all, if your heart were burning within you at the coming of His feet to bless you? Next time any temptation of this sort approaches, just look at your hand!

> Just to ask Him what to do all the day,
> And to make you quick and true to obey.
> Just to know the needed grace He bestoweth,
> Every bar of time and place overfloweth.
> Just to take thy orders straight
> From the Master's own command!
> Blessed day! when thus we wait
> Always at our Sovereign's hand.

December 19

REMARKABLE AND FAR-REACHING

And God saw . . . that every imagination of the thoughts of his heart was only evil continually. Genesis 6:5

There is real comfort in knowing that *every* imagination of the thoughts of the natural heart is *only* evil continually, because this shows how really He is working in us when we find Him putting and keeping holy things in our minds. We may be quite sure no Godward thought comes natural to us; but His new covenant is, "I will put My laws into their mind, and write them in their hearts." The words are very remarkable and far-reaching. We feel that they go to the very depths, that it is our whole mental being which is to be thus pervaded with the incense of consecration; not that it is to be kept only in some inner recess of the heart, and not equally so in the mental consciousness. "Keep this for ever in the imagination."

> Such mystery of iniquity within,
> That we must loathe our very tho'ts, but for the cure
> He hath devised — the blessed Tree
> The Lord hath shown us, that, cast in, can heal
> The fountain whence the bitter waters flow.
> Divinest remedy whose power we feel,
> Whose grace we comprehend not, but we know.

December 20

"AFTERWARD" — NOW AND ALWAYS

Now no chastening for the present seemeth to be joyous, but grievous: nevertheless afterward it yieldeth the peaceable fruit of righteousness unto them which are exercised thereby. Hebrews 12:11

There are some promises which we are apt to reserve for great occasions, and thus lose the continual comfort of them. Perhaps we read this one with a sigh, and say: "How beautiful this is for those whom the Lord is really chastening! I almost think I should not mind that, if such a promise might then be mine. But the things that try me are only the little things that turn up every day to trouble and depress me." Well, now, does the Lord specify what degree of trouble, or what kind of trouble is great enough to make up a claim to the promise? And if He does not, why should you? He only defines it as "not joyous, but grievous." Perhaps there have been a dozen different things today which were "not joyous, but grievous" to you. And though you feel ashamed of feeling them so much, and hardly like to own to their having been so trying, and would not think of dignifying them as "chastening," yet, if they come under the Lord's definition, He not only knows all about them, but they were, every one of them, chastenings from His hand; neither to be despised and called "just nothing," when all the while they *did* grieve you; nor to be wearied of; because they are working out blessing to you and glory to Him. Every one of them has been an unrecognized token of His love and interest in you; for "whom the Lord loveth He chasteneth."

"There is no 'afterward' on earth for me!"
Beloved, 'tis not so!
That God's own "afterwards" are pledged to thee,
Thy life shall show.

But living fruit of righteousness to Him
His chastening shall yield,
And constant "afterwards," no longer dim,
Shall be revealed.

Is it no "afterward" that in thy heart
His love is shed abroad?
And that His Spirit breathes, while called apart,
The peace of God?

December 21

A HIGHER MOTIVE

He hath put a new song in my mouth, even praise unto our God.
Psalm 40:3
O sing unto the Lord a new song: sing unto the Lord, all the earth.
Psalm 96:1

It is not only for the sake of the unsaved that we want them so much to come to the Saviour. Our earnestness has a stronger spring than even that. We love our Lord, so that we cannot bear Him not to be esteemed aright. We cannot bear Him to be thought little of, and to be misunderstood; it is pain, real pain, to us when He is not appreciated and loved and adored—when all that He has done is treated as not worth whole-hearted gratitude and love—when His great and blood-bought salvation is neglected. For His own beloved sake, for His own glory's sake, we want others to come, that they too may love, and bless, and glorify Him!

Do ye doubt our feeble witness? Though ye scorn us, come and see!
Come and hear Him for yourselves, and ye shall know that it is He!
Ye shall find in Him the Center, the very Truth and Life,
Resplendent resolution of the endless doubt and strife.

December 22

Nothing shall by any means hurt you. Luke 10:19

Is not this one of those very strong promises which we are apt to think are worded a little too strongly, and off which we take a great discount? Now, instead of daring a "Yea, hath God said?" let us just take all the comfort and rest and gladness of it for ourselves. Let us believe every word, just as our beloved Master uttered it to the simple-hearted seventy who were so surprised to find His name so much more powerful than they expected. Nothing? If He said "nothing," have we any right to add, "Yes, but except . . ."? Nothing can hurt those who are joined to Christ, "for with Me thou shalt be in safeguard," unless anything can be found which should separate us from Him. And "who shall separate us?" Earthly tribulations, even the most terrible, shall not do it, for "in all these things we are more than conquerors through Him that loved us." Yet a farther-reaching and indeed, entirely exhaustive list is given, none of which, "nor any other creature, shall be able to separate us."

> Our Father, our Father, who dwellest in light,
> We lean on Thy love, and we rest on Thy might;
> In weakness and weariness joy shall abound,
> For strength everlasting in Thee shall be found:
> Our Refuge, our Helper in conflict and woe,
> Our mighty Defender, how blessed to know
> That Thine is the power!

December 23

And the king commanded . . . saying, Deal gently for my sake with the young man, even with Absalom. 2 Samuel 18:5

Even with Absalom! Even with the heartless, deliberate traitor and rebel. We must recollect clearly what he was, to appreciate the exquisite tenderness of David in such a command to his rough war captains in such untender times. For the sake of his people and his kingdom, he must send them forth against him, but the deep love gushes out in the bidding, "Deal gently for my sake." It was no new impulse. When Amnon was murdered, the king wept very sore and mourned for his son every day, and yet, when the fratricide had fled, the soul of

King David longed to go forth unto him, and the king's heart was toward Absalom. And when God's own vengeance fell upon the wicked son, David's lamentation over him is perhaps unparalleled in its intensity of pathos among the records of human tenderness. Turn to the Antitype, and see the divine tenderness of our King. Again and again it gleams out, whether He Himself wept, or whether He said, "Weep not"—whether in the tender look, the tender word, or the tender touch of gentlest mercy. May we not recognize a command in this, as well as a responsibility to follow the example of the gentleness of Christ? Perhaps next time we are tempted to be a little harsh or hasty with an erring or offending one, the whisper will come, "Deal gently, for My sake!"

> Return!
> O erring, yet beloved!
> I wait to bind thy bleeding feet, for keen
> And rankling are the thorns where thou hast been;
> I wait to give thee pardon, love, and rest;
> Is not My joy to see thee safe and blest?
> Return! I wait to hear once more thy voice,
> To welcome thee anew, and bid thy heart rejoice!

December 24

SIMPLE TRUST FOR INFINITE REST

The word of my lord the king shall now be "for rest."
2 Samuel 14:17 (margin)

Here is the whole secret of rest from the very beginning to the very end. The word of our King is all we have and all we need for deep, utter heart-rest, which no surface waves of this troublesome world can disturb. What gave "rest from thy sorrow and from thy fear" at the very first, when we wanted salvation and peace? It was not some vague, pleasing impression, some indefinable hush that came to us (or if it was, the unreality of the rest was soon proved), but some word of our King which we saw to be worthy of all acceptation; we believed it, and by it Jesus gave us rest. There is no other means of rest for all the way but the very same. The moment we simply believe any word of the King, we find that it is truly "for rest," about the point to which it refers. And if we would but go on taking the King's word about every single thing, we should always find it, then and there, "for rest."

> The Master hath said it! Rejoicing in this,
> We ask not for sign or for token;
> His word is enough for our confident bliss,
> "The Scripture cannot be broken!"

December 25

His name shall be called Wonderful. Isaiah 9:6

All the other names of Jesus are nouns. But here is a name that is an adjective; so we may use it not only as a name by itself, but as an adjective to all His other names; and the more we know Him and love Him the more we shall delight in this.

If we know Jesus as our Saviour at all, we shall be quite sure that He is a Wonderful Saviour. And if we grow in grace and in the knowledge of our Lord and Saviour Jesus Christ, we shall find more and more, year by year, and even day by day, what a Wonderful Friend, and Wonderful Gift, and Wonderful High Priest, and Wonderful everything else He is.

When you see a wonderful sight, don't you always want others to see it first thing? And if you cannot bring them to see it, don't you want to tell about it, try to give them an idea of it? So I think one proof that we have really found Jesus is that we shall want others to come and see what a Wonderful Saviour we have found.

Jesus is Wonderful in what He is. Even the angels must have wondered to see the Son of God, whom they all worship, lying in a manger as a little baby. But I think they must have wondered more still when they saw "Him taken and by wicked hands crucified and slain." They must have marvelled indeed then at the love of Christ which passeth knowledge, yet He was not dying for them but for you, so you may say, "Thy love to *me* was wonderful."

Everything that He did was wonderful. Isaiah said that many should be astonished at Him; and I want you to see how exactly that was fulfilled. Look in the first seven chapters of Mark, and you will see it five times mentioned that they were astonished or amazed at Him.

And His words were not less wonderful. Look in the 4th chapter of Luke, and you will see how even those who did not love Him wondered, and were astonished and amazed at His words. If we wonder at His gracious words to us now, how much more shall we wonder when we see Him on the throne of His glory, and hear His own voice.

O Bringer of Salvation, who wondrously hast wrought,
Thyself the revelation of love beyond our thought:
We worship Thee, we bless Thee, to Thee alone we sing;
We praise Thee, and confess Thee, our gracious Lord and King!

December 26

WE — THY BONE AND THY FLESH
The king is near of kin to us. 2 Samuel 19:42

Not only in the Prophet raised up "from the midst of thee, of thy brethren," and in the High Priest, "thy brother," taken from among men, do we see the kinship of Christ; but in the divinely chosen King the same wonderful link is given—"One from among thy brethren shalt thou set king over thee: thou mayest not set a stranger over thee, which is not thy brother." When we have exhausted all that is contained in the very full and dear idea of brother, we are led beyond, to realize One who "sticketh closer than a brother." . . . The King is so near of kin, that we may come to Him as the tribes of Israel did, and say, "Behold, we are Thy bone and Thy flesh." So near of kin, that He is "in all things" "made like unto His brethren." So "near of kin to us," and yet God! Is this not worth thinking out?

Oh let me sing . . . For very joy, because Thou art my King;
Oh let me praise . . . Thy love and faithfulness thro' all my days.

December 27

ON GIVING

Every man shall give as he is able, according to the blessing of the Lord thy God which he hath given thee. Deuteronomy 16:17

There is always a danger that just because we say "all," we may practically fall shorter than if we had only said "some," but said it very definitely. God recognizes this, and provides against it in many departments. For instance, though our time is to be "all" for Him, yet He solemnly sets apart the one day in seven which is to be specially for Him. Those who think they know better than God, and profess that every day is a Sabbath, little know what flood-gates of temptation they are opening by being so very wise above what is written. God knows best, and that should be quite enough for every loyal heart. So, as to money, though we place it all at our Lord's disposal, and rejoice to spend it all for Him directly or indirectly, yet I am quite certain it is a great help and safeguard, and, what is more, a matter of simple obedience to the spirit of His commands, to set aside a definite and regular proportion of our income or receipts for His direct service.

I gave My life for thee, My precious blood I shed,
That thou might'st ransomed be, and quickened from the dead.
I gave My life for thee; what hast thou given for Me?

December 28

HEARTS FILLED AND FIXED

His heart is fixed, trusting in the Lord. Psalm 112:7

Whose heart? An angel's? A saint's in glory? No! Simply the heart of the man that feareth the Lord, and delighteth greatly in His commandments. Therefore yours and mine, as God would have them be; just the normal idea of a God-fearing heart, nothing extremely and hopelessly beyond attainment.

"Fixed, trusting in the Lord." Here is the means of the fixing—trust. He works the trust in us by sending the Holy Spirit to reveal God in Christ to us as absolutely, infinitely worthy of our trust. When we "see Jesus" by Spirit-wrought faith, we cannot but trust Him; we distrust our hearts more truly than ever before, but we trust our Lord entirely, because we trust Him *only*. For, entrusting our trust to Him, we know that He is able to keep that which we commit (i.e., entrust) to Him. It is His own way of winning and fixing our hearts for Himself.

> Nor can the vain toil cease,
> Till in the shadowy maze of life we meet
> One who can guide our aching, wayward feet
> To find Himself, our Way, our Life, our Peace.
> In Him the long unrest is soothed and stilled;
> Our hearts are filled.

December 29

PLEDGE ALLEGIANCE

Ye sought for David in times past to be king over you: Now then do it. 2 Samuel 3:17-18

Well we might, for the bondage of any other lord was daily harder. Well we might, with even a dim glimpse of the grace and glory of the King who waited for our homage. We sought, first, only for something—we hardly knew what—restlessly and vaguely; then, for Someone, who was not merely the desire of all nations, but our own desire. And yet we did not come to the point: we were not ready for His absolute monarchy, for we were loving and doing the will of our old tyrant. We come face to face with a great "NOW!" "Now then do it!" He does not force allegiance—He waits for it. The crown of our own individual love and loyalty must be offered by our own hands. We must do it. When? Oh, now! Now let us, first in solemn heart-surrender, and then in open and unmistakable life-confession, yield ourselves to Him as our Sovereign, our Ruler. What a glorious life of victory and peace opens before us when this is done! What a silencing of our fears lest the time to come should nevertheless be as the time past!

God's "Now" is sounding in your ears; oh, let it reach your heart!
Not only from your sinfulness He bids you part;
Your righteousness as filthy rags must all relinquished be,
And only Jesus' precious death must be your plea.

December 30

A CHANNEL FOR BOUNDLESS LOVE

The love of God is shed abroad in our hearts by the Holy Ghost which is given unto us. Romans 5:5

When the Holy Spirit reveals the love of Christ, and sheds abroad the love of God in our hearts, this (natural) love is penetrated with a new principle, as it discovers a new Object. Everything that it beholds in that Object gives it new depth and new colors. As it sees the holiness, the beauty, and the glory, it takes the deep hues of conscious sinfulness, unworthiness, and nothingness. As it sees even a glimpse of the love that passeth knowledge, it takes the glow of wonder and gratitude. And when it sees that love drawing close to its deepest need with blood-purchased pardon, it is intensified and stirred, and there is no more time for weighing and measuring; we must pour it out, all there is of it, with our tears, at the feet that were pierced for love of us.

And what then? Has the flow grown gradually slower and shallower? Has our Lord reason to say, "My brethren have dealt deceitfully as a brook, and as a stream of brooks they pass away"? It is humiliating to have found that we could not keep on loving Him, as we loved in that remembered hour when "Thy time was the time of love." We have proved that we were not able. Let this be only the steppingstone to proving that He is able!

Are you shining for Jesus, dear one?
You have given your heart to Him;
But is the light strong within it,
Or is it but pale and dim?
Can everybody see it—
That Jesus is all to you?
That your love to Him is burning
With radiance warm and true?
Is the seal upon your forehead,
So that it must be known
That you are "all for Jesus,"—
That your heart is all His own?

December 31

He will rejoice over thee with joy; he will rest [be silent] in his love, he will joy over thee with singing.

Zephaniah 3:17

With a passing guest or ceremonial acquaintance you feel under an obligation to talk; you make effort to entertain them as a matter of courtesy; you may be tired or weak, but no matter, you feel you must exert yourself. But with a very dear and intimate friend sitting by you, there is no feeling of the kind. To be sure, you may talk if you feel able: pouring out all sort of confidences, relieved and refreshed by the interchange of thoughts and sympathies. But if you are very tired, you know you do not need to say a word. You are perfectly understood, and you know it. You can enjoy the mere fact of your friend's presence, and find that does you more good than conversation. The sense of that present and sympathetic affection rests you more than any words. And your friend takes it as the highest proof of your friendship and confidence, and probably never loves you so vividly as in these still moments. Even so we may be silent to the Lord; because we know He loves us and understands us so thoroughly! There is no need when very weary, bodily or mentally, or both, to force ourselves to entertain Him, so to speak; to go through a sort of duty-work of a certain amount of uttered words or arranged thoughts. That might be if He were only to us as a wayfaring man that turneth aside to tarry for a night, but not with the beloved and gracious One who has come in to abide with us, and is always there! If this is His relation to us, there is no fear but what there will be, at other times, plenty of intercourse; but now, when we are "so tired," we may just be silent to Him, instead of speaking to Him.

Love culminates in bliss when it doth reach
A white, unflickering, fear-consuming glow;
And, knowing it is known as it doth know,
Needs no assuring word or soothing speech.
It craves but silent nearness, so to rest,
No sound, no movement, love not heard but felt,
Longer and longer still, till time should melt,
A snowflake on the eternal ocean's breast.
Have moments of this silence starred thy past,
Made memory a glory-haunted place,
Taught all the joy that mortal ken can trace?
By greater light 'tis but a shadow cast—
So shall the Lord thy God rejoice o'er thee,
And in His love will rest, and silent be.

ADVENT SONG

Thou art coming! rays of glory
Through the veil Thy death has rent,
Touch the mountain and the river
With a golden glowing quiver,
Thrill of light and music blent.
Earth is brightened when this gleam
Falls on flower and rock and stream;
Life is brightened when this ray
Falls upon its darkest day.

Not a cloud and not a shadow,
Not a mist and not a tear,
Not a sin and not a sorrow,
Not a dim and veiled tomorrow,
For that sunrise grand and clear!
Jesus, Saviour, once with Thee,
Nothing else seems worth a thought!
Oh, how marvellous will be
All the bliss Thy pain hath bought.

FINIS

Another little volume filled with varied verse and song,
Should wake another note of praise, unheard, but deep and
    strong;
For He who knows my truest need, and leads me day by day,
Has given the music that hath been such solace on my way.

I bless Thee, gracious Father, who hast moulded praise from
    pain,
And turned a wail of mourning to a trustful, calm refrain,
To many a sorrow giving me an afterward of song,
And wafting it to other hearts in comfort true and strong.

I bless Thee, gracious Father, for Thy pleasant gift to me,
And earnestly I ask Thee that it may always be
In perfect consecration laid at Thy glorious feet,
Touched with Thine altar-fire, and made an offering pure and
    sweet.